Non-Democratic Regimes

Theory, Government and Politics

Paul Brooker

palgrave
macmillan

First published 2000

Published by
PALGRAVE MACMILLAN
Houndmills, Basingstoke, Hampshire RG21 6XS and
175 Fifth Avenue, New York, N.Y. 10010
Companies and representatives throughout the world

PALGRAVE MACMILLAN is the global academic imprint of the Palgrave Macmillan division of
St. Martin's Press, LLC and of Palgrave Macmillan Ltd. Macmillan® is a registered trademark
in the United States, United Kingdom and other countries. Palgrave is a registered trademark
in the European Union and other countries.

ISBN-13: 978-0-333- 66079-9
ISBN-10: 0-333-66079-X paperback

This book is printed on paper suitable for recycling and
made from fully managed and sustained forest sources.

A catalogue record for this book is available from the British Library.

First published in the United States of America by
ST. MARTIN'S PRESS, LLC.,
Scholarly and Reference Division,
175 Fifth Avenue, New York, N.Y. 10010

ISBN 0-312-22755-8 (paper)

Printed and bound in Great Britain by
Biddles Ltd., King's Lynn, Norfolk

COMPARATIVE GOVERNMENT AND POLITICS
Founding Series Editor: The late **Vincent Wright**

Published

Rudy Andeweg and Galen A. Irwin
Governance and Politics of the Netherlands (2nd edition)

Tim Bale
European Politics: A Comparative Introduction

Nigel Bowles
Government and Politics of the United States (2nd edition)

Paul Brooker
Non-Democratic Regimes: Theory, Government and Politics

Robert Elgie
Political Leadership in Liberal Democracies

Rod Hague and Martin Harrop
*Comparative Government and Politics: An Introduction (6th edition)

Paul Heywood
The Government and Politics of Spain

B. Guy Peters
Comparative Politics: Theories and Methods
[Rights: World excluding North America]

Tony Saich
Governance and Politics of China (2nd edition)

Anne Stevens
Government and Politics of France (3rd edition)

Ramesh Thakur
The Government and Politics of India

Forthcoming

Judy Batt
Government and Politics in Eastern Europe

Robert Leonardi
Government and Politics in Italy

* Published in North America as **Political Science: A Comparative Introduction (4th edition)**

Comparative Government and Politics
Series Standing Order
ISBN 0–333–71693–0 hardcover
ISBN 0–333–69335–3 paperback
(outside North America only)

You can receive future titles in this series as they are published by placing a standing order. Please contact your bookseller or, in the case of difficulty, write to us at the address below with your name and address, the title of the series and the ISBN quoted above.

Customer Services Department, Macmillan Distribution Ltd
Houndmills, Basingstoke, Hampshire RG21 6XS, England

321.9
BRO

Contents

List of Tables, Figures and Exhibits

Tables

Figures

Exhibits

Introduction

Studying Non-Democratic Regimes – Why and How

Although the world has entered an 'age of democracy', non-democratic regimes continue to be of more than just historical interest to students of comparative government and politics. One reason is simply that the global wave of democratisation lost momentum in the early 1990s and left some important non-democratic regimes in place. They still govern a significant proportion of the world's population, with the Chinese communist regime alone ruling a quarter of humanity, and they are still a source of international tension, as in the case of Saddam Hussein's regime in Iraq. A second reason is that there may be a revival of non-democratic rule, on a regional or even global scale, in the twenty-first century. It is therefore as well to be forewarned and forearmed by past experiences of how and why non-democratic regimes emerge.

Thirdly, non-democratic regimes have played a very influential role in the history and development of politics and government. Non-democratic government, whether by elders, chiefs, monarchs, aristocrats, empires, military regimes or one-party states, has been the norm for most of human history. As late as the 1970s non-democratic government was more common than democracy, and for a large part of the twentieth century first fascism and then communism seemed to have replaced democracy as the 'wave of the future'. Furthermore, the era of non-democratic rule has had an important influence on the development of government and politics. In particular, many newly emerged democracies are still experiencing the after-effects of dictatorship, as in formerly military-ruled Latin America and formerly communist Eastern Europe.

Fourthly, the prominent role that non-democratic regimes

1

have played in twentieth-century history has been reflected in the amount of attention that they received from leading Western political scientists. Theorists and analysts of totalitarianism, authoritarianism, one-party states, military regimes and personal dictatorship made a major contribution to the development of political science. This impressive heritage remains a source of inspiration for later analysts of non-democratic regimes and a source of comparisons and contrasts for theories of democracy.

Finally, the study of non-democratic regimes offers a comparative perspective on democracy. Comparisons between non-democratic and democratic regimes can be made across a wide range of areas, such as the consolidation of new regimes, degeneration into personal rule, government policies and performance, policy-making and even style of government. A more direct comparison arises when the demise of a non-democratic regime overlaps with the birth of a democracy, as was especially common during the 1970s–90s wave of democratisation that removed most of the world's dictatorships. There is also an almost overlapping, grey area where flawed democracy or semi-democracy verges on the semi-dictatorship that is produced by the use of semi-competitive elections to disguise a dictatorship.

This book therefore aims to provide a wide-ranging basis for comparison with democratic regimes as well as a thematic analysis of past, present and future non-democratic regimes and an account of previous theories or analyses of these regimes. It will focus on the *modern* form of non-democratic regime, that is, on dictatorship by a political party or the military rather than rule by a chief or monarch. For during the twentieth century these dictatorships became (and still are) the most influential form of non-democratic regime; they are the most likely form to emerge in the future; they are the focus of most of the theorising about non-democratic regimes; and they offer more opportunity for comparison (for identifying similarities as well as differences) with modern democracies than do the pre-modern regimes of chiefs, kings, aristocracies and empires.

The opening, theory chapters of the book will examine theories of totalitarian and authoritarian forms of modern non-democratic government and will then look at less ambitious approaches that have sought to analyse a particular type of regime, whether party, military or personal dictatorship. (Readers who find such theorising daunting or of little interest are recommended to skip or skim Chapters 1 and 2 and view them as a misplaced Appendix!) But the next chapters will tackle the eminently practical issues of how military and party dictatorships emerge, how they attempt to consolidate their hold on power, and how often they degenerate into personalist dictatorships. A chapter on government policies and performance will also look at the policy-making processes and governing style of dictatorships. The demise of dictatorships will be covered in a chapter that focuses on the 1970s–90s wave of democratisation, while the following chapter will examine semi-dictatorship and semi-democracy. Finally, there will be brief discussion of the failure of modern dictatorship and of its future prospects.

The Modern Form of Non-Democratic Regime – the Military and Party Dictatorships

The modern form of non-democratic regime combines dicta-torship by an organisation (or its leader) with a claim to be committed to democracy. The organisation is normally the military or a political party but the claim to favour democracy has come in a variety of shapes and sizes. A plebiscite or elec-tion may be conducted to show popular support for the regime, the official ideology may claim that the regime embodies a type of democracy, such as 'proletarian' democracy, or the regime may claim that it intends to establish/restore democracy. But such protestations of innocence or good intent are seeking to conceal a political and usually legal offence – the theft of pub-lic office and powers. A political party or the military has undemocratically usurped power by seizing public offices/powers or by misappropriating the public offices that it had acquired democratically.

This modern form of non-democratic regime emerged with Napoleon Bonaparte's use of plebiscites (referendums) to legit-imise his military dictatorship and eventual assumption of the title of Emperor. A military commander's seizure of power was nothing new in world history. The Imperial throne of the an-cient Roman Empire had often been fought over by military commanders, and the monarchical title of Emperor is derived from the Latin *imperator* (commander). But Bonaparte had put forward a new answer to the problem of how to legitimise a military seizure of power; he had hypocritically adopted the 'will of the people' principle espoused by the democratic ideology of the American and French revolutions. Military regimes hypo-critically claiming to be democratic in nature or intent became quite common in nineteenth-century Latin America, and would be the most common form of non-democratic regime in the twentieth century. But a newer form of dictatorship – the truly twentieth-century form – has had a more momentous influence than the military regimes on this century's political history.

The newer form was dictatorship by a political party, often accompanied by an ideology. As in the case of Bonaparte's plebiscites, political tools that had been developed in more democratic regimes – ideology and the organised political party – were put to a new, dictatorial use. First came the communist party dictatorship which emerged from the October 1917 rev-olution in Russia (renamed the 'Soviet Union'). Its Marxist-Leninist ideology espoused not only socialism but also 'leader-ship' by the Communist Party over state and society. During the 1920s–30s, though, communism was overshadowed by the emergence of fascist party dictatorships – Mussolini's Fascist regime and Hitler's Nazi regime – whose nationalist/racist ideol-ogy espoused personal dictatorship by the party leader over state and society. But the Second World War led to the de-struction of the fascist regimes and to a huge expansion in the number of communist party dictatorships. By the end of the 1940s they had been established throughout Eastern Europe and in China and North Korea. The only major additions to the ranks of communist regimes in the 1950s–60s were North Vietnam and Cuba. On the other hand, Africa was producing so many examples of a new type of party dictatorship (with an ideology espousing some degree of socialism and party leader-ship of state and society) that the 'African one-party state' became as common as communist regimes.

However, the 1960s–70s spread of military dictatorships through Africa as well as Latin America and Asia destroyed many party dictatorships as well as democracies. The Third World therefore came to be dominated by the military rather than party type of dictatorship, though in some cases by an updated form of military dictatorship that boasted an official party and even an ideology. But already a wave of democratisation was beginning to build and in the 1980s–90s it swept away most military and party dictatorships – only a few years after these modern non-democratic regimes had reached their numerical peak.

Differences between Military and Party Dictatorships

A political party and the military arm of a modern state are very different types of organisation, designed for quite different purposes, and this is reflected in major differences between the military and party types of dictatorship. For example, a usurping military is much more likely than a party actually to seize rather than misappropriate power. Similarly, a distinctive feature of the military type of dictatorship is that discontent within the ruling organisation often takes the form of a violent revolt against its political leader(s). Countercoups by soldiers discontented with the existing military government are so frequent that attempted coups are actually twice as common in military regimes as in civilian regimes (Nordlinger, 1977: 140). But a more important aspect of the distinctive instability of military rule is the frequency with which the military peacefully relinquish power to civilians and 'return to the barracks'. The average life of military regimes has been calculated to be only about five years, with in most cases the regime being ended by the military's voluntary withdrawal from power (*ibid.*: 139).

One reason why military rule tends to be of shorter duration than party dictatorship is that the military is more likely than a usurping party to have quite limited and only short-term political goals for its regime – and often seems to have intended to retain power for only a few years (*ibid.*: 142–3). In the many cases where the military has such limited goals, its seizure of power may have little effect upon the lives of ordinary citizens, in the sense of those who are not involved in politics and are not viewed as enemies by the new regime.

The same could be said of the onset of some party dictatorships, despite their seemingly more ambitious goals. Even the self-proclaimed 'totalitarian' Fascist regime had little effect upon the underdeveloped southern half of Italy; one southern party boss complained that the people of his province had been given no tangible indication that they were living in a Fascist era (Brooker, 1991: 289). The Nazi regime in more economically developed Germany established a more extensive and invasive presence but it, too, often failed to have much effect upon the 'hearts and minds' of its ordinary citizens. Local Nazi leaders could compel their fellow townspeople 'to attend meetings and pretend enthusiasm, but that was largely a mutually agreed charade' (Allen, 1984: 104). Later, when the country was facing the prospect of military defeat, some elderly workers provided an ordinary citizen's view of such dramatic political changes as the onset of Nazi rule. They commented 'that they had little concern for the future: that they had had to work hard under the [monarchical] Kaiser, in the [democratic] Weimar Republic, and in the [Nazi] Third Reich, and had probably no more and no less to expect from [communist] Bolshevism than hard work and low wages' (Kershaw, 1983: 314).

On the other hand, many of their fellow citizens had more reason to fear the coming of communist dictatorship. Peasant farmers and small-businessmen, as well as wealthy landowners and industrialists, were likely to lose their land or businesses through communist collectivisation of agriculture and expropriation of the private sector. More importantly, the small Jewish minority of their fellow citizens had already suffered greatly from the Nazi dictatorship, with many having lost their lives as well as their livelihood. And this intent of some dictatorships to take away or reshape human life is perhaps the most important reason for studying the emergence of modern non-democratic regimes and the possibility of their resurgence in the next century.

1

Theories of Non-Democratic Government

Although there are no widely recognised general theories of non-democratic government, there are many theories of such particular forms of non-democratic government as totalitarianism, authoritarianism, communism and fascism. Being concerned with forms of government, these theories are less interested in the traditional regime-defining question of 'who rules?' than in the wider question of '*how* do they rule?', which involves such issues as the regime's methods and degree of control over society, its ideological or other claims to legitimacy, its political and administrative structure, and the goals that it seeks to attain.

Therefore, although such terms as 'totalitarian', 'authoritarian', 'communist' and 'fascist' are used to describe regimes as well as forms of government, these labels say much more about a regime than whether it is a military or a party dictatorship (and in fact the term 'authoritarian' can be applied to both types of dictatorship). In contrast, to label a dictatorship as a 'military' or 'party' regime is to describe only the type of regime, in the sense of military or party rule, not the form of government – which in the case of party rule could be either totalitarian or authoritarian, communist or fascist.

Only theories of totalitarian and authoritarian forms of government will be examined in this chapter. The notions of 'totalitarianism' and 'authoritarianism' are general enough to have been applied (not necessarily very successfully) to a relatively wide range of regimes, including those labelled communist and fascist. Moreover, the distinctive features of communist and fascist forms of government will be described in later chapters, especially those on legitimacy and control (Chapter 5) and on policy and performance (Chapter 6).

Totalitarianism

The theories of totalitarianism are the most distinctive and imaginative of those developed by theorists of non-democratic government (see Table 1.1). The term 'totalitarianism' emerged in the 1920s–30s as part of the ideology of Fascist Italy: the Fascist 'totalitarian' state was pithily described by Mussolini as 'everything in the State, nothing outside of the State, nothing against the State'. But in the 1950s totalitarianism reemerged as a prominent concept in Western political science and was used to describe communist as well as fascist regimes. The classic works of Arendt and of Friedrich and Brzezinski provided descriptive *theories* of totalitarianism (in the sense of offering a much broader as well as a deeper understanding of the concept) which claimed that it was a quite new and 'total' form of dictatorship. In fact theories or concepts of totalitarianism were for years the leading or most dynamic approach to the study of non-democratic regimes; but from as early as the 1960s onwards there was a growing body of opinion that the notion of totalitarianism had outlived its usefulness. And, despite the work of such second-generation theorists as Schapiro, the notion of totalitarianism has never recovered the prominence that it enjoyed in the 1950s–60s.

Arendt's Classic Theory

Arendt's 1951 pioneering work, *The Origins of Totalitarianism*, depicted totalitarianism as a new and extreme form of dictatorship. In her view there had been only two examples of totalitarian dictatorship – Hitler's Nazi regime and Stalin's communist regime. More precisely, totalitarianism had existed in the 1938–45 years of Hitler's Nazi dictatorship in Germany, in the post-1929 years of the communist dictatorship in the Soviet Union, and in post-Second World War Eastern Europe, whose newly established communist regimes were viewed by Arendt as only extensions of the Soviet-based communist movement (1962 [1951]: 419, 308 n. 10).

She downplayed the ideological/policy differences between the rightist Nazis and leftist communists, declaring that in practice it made little difference whether totalitarians organised the masses in the name of race or of class (*ibid.*: 313). In contrast, only a year later Talmon emphasised the distinction between Left and Right totalitarianism in his famous work on what he termed the 'totalitarian democracy' associated with the French Revolution (1952: 1–2, 6–7). He argued that only totalitarianism of the Left was a form of totalitarian democracy, for the Right totalitarians were concerned with such collective/historic entities as state, nation or race and viewed force as permanently required for maintaining order and social training. The significance of the differences between left-wing (communist) and right-wing (fascist) variants of totalitarianism has remained an awkward issue for theorists and users of the concept of totalitarianism.

Although Arendt did not view totalitarian regimes' ideological differences (or even ideological content) as very significant, she noted that ideology plays an important role in such regimes (1962: 325, 458, 363). Totalitarian ideology's desire to transform human nature provides the regime with a reason as well as a road map for the all-pervading totalitarian organisation of human life, as only under a totalitarian system can all aspects of life be organised in accordance with an ideology. Furthermore, ideology in turn provides a means of internally, psychologically dominating human beings and therefore plays an important role not only in the totalitarian organisation of all aspects of human life, but also in attaining the ultimate totalitarian goal of total domination.

One of the features of Arendt's theory of totalitarianism is the extreme and total goal that she ascribed to this form of dictatorship. For totalitarianism seeks 'the permanent domination of each single individual in each and every sphere of life' and 'the total domination of the total population of the earth' (*ibid.*: 326, 392). A totalitarian movement's seizure of power in a particular country therefore only secures a base for the movement's further global expansion. But taking control of a country also offers the opportunity to experiment with organising and dominating human beings more intensively as well as extensively, and thereby subjecting society to 'total terror' (*ibid.*: 392, 421–2, 430–5, 440). After the secret police have liquidated all open or hidden resistance, they begin to liquidate ideologically defined 'objective enemies', such as Jews or supposed class enemies. This uniquely totalitarian level of terror is in turn replaced by a third, fully totalitarian stage. Now everyone seems to be a police informer and the secret police not only seek to remove all trace of their victims, as if these people had never existed, but also randomly select their victims. However, the ultimate 'laboratories' for experimenting with total domination are the regime's concentration, extermination or labour camps, where terror and torture are used to liquidate spontaneity and reduce human beings to only animal-like reactions and functions (*ibid.*: 436–8, 441, 451–6).

Unlike most later theorists of totalitarianism, Arendt was willing to take on the difficult task of explaining the origins of totalitarian regimes (though her explanations have never found favour with historians). She argued that these regimes arise from totalitarian movements' organisation of 'masses', in the sense of people who are experiencing social atomisation and extreme individualisation – the main characteristic of 'mass man' is social isolation created by the lack of normal social relationships (*ibid.*: 308–17). Such people are more easily attracted by totalitarian movements than are the sociable, less individualistic people who support normal political parties. If socially atomised masses also constitute (or are joined by) masses in the sense of sheer numbers, they can produce such a powerful totalitarian movement that a totalitarian regime can be established.

Socially atomised masses were created in a very different fashion in the Soviet Union than in Germany (*ibid.*: 313–24, 378–80). The Nazi movement came to power by winning the support of socially atomised masses that were created by the economic, social and political crises afflicting democratic Germany in the early 1930s. But in the Soviet Union the socially atomised masses were created *after* the communist movement had established a one-party dictatorship. Under its new leader, Stalin, the communist dictatorship created such masses by the destruction of the semi-capitalist class structure and by extensive political purges. Paradoxically, the victims sought relief from their social atomisation by offering total loyalty to the Communist Party, even though it was dominated by the perpetrators of the purges – Stalin and the political police.

The prominent role played by the political/secret police (as elite formations and super-party) is a unique structural feature of totalitarian regimes, but the key and most distinctive structural feature is the functionally indispensable leader figure – the Stalin or Hitler (*ibid.*: 380, 413, 420, 374–5, 387). A totalitarian regime and movement is so closely identified with the leader and his infallibility (as interpreter of the infallible ideology) that any move to restrain or replace him would prove disastrous for the regime and movement. His subordinates are not only aware of his indispensability, but have also been trained for the sole purpose of communicating and implementing his commands. Therefore the leader can count on their loyalty to the death, monopolise the right to explain ideology and policy, and behave as if he were above the movement.

Friedrich and Brzezinski's Classic Theory

Friedrich and Brzezinski's 1956 *Totalitarian Dictatorship and Autocracy* provided a more detailed and widely applicable descriptive theory than Arendt's (see Table 1.1). The newer theory's examples included post-1936 Nazi Germany, Fascist Italy and communist Soviet Union plus the newly established communist regimes in Eastern Europe and China (though it was acknowledged that Fascist Italy was a borderline case). But the most distinctive and important aspect of the theory was its claim that the 'character' of totalitarian dictatorship was to be found in a *syndrome* of six interrelated and mutually supporting features or traits (1961 [1956]: 9):

1. an ideology;
2. a single party, typically (that is, not always) led by one person;
3. a terroristic police;
4. a communications monopoly;
5. a weapons monopoly; and
6. a centrally-directed economy.

However, it was acknowledged that the six-point syndrome had shown 'many significant variations', such as the striking variation in economic structure arising from the fascist regimes' retention

TABLE 1.1

Theories of totalitarianism

Theories	Examples	Origins	Goals	Structure	Evolution
Arendt (1951)	Only Nazi Germany and Stalin's Communist Soviet Union (plus subsidiary East European communist regimes)	Political exploitation of the masses (of socially 'atomised' isolated individuals) created by preceding democracy's economic/social crisis or by preceding one-party dictatorship's political purges and destruction of social classes	Ideology-directed goal of dominating every individual in every sphere of life (use of terror)	1. Leader (functionally indispensable) 2. Secret police 3. Party/movement	
Friedrich and Brzezinski (1956)	Nazi Germany, Communist Soviet Union and Eastern Europe plus Fascist Italy and Communist China	Era of mass democracy and modern technology	Ideology-directed political, social, cultural and economic revolution with 'violent passion for unanimity' (use of terror and propaganda)	Party typically led by an individual leader 1. leader (absolutist) 2. party (of leader's followers) 3. terroristic police 4. politicisation of military by totalitarian movement	Long-term, 1. decline in need for terror and 2. possibility of post-leader collective leadership (small group) by party bureaucrats

Schapiro (1972)	Nazi Germany, Communist Soviet Union, Eastern Europe, China and Cuba – also Fascist Italy and Nkrumah's Ghana as weak cases	Ideology-accompanied domination of state, society and individual – 1. outward mass enthusiasm/support and 2. either preparation for war or building Communism	1. Party leader (personalised rule) 2. Party 3. State's administrative machinery 4. Police and army	Long-term possible post-leader transitional era with some pluralism of institutions; e.g. incipient pressure-group activity by military or industrial managers

of a form of private-ownership economy instead of shifting to a state-owned/collectivised economy as the communists had done in the Soviet Union (*ibid.*: 10).

In fact Friedrich and Brzezinski, unlike Arendt, went on to address the awkward issue of whether the differences between communist and fascist regimes outweigh the totalitarian similarities (*ibid.*: 7–8, 10–11, 68, 57, 77). They argued that communist and fascist totalitarian regimes are basically alike but by no means wholly alike, and they pointed to differences in origins, political institutions and proclaimed goals. In a later discussion of totalitarian ideology's link to international revolutionary appeals (and to the leader's ambitions for world rule), they again pointed to the difference between communism's supposedly global, class-based appeal and fascism's appeal to a particular people. Yet despite these significant differences, Friedrich and Brzezinski maintained that communist and fascist regimes were sufficiently similar to be classed together as totalitarian dictatorships and to be distinguished from older types of autocracy, none of which had displayed the totalitarian six-feature syndrome.

Like Arendt, these two later theorists viewed totalitarianism as an extreme, ideologically driven and terror-ridden form of dictatorship (Friedrich and Brzezinski, 1961: 130–2, 150, 137). The regime's ideology is the ultimate source of the goals that the totalitarians seek to attain through a political, social, cultural and economic revolution. Totalitarianism is in fact an actual system of revolution, requiring a state of 'permanent revolution' that will extend for generations and applies to even such prosaic matters as fulfilling economic Five-Year Plans.

The use of terror is stimulated not only by the ideology's extensive revolutionary goals, but also by its supposed infallibility. The totalitarians' commitment to their ideology's infallibility produces a 'violent passion for unanimity'; after the destruction of the regime's obvious enemies, the terroristic police turn their attention to the rest of society and even to the totalitarian party itself – 'searching everywhere for actual or potential deviants from the totalitarian unity' (*ibid.*: 132, 137, 150).

But Friedrich and Brzezinski took a less extreme view than Arendt of totalitarian terror. They pointed to 'islands of separateness', such as the churches and universities, where a person could remain aloof from the terror-accompanied 'total demand for total identification' (*ibid.*: 231, 239). And they argued that the level of police-inflicted terror may eventually decline as terror is internalised into a habitual conformity and new generations of society are raised as fully indoctrinated supporters of the regime (*ibid.*: 138).

In fact the regime relies on its 'highly effective' propaganda/ indoctrination system as well as terror to instil a totalitarian atmosphere in society (*ibid.*: 107, 116–17). The propaganda/ indoctrination system uses not only mass communications, notably radio and newspapers, but also face-to-face communication by thousands of speakers and agitators deployed by the party and such mass-member organisations as the regime's youth and labour movements.

Like most other post-Arendt theorists of totalitarianism, Friedrich and Brzezinski did not examine the origins of totalitarian regimes. However, they identified mass democracy as among the 'antecedent and concomitant conditions' for totalitarianism, argued that totalitarian movements and ideologies are 'perverted descendants' of democratic parties and their party platforms, and emphasised the significance of modern technology for totalitarianism – pointing out that four of the syndrome's six traits have a technological dimension (*ibid.*: 6–7, 11, 13).

Their description of the structure of totalitarian regimes was wide-ranging and showed some obvious similarities with Arendt's analysis. In particular, Friedrich and Brzezinski considered the totalitarian absolutist leader to be a unique feature of the regime's structure

1. possessing 'more nearly absolute power than any previous type of political leader';
2. embodying a unique form of leadership that involves a pseudo-religious or 'pseudo-charismatic' emotionalism and a mythical/ mystical identification of leader and led;
3. subordinating the regime's political party to a wholly dependent status so that it is more the leader's following than an organisation in its own right (*ibid.*: 25–6, 29).

However, they also acknowledged that the extensive role allotted to the party in a communist regime was a significant structural difference between communist and fascist totalitarianism (*ibid.*: 273–4, 279–81, 32, 34–6). They described how the communist movements carried out a markedly more extensive politicisation of the military than the fascist movements sought to do, and pointed to a similar contrast between fascist and communist parties' relationships with their regime's (civilian) state apparatus. In fascist regimes the party was allotted a relatively limited administrative role and was no more than equal in power to the state. In contrast, in communist regimes the party bureaucracy plays a vital role in the state-owned/controlled economic system, and in the post-Stalin Soviet Union it had become a super-bureaucracy, penetrating and controlling the state's administrative apparatus.

Friedrich and Brzezinski had more to say than Arendt on the issue of whether a totalitarian regime continues to evolve after it has established totalitarianism (*ibid.*: 6, 151, 50–7). (However, they had the benefit of observing the changes that had occurred in the Soviet Union after Stalin's death in 1953, too late for Arendt to consider in her book.) They contended that the communist Soviet Union had passed through phases of totalitarian development which had never had time to emerge in the short-lived Nazi and Fascist totalitarian regimes.

These later evolutionary phases or stages had seemed to produce a more moderate version of totalitarianism, with a decline in terror and an end to absolutist individual rule. As was mentioned earlier, Friedrich and Brzezinski argued that the level of police-inflicted terror might eventually decline (as it had in the Soviet Union after Stalin's death), and in their discussion of the post-leader succession problem they acknowledged that after Stalin's death the highest-ranking officials of the Communist Party had established a collective form of leadership. They argued that it was likely such collective leadership would eventually be replaced by a return to rule by an individual, personal leader. But, as the years passed without the rise of a new Stalin (and as the Stalinist terror became a distant memory), the next generation of theorists of totalitarianism had to take a more flexible approach to the issue of regime evolution and made some significant modifications to the classical conception of totalitarianism.

Second-Generation Theories of Totalitarianism

The differences between the two classic theories of totalitarianism were only a foretaste of the different interpretations and definitions that the term 'totalitarian' soon acquired. With nearly a dozen theorists having coined their own definitions, with researchers having applied it to more than a dozen pre-twentieth century regimes, and with politicians employing it in anti-communist polemics, it is not surprising that some scholars believed that such a loosely used term should be avoided or abandoned (Barber, 1969; Rigby, 1972). However, others sought instead to build upon the contribution made by the two classic works of Arendt and Friedrich and Brzezinski. They offered second-generation theories of totalitarianism that could accommodate the criticisms and changing circumstances that were undermining the standing of the classic conception of totalitarianism.

Schapiro's (1972) book *Totalitarianism* is an accomplished example of such second-generation theorising (see Table 1.1). He espoused an Arendt-like view of totalitarianism as being a form of personalised rule by a leader, aided by a subordinate elite and ideology, who seeks to dominate – in fact to totally control – state, society and individual (1972: 102, 119). But Schapiro also adopted a similar approach to Friedrich and Brzezinski's six-point syndrome by identifying totalitarianism's five characteristic features or 'contours', and three distinctive instruments of rule or 'pillars' (see Table 1.2). Together, his two lists covered similar territory to the six-point syndrome but with the significant addition of mobilisation (see Exhibit 1.1) as a characteristic feature, and the significant omission of the terroristic police as a distinctive instrument of rule (*ibid.*: 20, 45, 119, 38).

Like other second-generation theorists of totalitarianism, Schapiro had to take into account the criticisms that had been directed at the concept. He tackled a key criticism head-on by presenting and responding to Curtis's argument that the concept of totalitarianism was no longer applicable to the Soviet Union, nor automatically applicable to the now diverse range of regimes to be found among the other communist countries (Schapiro, 1972: 107; Curtis, 1969). In fact political scientists dissatisfied with theories of totalitarianism had developed a host of new concepts or models of contemporary communist systems: the administered society, the command society, the organisational or mono-organisational society, the ideological system, the monist system, the mobilisation system, and, most fruitfully, the bureaucratic system; they had also begun to apply to

TABLE 1.2

Characteristic features of totalitarianism and authoritarianism

Totalitarianism: classic theorists, Friedrich and Brzezinski	*Totalitarianism:* second generation theorist, Schapiro	*Authoritarianism:* classic theorist, Linz
Six-point syndrome	'Contours'	1. Limited political
1. Ideology	1. The Leader	pluralism
2. Single party typically led by an individual	2. Subjugation of the legal order	2. Distinctive mentalities instead
3. Terroristic police	3. Control over	of elaborate and
4. Communications monopoly	private morality	guiding ideology
5. Weapons monopoly	4. Continuous mobilisation	3. Absence of intensive/extensive
6. Centrally-directed economy	5. Legitimacy based on mass support	mobilisation
		4. Leader or (occasionally) small
	'Pillars'	group of leaders
	1. Ideology	exercise power
	2. Party	within predictable
	3. Administrative machinery of the state	limits

communist systems the factional-conflict and interest-group approaches originally developed as models of Western or democratic politics (Hough and Fainsod, 1979: 523–4; Hough, 1977: 49–51).

In response, Schapiro argued that while there had been changes in the Soviet Union and other communist regimes, these developments did not mean that the concept of totalitarianism was outmoded. He acknowledged that the Soviet Union no longer suffered from a totalitarian leader and terror, and had seen a decline in ideological commitment, the emergence of dissenters, and some signs of pluralism in the form of such interests as the military establishment and the industrial managers emerging as 'incipient' pressure groups (1972: 109, 112–13, 115). But he contended that the essence of totalitarian rule still persisted, namely an ever-present total control over the individual (*ibid.*: p. 117).

As for the diversity to be seen among communist regimes, he argued that so long as these regimes shared certain fundamental and distinctive features they can be classed together as

Exhibit 1.1 Mobilising the Masses

Although no longer much used, the term (political) 'mobilisation' was quite commonly used by political scientists in the 1960s–70s and was included in some theories of totalitarianism and authoritarianism. The concept was originally a military term meaning the preparation of an army for war by calling up the reserves and moving forces to the front line. As later recast into a political term it would mean dictatorships' attempts 'to activate their peoples in support of official norms and goals', and it was used in this sense by fascist and communist regimes themselves long before the notion of mobilisation entered the theoretical vocabulary of political science (Unger, 1974: 5).

In the Soviet Union the emphasis was on economic attitudes and behaviour, especially the labour productivity and discipline needed to meet the production targets of the economic Five-Year Plans (*ibid.*: 266, 126). As will be seen in Chapter 7 mobilisation of the public in support of economic goals was taken even further by some other communist regimes, notably North Korea, and it was experimented with by a few African one-party states of the 1960s. In fact, the one-party states in Guinea, Mali and Ghana were included along with communist regimes as examples of 'mobilisation systems' in a leading 1960s work on the politics of modernisation, and the concept was briefly adopted by some analysts of communist politics (Apter, 1965; Rigby, 1972). Mobilising regimes also employed their official parties and mass-member organisations to mobilise the public in support of non-economic goals, such as community health and/or birth-control programmes, self-proclaimed cultural revolutions, or instilling the official ideology in the hearts and minds of the public.

The minimal and most common form of political mobilisation, though, is simply the activation of the public to express support for the regime itself. For example, the Cuban communist regime's ability to draw a crowd of over a million people to political gatherings in Revolution Square has been based on a highly organised mobilisation of the public at neighbourhood and workplace level by the local Committees for the Defence of the Revolution and by the official trade union movement (Aguirre, 1989: 389–90). To what extent this support-expressing behaviour reflects a positive attitude to the regime is always difficult to judge against the coercive/repressive background of a non-democratic regime (as research into the defunct Nazi case has confirmed) (Unger, 1974: 102–3; Allen, 1984, chs 17, 19). Such political 'participation' is very different from that 'mobilised' by parties and interest groups in a democratic system.

totalitarian despite their diversity in other respects (*ibid.*: 112). Moreover, in typical second-generation fashion he gave the concept more flexibility by suggesting that totalitarianism actually varies in intensity and totality, and that even when one or more characteristic features is weak or absent, the totalitarian nature of a regime is still clearly discernible (*ibid.*: 124).

Outmoded or Unfashionable?

Despite the efforts of the second-generation theorists, the notion of totalitarianism never regained its earlier prominence. In the 1970s most analysts of their contemporary communist regimes continued to prefer one of the newer models or approaches, notably the bureaucratic politics model, or to develop new approaches focused on the policy-making issue, such as Hough's notion of institutional (or institutionalised) pluralism (Hough, 1977, ch. 2; Hough and Fainsod, 1979: 547–8). By the 1980s it was also becoming increasingly clear that even such classic examples of totalitarianism as Nazi Germany had in reality fallen well short of the totalitarian 'ideal'. Historical research into Hitler's Germany and Stalin's Soviet Union was revealing that (a) control over society and individual, especially over 'hearts and minds', had been far from total, and (b) the leader had exercised far from total political control over his subordinates and the regime's institutions/organisations (Allen, 1984; Kershaw, 1983; Broszat, 1981; Getty, 1985). In fact, decades earlier some historical research had already suggested that there had been surprisingly weak 'totalitarian' control over behaviour, let alone attitudes, particularly in the rural areas of Hitler's Germany and Stalin's Soviet Union (Peterson, 1969; Fainsod, 1958). And this dawning awareness in the 1960s that even such horrific regimes as Hitler's and Stalin's had fallen short of the classic conception of totalitarianism may explain why there was so little enthusiasm for applying the concept to some of the new Third World dictatorships, particularly the rash of African one-party states that had emerged in the 1960s.

Schapiro did classify the short-lived African one-party state developed by Kwame Nkrumah in Ghana as a case of weak/failed totalitarianism (1972: 124). He argued that before its fall to military coup in 1966, Nkrumah's regime had been moving down the road to totalitarianism but that Nkrumah had failed to establish party control over the state or to arouse a more than play-acting public enthusiasm for the official ideology and leader cult (*ibid*.: 122). By categorising Nkrumah's regime as a form of totalitarian dictatorship – however weak and short-lived – Schapiro was reaffirming that the concept was not outmoded and was also implicitly offering a solution to the problem of how to categorise those African one-party states, notably Touré's mass-mobilising regime in Guinea, which seemed to display characteristic features of totalitarianism (Rivière, 1977). Yet he did not develop this approach in any depth or with much enthusiasm. Nor would many other theorists, or many writers on Africa, show any interest in applying the concept of totalitarianism to African or other Third World, non-communist dictatorships.

Even political biases or expediency did not lead to the concept being extended to Third World regimes. In her controversial article calling for US foreign policy to take into account the distinction between traditional/authoritarian and revolutionary/totalitarian autocracies, Kirkpatrick (1979) did mention the (self-proclaimed Marxist-Leninist) regime in Angola and the revolutionary regime in Nicaragua among her examples of actual or potential revolutionary/totalitarian regimes. But her other examples were the typically communist cases of Cuba, China, North Korea and Vietnam, and the controversy aroused by the article revealed the lack of enthusiasm for applying the concept of totalitarianism to contemporary regimes. Furthermore, neither Qadhafi's regime in the 1980s nor Saddam Hussein's regime in the 1990s were denounced as 'totalitarian' by their Western critics, even though some US politicians and officials were prepared to go to extreme lengths to express their disapproval. Saddam Hussein may have been compared to Hitler, but his regime was not labelled as totalitarian despite its showing such characteristic features as an absolutist party leader and the extensive use of terror.

Authoritarianism

While theories of totalitarianism may seem to cover too rare a form of modern non-democratic government, theories of authoritarianism face quite the opposite problem. The term 'authoritarian' is so widely applicable that it is difficult to develop a theory which can cover so many diverse cases without becoming either banal or incoherent. In a general sense the term 'authoritarian' could be said to describe a situation where (a) freedom is restricted in favour of obedience to authority, and (b) this authority is itself exercised with few restrictions (Schapiro, 1972: 39).

However, the notion of 'authoritarian government' is often used as virtually a synonym for 'non-democratic government'. It is more widely applicable than the notion of dictatorship, which at least is not applied to monarchies and traditional forms of government. In fact the possible inclusion of tribal chiefs, priest-kings, and medieval monarchs as examples of authoritarian government has led some theorists of authoritarianism to redefine the term to specifically exclude such premodern forms of non-democratic government or regime. Some of these definitions of authoritarianism have also excluded totalitarianism, on the grounds that it is too extreme or distinctive a form of non-democratic government to be included in the same category with the more normal forms. Yet even when using these narrower definitions, theorists have been plagued by the problem of how to cover what is still a very diverse range of non-democratic regimes and forms of government. Even the classic works have either not been sufficiently coherent and systematic, or not been sufficiently broad and applicable.

Linz on Authoritarianism

Linz's pioneering 1964 analysis of authoritarianism, 'An Authoritarian Regime: Spain', excluded totalitarianism as well as traditional monarchies and other traditional systems from his conception of authoritarianism (Linz, 1970 [1964]: 269–70). But he rejected any notion that authoritarian regimes form only a residual category, such as the class of (modern) regimes that are neither democratic nor totalitarian. Instead, Linz stressed the distinctive nature of the authoritarian type of regime and presented a broad and multifaceted coverage of authoritarianism that was comparable to the theories of totalitarianism (see Table 1.3). However, the signs of strain that are evident in this descriptive theory (and in his definition of authoritarianism) are evidence of how difficult it is to incorporate so many varieties of non-democratic government into a single theory of authoritarianism.

The prominence that Linz gave to military dictatorships in his description of authoritarianism highlighted the distinction between authoritarian and totalitarian regimes. Both the classic works on totalitarianism had noted that the military played a relatively minor role in a totalitarian dictatorship (Arendt, 1962: 420; Friedrich and Brzezinski, 1961: 273); in contrast, Linz pointed out that the military enjoys a 'privileged position' in most authoritarian regimes and that its position is likely to be further enhanced if the regime had been established by a military coup (1970: 267).

By also including party dictatorships within his conception of authoritarianism Linz provided a solution to the problem of how to classify less-than-totalitarian and post-totalitarian party regimes. The number of Third World party dictatorships (particularly the many one-party states created in Africa in the 1960s) which it had seemed inappropriate to classify as totalitarian could be classed as authoritarian, as could the many communist regimes that had passed through and beyond their (most) totalitarian phase. For Linz suggested that totalitarian regimes might appear more like some authoritarian regimes 'if their ideological impetus is weakened, apathy and privatization replace mobilisation, and bureaucracies and managers gain increasing independence from the party' (*ibid.*: 281).

But it is difficult to provide a concise and coherent definition of authoritarianism that covers both the military and party types of dictatorship and yet still distinguishes authoritarianism from totalitarianism. Linz's definition pointed to four distinctive elements or features that define an authoritarian regime. Although they can be listed in similar form to totalitarian theorists' six-point syndrome or eight contours/pillars (as in Table 1.2), Linz's four defining elements or features of authoritarianism require some accompanying explanation:

1. Presence of 'limited, not responsible, political pluralism' (1970: 255–6). Linz viewed this *limited* political pluralism as the most distinctive feature of authoritarianism. The limits may be (a) severe or moderate, (b) legal or *de facto*, and (c) applied only to parties and political groups or to interest groups as well. But the crucial point is that there are groups which

TABLE 1.3

Theories of authoritarianism

Theorist	Examples	Origins	Goals	Structure	Evolution
Linz (1964)	Military regimes and non-totalitarian party dictatorships	1. Lack of 'popular consensus' under a democratic government, or actual organised political strife or even aborted revolution, *or* 2. Lack of political mobilisation of the masses by previous regime – e.g. by traditional monarchy, oligarchic democracy or colonial rulers	1. Political demobilisation or depoliticisation, *or* 2. Socially progressive or conservative policies that require some mass mobilisation	1. Regimes without a party, *or* 2. Regimes with a party in both cases: (i) Individual leader or occasionally small group of rulers (collective leadership) (ii) Military usually has 'privileged position'	Long-term: decline of any leader's charisma; civilianisation of any military rule; decline in level of any political mobilisation present in early stages of regime but only rarely evolution into democratic regime

| O'Donnell (1978) on Bureaucratic Authoritarianism (as distinct from traditional and populist types of authoritarianism) | Argentinian, Brazilian, Greek and Spanish military regimes of 1960s and early 1970s | Coup coalition of military and civilian technocrats confident they can solve economic and other social problems (see goals) | 1. Solve economic problem: shift *from* import-substituting/consumer-goods industrialisation *to* more 'intensive' industrialisation involving production of capital goods → socially 'painful' economic policies requiring political exclusion and deactivation of popular sector
2. solve political-social problem of polarisation between popular sector and propertied sector → political exclusion/deactivation
3. solve political problem of 'mass praetorianism' → political exclusion/deactivation | 'Bureaucratic' in sense of key role played by public bureaucracies (military, etc.) and private bureaucracies – but 'inconsequential' whether military govern | Long-term tendency towards political isolation of coup/ruling coalition and possible problems in attaining goals → split in coalition over whether to withdraw from power – but any withdrawal leaves resulting democracy plagued by pre-coup problems |

are independent of the regime and have some political influence. At one extreme is General Franco's absolutist regime in Spain allowing independence and influence to the Catholic Church; at the other extreme is the officially liberal-democratic party dictatorship in Mexico actually encouraging some degree of political participation by a limited number of independently existing parties and groups.

2. *Absence* of 'elaborate and guiding ideology' and instead 'distinctive mentalities' (*ibid.*: 255–8). Mentalities are apparently more emotional than rational and are not as future-oriented as the utopianism of ideologies. But Linz acknowledged that ideologies were by no means unknown among authoritarian regimes (though more commonly found among party than military dictatorships), and that in fact an ideology may be loudly proclaimed by an authoritarian regime.

3. *Absence* of intensive or extensive 'political mobilization' throughout most of a regime's history (*ibid.*: 255, 259). Political mobilisation is the exception rather than the rule in the case of authoritarian dictatorships. The exception occurs in the early stages of some authoritarian regimes during which there may be considerable and even very intensive (controlled) popular participation.

4. A 'leader (or occasionally a small group) exercises power within formally ill-defined limits but actually quite predictable ones' (*ibid.*: 255). Even when the regime's leader or leaders may seem to be absolutist, in practice this power is exercised within predictable limits rather than in a wholly discretionary or arbitrary fashion. Linz refers to the military junta as an example of occasions where power is exercised by a small group of leaders, and presumably another example would be the party political committee, such as the Communist Party Politburo.

That all four of these features are either quite complex or have significant exceptions is an indication of the problems involved in generalising about authoritarian regimes. However, Linz attempted to make his conception of authoritarianism more systematic by classifying the exceptions to the absence-of-mobilisation feature as a separate subtype. He described these mobilising exceptions as 'populistic' regimes, whose level of mobilisation falls short of 'the pervasiveness and intensity of the totalitarian model', but is still quite exceptional when compared to the lack of political mobilisation usually found in authoritarian regimes (*ibid.*: 260). These populistic regimes therefore form what is probably best described as the *higher-*mobilisation subtype; the more usual examples of authoritarianism form their own subtype, comprising the low-mobilisation regimes.

It appears at first glance that this distinction between subtypes also involves an important distinction in political structure – the absence or presence of an official party. For, as the low-mobilisation subtype is described by Linz as including regimes *without* parties, the higher-mobilisation subtype presumably comprises authoritarian regimes that do have an official party (*ibid.*). (The without-party/with-party distinction does not distinguish between military and party dictatorships; there have been many cases where a military regime has had an official party.) However, some with-party regimes clearly belong in the low-mobilisation subtype. And Linz suggested that some of the more 'populistic', mobilising one-party states in Africa might eventually experience a decline in the degree of political mobilisation – with their parties being transformed into patronage rather than mobilising organisations (*ibid.*). In fact he viewed such depoliticisation as characteristic of any 'stabilized' authoritarian regime, with or without a party (*ibid.*: 259–60).

His wide-ranging account of regime evolution was more impressive than his typology of authoritarian regimes (*ibid.*: 269, 271–2, 280–1). As well as the decline in levels of mobilisation, he identified several other trends in the long-term evolution of an authoritarian regime, including the decline of any charisma initially possessed by a leader; the institutionalising of the exercise of power through the development of general rules; and the civilianisation of the military dictatorships. Yet, while an authoritarian regime might therefore undergo some considerable changes over the long term, Linz noted that only rarely had such a regime evolved into a stable democracy.

Linz also provided a wide-ranging, if somewhat complex, account of the origins of authoritarian regimes (*ibid.*: 260–1, 267). The lack of popular consensus which he considered to be a precondition seems to occur in two very different situations: either

1. there has been a period of abortive revolutions, organised political strife, or simply lack of consensus (under a democratic government); or
2. the preceding regime has not politically mobilised the masses, as when the preceding regime has been a colonial administration, a traditional monarchy or an oligarchic democracy.

These situations in turn create two very different forms of opportunity for authoritarianism:

1. an authoritarian depoliticisation of society that is 'one way to reduce the tension in the society and achieve a minimum of re-integration' (*ibid.*: 261);
2. the masses are initially easy to manipulate by a (populistic) authoritarian regime because they have not previously been won over by any organised movement.

Similarly, Linz identified two alternative and very different types of goals that have been pursued by authoritarian regimes (*ibid.*: 261–4). Many of them have sought an actual demobilisation or depoliticisation of society and, consciously or unconsciously, have encouraged a process that Linz termed 'privatization', in the sense of citizens shifting their attention from public affairs to private matters. In contrast, other authoritarian regimes have sought instead to implement socially progressive or conservative policies that require a degree of mass mobilisation if they are to be efficiently or effectively implemented.

As with the relationship between regime structure and subtype, there seems to be no consistent connection between origins and goals – a particular type of goal is not associated with a particular type of origin. It is true that in many cases an authoritarian regime that has originated in a period of political or social strife has also had the goal of depoliticising or demobilising its society. However, Linz's case study of authoritarianism – Franco's military-party regime in Spain – originated from the intense social and military strife of the Spanish Civil War, but initially sought to attain fascist-style social goals that required high levels of mobilisation.

In the light of these anomalies and complexities, it is not surprising that Linz did not attempt to present his theory more systematically – such as by presenting it in the form of two alternative subtypes of authoritarianism that differ from each other in origins, goals and structure. But the lack of a systematic and coherent framework may also explain why his multifaceted theory of authoritarianism has been much less widely used than his more concise (and seemingly straightforward) four-feature definition of authoritarianism.

O'Donnell's Bureaucratic Authoritarianism

O'Donnell's 1973 classic work, *Modernization and Bureaucratic Authoritarianism: Studies in South American Politics*, used Linz's definition of authoritarianism as the basis for a more narrowly focused theory that was aimed at a particular variety of authoritarian regime, which he labelled 'bureaucratic authoritarianism' (see Table 1.3). O'Donnell viewed authoritarianism (as defined by Linz) as being the genus to which belonged three species of authoritarianism – the traditional, the populist and the bureaucratic types (O'Donnell, 1979 [1973]: 91, 91 n. 76).

O'Donnell's typology also differed from Linz's in being linked to levels of modernisation rather than mobilisation (*ibid.*: 108–9). The traditional type of authoritarianism is associated with a *low* level of modernisation, as in his example of Stroessner's regime in Paraguay (see Chapter 6), but he specifically excludes any traditional monarchy or other traditional forms of government. The populist type of authoritarianism, such as Perón's regime in Argentina (see Chapter 9), is associated with *medium* levels of modernisation. It seems somewhat similar to Linz's higher-mobilisation subtype, for the leaders of populist-authoritarian regimes attempt to politically activate and 'incorporate' – under tight control – segments of the 'popular sector', namely the working class and sections of the lower-middle class.

O'Donnell was primarily concerned with the *high*-modernisation type of authoritarianism – the 'bureaucratic' type (*ibid.*: 90). As he implies, this type is somewhat similar to Linz's depoliticising, low-mobilisation subtype because the bureaucratic type seeks to politically exclude and deactivate the popular sector. The description 'bureaucratic' is not exactly self-explanatory but had been borrowed from Janos's recent analysis of non-democratic government in Eastern Europe in the 1930s. Janos had argued that in Yugoslavia, Hungary, Romania and Poland an 'administrative-military complex' of civil service and military (together with some middle-class camp followers) had formed a dominant political class which he labelled 'bureaucratic' (Janos, 1970: 205).

Although the military component of O'Donnell's bureaucratic type seems particularly strong, this is largely because he used the military regimes established in Argentina and Brazil in the 1960s as his case studies or primary examples of bureaucratic authoritarianism. He specified that the presence or absence of military government was irrelevant typologically, and therefore bureaucratic authoritarianism can presumably also occur under a party dictatorship (O'Donnell, 1979: 108).

As for the description 'bureaucratic', O'Donnell argued that the term suggested the typical features of the high-modernisation type of authoritarianism. These included not only the key role played by large public bureaucracies (military and civil service) and private bureaucracies (business corporations), but also the role played by technocrats, the organisational strength of many social sectors, and the government's attempts to control social sectors by 'encapsulation' – by encapsulating their political representation into government-dependent interest groups and/or political parties (*ibid.*: 91, 51). This encapsulation is in turn linked to the government's attempt to politically exclude and deactivate the popular sector. The government may (a) eliminate the sector's organisational bases so that 'it can no longer make genuine political demands', and/or (b) eliminate the electoral arena by allowing 'only government-sponsored parties to participate' or by simply suppressing all electoral activities (*ibid.*: 51–2, 52 n. 1).

Therefore O'Donnell had linked his high-modernisation subtype to a particular structure, the bureaucratic, and to a particular goal, that of political exclusion and deactivation. But the depth as well as multifaceted nature of his account of bureaucratic authoritarianism is most evident in his explanation of how political exclusion and deactivation is only an intermediate goal – a means to an end – that has to be attained in order to achieve a wider and much more ambitious goal. For the bureaucratic authoritarian regime's ultimate goal is to solve major economic and political-social problems which had played a vital role in the origins of the regime.

The underlying problem was economic in nature and likely to be found in only highly modernised economies. Essentially the problem was that the country had exhausted the possibilities offered by the relatively easy, import-substituting/consumer-goods stage of industrial growth and was therefore suffering from a lack of economic growth, high inflation and foreign-exchange problems (*ibid.*: 57–64). To shift to a more 'intensive' form of industrialisation ('the vertical integration of domestic industry for the production of a wide range of raw, intermediate, and capital goods') would require 'quite painful' economic policies which could not be implemented unless there was a reduction in the popular sector's demands for consumer goods and for participation in political power (*ibid.*: 59–60, 63, 67–9). The political exclusion and deactivation of the popular sector was the obvious authoritarian solution to this preliminary, political aspect of the economic problem.

It was also the obvious authoritarian solution, even if only a temporary or stop-gap solution, to the two political-social problems facing the country. The popular sector's demands for consumer goods and political power had led to a social, class-conflict 'polarization' between the propertied sectors and the popular sector – a polarisation which had been intensified by the recent example of social revolution in Cuba (*ibid.*: 69). The second political-social problem was a situation described by some political scientists as 'mass praetorianism' (see also Chapter 2 and Exhibit 2.1), in which a society's political institutions are unable to cope with political participation by the urban lower class (*ibid.*: 73).

The bureaucratic-authoritarian regime is established by a 'coup coalition' of officers and civilians that intends to make and implement policies which will effectively deal with these problems (*ibid.*: 74, 81–5). The coup coalition tends to be dominated by technocratic officers and civilians who share not only a common jargon and approach, but also a common self-confidence in their capabilities, believing that 'their combined expertise can ensure effective problem-solving throughout a broad range of social problems' (*ibid.*: 83).

O'Donnell also examined in some detail the evolution of these technocrats' bureaucratic-authoritarian regimes (*ibid.*: 85, 105). Apparently the coup coalition can count on at least the acquiescence of many sectors of society when it stages a coup and when it carries out its initial policy of political exclusion and deactivation. But this now ruling coalition (a) will become more isolated as it moves on to implement policies with high

social and economic costs, and (b) may be only partly successful in implementing its exclusionary and economic policies.
Such difficulties and failures will lead to a split within the ruling
coalition over the issue of whether to press on or whether to
withdraw from power and return the country to democracy.
However, even if there is a withdrawal from power, the resulting democracy will be plagued by the pre-coup problems which
bureaucratic-authoritarian government failed to solve.

With his coverage of evolution, origins, goals and structure,
O'Donnell had presented a multifaceted account of bureaucratic authoritarianism that was more coherent and systematic
than Linz's general theory of authoritarianism. O'Donnell's
theory was much more closely linked to the regime's characteristic
feature – a high level of modernisation – and it also provided
a much deeper and coherent account of the regime's origins.
Therefore, it is not surprising that 'bureaucratic authoritarianism' soon became one of the most widely known concepts in
political science and one of the most widely used by analysts
of South American non-democratic government.

On the other hand, any theory focused on only one type of
authoritarianism could be expected to be more detailed and
coherent than an attempt to cover authoritarianism in general. Moreover, by providing such a specific, detailed coverage
of the bureaucratic-authoritarian regime's origins and goals,
O'Donnell markedly reduced the applicability of his theory of
high-modernisation authoritarianism.

In fact the number of authoritarian regimes which meet the
origins/goals criteria for bureaucratic authoritarianism may be
as few as Arendt's examples of totalitarianism. O'Donnell's two
examples from outside South America, the Spanish and Greek
military regimes, do not seem to have been responding to this
particular set of economic and political problems. The 1930s
regimes in Eastern Europe from which the notion of 'bureaucratic' regimes was first derived had not yet reached a high
level of modernisation (Janos, 1970). And none of the new
high-modernisation dictatorships that emerged in South America
in the 1970s seem to have followed the same path as O'Donnell's
two examples.

Although the notion of bureaucratic authoritarianism was the
point of departure for a survey of the new authoritarianism in
Latin America (Collier, 1979), not all of the contributors to

the book wholly accepted the bureaucratic-authoritarian 'model', particularly its economic aspect. Doubts were raised about the link between bureaucratic-authoritarian policies and the high modernisation stage of economic development, and it was stressed that there was no 'objective' economic need for high-modernisation countries to adopt these political and economic policies. One contributor pointed out that such countries as Venezuela and Colombia had internationalised their production without the need for bureaucratic authoritarianism, and he contended that the economic successes of even O'Donnell's Brazilian example had not required an authoritarian government (Sera, 1979). Another contributor (Kaufman, 1979) pointed to the Mexican case as evidence that some countries had achieved comparable economic successes to O'Donnell's Brazilian and Argentinian examples without the need for bureaucratic authoritarianism. Kaufman also pointed to significant differences in economic policies among high-modernisation authoritarian regimes, and suggested that the common feature of such regimes' economic programmes was actually export diversification, not vertically integrated intensification or 'deepening' of industrialisation.

During the 1980s and into the 1990s, the bureaucratic-authoritarian 'model' faced a growing body of work criticising or discounting it. For example, it was shown to be seriously inapplicable to cases of personalist rule, such as General Pinochet's high-modernisation authoritarian regime in Chile (Remmer, 1989). And its analysis of high-modernisation economic problems and goals continued to be discounted. For example, an analysis of the economic policies of the high-modernisation authoritarian regimes established in Argentina, Chile and Uruguay in the 1970s argued that they had implemented a 'neoconservative' programme of economic restructuring which was monetarist, efficiency-oriented, and free-market – sharing 'few features, if any, with the bureaucratic-authoritarian economic model' (Schamis, 1991: 209–10).

Yet, the notion of bureaucratic authoritarianism was not deemed by conventional wisdom to be an outmoded concept, even though its two model examples were defunct and no equivalents ever emerged in South America or elsewhere, and the term 'bureaucratic authoritarianism' remained a convenient label to attach to high-modernisation dictatorships. For example, although Im (1987) acknowledged that the Park regime of 1970s South

Korea had a different economic, social and political background from the O'Donnell examples, this did not prevent him from labelling the regime as a case of bureaucratic authoritarianism. Therefore the notion of bureaucratic authoritarianism made an important contribution to the continuing prominence of the concept of authoritarianism, as reflected also in such works as Perlmutter's analysis of modern authoritarianism.

Perlmutter on Authoritarianism

Perlmutter's (1981) work, *Modern Authoritarianism: A Comparative Institutional Analysis,* differed markedly from Linz's approach. Perlmutter did not exclude premodern forms of non-democratic government from his definition of 'authoritarianism', preferring instead to draw a distinction between modern and older forms by pointing out that the older regimes had seen rule by the few in the name of the few, but that the modern regimes have instead seen rule by the few in the name of the many (*ibid.*: 2). Perlmutter also differed from Linz (and reflected the increasing disillusionment with the notion of totalitarianism) by including the classic cases of totalitarianism, Nazi Germany and the Soviet Union, among his examples of modern authoritarianism.

More importantly, Perlmutter emphasised the institutional-structural aspect of authoritarian regimes, arguing that this was the most useful way of explaining their political behaviour and dynamics (*ibid.*: 62–3). His structural analysis is not based, though, on the distinction between party and military regimes, but rather on the ways in which regimes employ particular structures or institutions as instruments for intervention, penetration and supervision. These instruments are:

1. 'the single authoritarian party';
2. 'the bureaucratic-military complex', which means basically the civil service and the military; and
3. 'the parallel and auxiliary structures of domination, mobilization, and control', such as political police, paramilitary forces, and militant youth movements (*ibid.*: 9, 11, 13).

Each of his many types or models of authoritarianism (such as the Bolshevik Communist, Nazi, Fascist, Corporatist and Praetorian models) apparently shows a distinctive or characteristic preference for one of these three institutional-structural instruments. For example, one type or model may dispense 'with the use of the single party and employ the military as the instrument of domination', while another may make 'extensive use of the political police, an auxiliary instrument, at the expense of the single party and the military' (*ibid.*: 9).

Perlmutter had therefore rectified a serious weakness in Linz's and O'Donnell's approaches to authoritarianism – the lack of attention paid to structural features. It is true that he did not provide an alternative theory of authoritarianism: his analysis lacked sufficient coverage of origins and goals to be properly compared with Linz's and O'Donnell's theories, however flawed and problematic they may have been. But his less ambitious approach seems the only way in which the study of authoritarianism can adequately and coherently cover the various types of regime that have governed their societies in an authoritarian fashion.

2

Types of Non-Democratic Regime

In this chapter attention will shift to less ambitious approaches to analysing non-democratic government. They focus on a particular type of modern non-democratic regime – military, party or personalist – rather than dealing with the wider topic of the form of government. As was pointed out in the previous chapter, theorists of non-democratic forms of government are primarily concerned with the question of how dictatorships rule, while analysts of particular types of non-democratic regime instead focus on the narrower question of who or what rules – the military, a party or a personal leader. And these approaches are also often less ambitious in the sense of presenting only a typology, an analytic framework for classifying types and subtypes of regime, rather than presenting a descriptive theory comparable to those of totalitarianism and authoritarianism.

However, the two classic works on the party type of non-democratic regime, Tucker's and Huntington's, were exceptions that in addition to providing a typology, covered a similar range of topics to theories of totalitarianism and authoritarianism. Moreover, both Tucker and Huntington envisaged their respectively 'single-party' and 'one-party' types of non-democratic regime as including not only cases of party rule, but also cases of military rule accompanied by an official party (which are actually cases of military rather than party dictatorship). In contrast, analysts of the military type of non-democratic regime have more strictly applied the traditional criterion of 'who rules?', and

36

have included only cases of military rule – of the military's or a military man's dictatorship.

But military rule has taken diverse forms that are sometimes far from straightforward. As an examination of Finer's classic structural typology of military regimes will show, military rule can take indirect and civilianised forms that are difficult to identify and/or to categorise. The many other typologies of military dictatorship have tended to be at least as concerned with the roles or goals of military regimes as with their varying structures, as will be seen in the case of Perlmutter's, Nordlinger's and Huntington's classic typologies of what they term 'praetorianism'.

Finally, any survey of types of modern non-democratic regime has to include the personalist type, with its personal rule by an individual leader rather than by his party or military. Personal rule has occurred in many modern dictatorships and is not confined to any particular variety, whether party or military, totalitarian or authoritarian, rightist or leftist. The presence of personal rule is usually viewed as being only a secondary or supplementary feature of a regime, not as a basis for classifying it as a personalist type of non-democratic regime. However, personalist types/typologies have been developed by Linz and by Jackson and Rosberg. Moreover, the two personalist elements of Weber's venerable typology of legitimate rule, charisma and patrimonialism, have been used to categorise as well as analyse some non-democratic regimes.

The Party Type of Non-Democratic Regime

Tucker's 'Movement-Regimes'

In his 1961 paper 'Towards a Comparative Politics of Movement-Regimes', Tucker provided a 'user-friendly' typology of single-party regimes that was based on the familiar, commonly used categories of communist, fascist and nationalist (see Figure 2.1). He argued that the concept of totalitarianism needed to be supplemented by a wider category that would take into account the resemblances that communism and fascism shared with the 'large and still growing number of revolutionary nationalist regimes under single party auspices' (1961: 283). He identified Kemalist Turkey, Nationalist China, Bourguiba's Tunisia, Nasser's

FIGURE 2.1
Tucker's and Huntington's typologies of single-party or one-party regimes

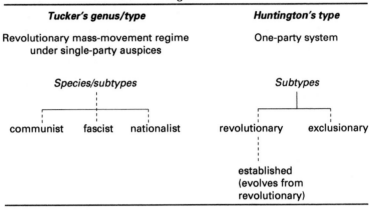

Egypt, and Nkrumah's Ghana as a few of the many examples of single-party nationalist regimes. (As can be seen from his inclusion of the Turkish and Egyptian military regimes, Tucker was not concerned with whether the single party actually ruled or was only a subordinate part of the regime.)

The nationalist 'single-party systems' were authoritarian rather than totalitarian, but they displayed sufficient similarities with communist and fascist regimes for Tucker to argue that the nationalist, communist and fascist regimes should be viewed as three species of the same political genus – which he labelled the 'revolutionary mass-movement regime under single-party auspices' or, more concisely and confusingly, the 'movement-regime' (*ibid.*). Moreover, Tucker provided a multifaceted exposition of this typology, describing the movement-regime's structure, goals and evolution as well as subtypes.

The single-party aspect of the movement-regime is a key component of the regime's structure (*ibid.*: 284–5, 288). Not only does the regime operate under single-party auspices, but the party also controls the mass movement that mobilises popular participation in support of the regime and revolution – and therefore provides the regime with a claim to be democratic. He depicted the party as governing the country and dominating the regime, but later acknowledged that the party had a much weaker position in the two fascist regimes. In fact he labelled

them 'fuehrerist' (leaderist) regimes because they were dominated by an autocratic/absolutist leader rather than by a party.

The revolutionary goals of a movement-regime are to be found
in its ideology (*ibid.*: 283–4). The ideology contains the phi-
losophy, programme and political orientation of the movement
and its revolution, and after coming to power the movement
attempts to maintain its regime's revolutionary momentum. Even
a nationalist revolutionary movement seeks not only national
independence as a sovereign state, but also the modernisation
of this new nation-state. Such a goal 'typically involves many
elements of an internal social revolution' as old social relations and activities are 'assailed in an internal revolution of
national renewal' (*ibid.*: 286).

The presence of revolutionary goals does not mean that these
regimes necessarily had revolutionary origins. For example,
Nkrumah's movement came to power in Ghana through an
electoral rather than revolutionary form of decolonisation, during
which he won several elections and held the equivalent of a
prime-ministerial post under British rule. His was only one of
many African nationalist single-party regimes that originated
in the 1950s–60s through electoral rather than revolutionary
means. However, Tucker did not explore the issue of how revolutionary regimes could originate in a non-revolutionary fashion.
In fact he was dubious about any attempts to account for why
and how such regimes originated, contending that the movement-regime was a 'political phenomenon to which no nation
and no part of the world is immune' (*ibid.*).

However, Tucker did make some innovative points about the
evolution of movement-regimes. He suggested that a movement-
regime could undergo a transformation, a 'metamorphosis', from
one species/type into another (*ibid.*: 289). His example was the
rise of Stalinism in the Soviet Union in 1928–38, which involved
the metamorphosis of an originally communist movement-regime
into a fuehrerist (fascist) type of movement-regime.

More importantly (and convincingly), he argued that movement-
regimes which have lost their revolutionary momentum should
be classed as 'extinct' movement-regimes (*ibid.*: 286–7). Although
they may continue in power long after they have lost their revolutionary purpose, they will no longer be revolutionary regimes.
It is not clear whether the revolutionarily 'extinct' movement-
regime constitutes a new species/type, or even a whole new

genus, of movement-regime, but some years after Tucker's work Huntington presented a more comprehensive typology/theory of party regimes that emphasised regime evolution and clearly specified that the fully evolved regime belonged to a new subtype.

Huntington's Typology of One-Party Systems

Huntington's typology appeared in his contribution to an edited work (Huntington and Moore, 1970) *Authoritarian Politics in Modern Society: The Dynamics of Established One-Party Systems* (see Figure 2.1). He defined a one-party system as a political system in which there was only one effective party – any other parties that might exist having 'little effect on the course of events' (1970: 5). Like Tucker, he did not exclude cases where the party was attached to a military regime, as in Franco's Spain and Ataturk's Turkey. But his three subtypes described below were much less familiar than Tucker's communist, fascist and nationalist species/types of movement-regime.

- *The revolutionary one-party system.* Of the Huntington typology's three subtypes, this is the most familiar, and apparently encompasses totalitarianism and Tucker's movement-regimes. It has the suitably revolutionary and extreme goal of seeking to liquidate or rapidly assimilate the politically subordinate section of its divided society (*ibid.*: 15). Huntington describes this social division as a 'bifurcation' in the sense of society being split into two sections on the basis of differences in class, race, religion or some other such category. The revolutionary type of one-party system includes the communist regimes, for they are seeking to eradicate class bifurcation by the elimination of the capitalist classes and the conversion of their former members into workers, peasants or intelligentsia. Huntington also categorised Nazi Germany as a revolutionary system, as the genocidal Nazi regime was seeking to eliminate the Jewish ethnic group rather than just exclude it from politics (*ibid.*: 17).

  The African and other Third World one-party states apparently fall into the revolutionary category, but Huntington noted that the African systems were seeking to emphasise national unity and minimise sources of social conflict, such as the differences between modernised elite and traditional masses (*ibid.*: 14). Although he argued that this approach was a reason why the African examples were 'weak' one-party systems, their emphasis on national unity did not affect their revolutionary credentials – as apparently the modernised elite was seeking to eradicate bifurcation by rapidly assimilating the traditional masses.

• *The exclusionary one-party system.* This second subtype is less familiar but, as was seen in Chapter 1, theories of authoritarianism have been very concerned with the issue of political exclusion or demobilisation. In Huntington's typology of one-party systems, the exclusionary type was described as seeking to suppress or restrict the political activity of the politically subordinate section of its divided (bifurcated) society (*ibid.*: 15). Although this type is much rarer than the revolutionary, Huntington mentioned a number of cases of exclusionary one-party system: Liberia, South Africa, the South of the United States, Northern Ireland, Kemalist Turkey, Kuomintang China, and Taiwan. The exclusionary systems are more moderate than the revolutionary in other respects than just preferring suppression/restriction rather than liquidation/assimilation, and Huntington contended that it was inappropriate to apply the notions of totalitarianism or movement-regime to them. He also suggested that an exclusionary system will in the long term adopt one (or more?) of the following strategies: retreat into isolation from the world community, rein in economic and social change, become more repressive, or evolve into a form of competitive party system (*ibid.*: 18–23).

• *The established one-party system.* Huntington's third subtype differed fundamentally from the other two in being only an evolved form of revolutionary one-party system and in lacking any obvious social or political goal.

The evolved, established one-party system is a complex regime that has several characteristic features (*ibid.*: 23, 40–1). It is not faced with the issue of a divided, bifurcated society (which has been dealt with by the preceding, revolutionary one-party system), and it has a more administrative than revolutionary character. There has been a decline in party-mobilised popular participation and in the importance of ideology in shaping goals and policy decisions. Political leadership tends to have lost its personalist, charismatic and autocratic quality and to have become oligarchical and bureaucratic. The party elite is no longer an initiator of policy but rather a mediator of policy initiatives coming from technocratic and managerial elites. The party as an organisation has become the regulator of a now pluralist political and social structure containing important interest groups. Huntington used the uniquely liberal and decentralised version of communism developed in Yugoslavia as his example of this type, but other communist regimes had also journeyed far along the evolutionary path to an established type of one-party system. He provided an extensive analysis of how a revolutionary one-party system evolved into an established one-party system, and gave a detailed description of the three phases in this evolutionary process – transformation, consolidation and adaptation (*ibid.*: 24–38).

Huntington's extensive coverage of regime evolution was the main part of a multifaceted account of one-party systems which was comparable in breadth and depth to the descriptive theories of totalitarianism and authoritarianism. He had provided a brief coverage of regime goals when he had described the revolutionary and exclusionary types' different approaches to dealing with social divisions. And he also provided innovative analyses of both the origins and structure of the revolutionary and exclusionary types.

The social origins of these one-party systems are closely linked to their goals, and are to be found in bifurcation between 'social-economic groups' or between 'racial, religious or ethnic' social forces (*ibid.*: 11). Moreover, it is crucial that these social bifurcations be 'pronounced' and 'intense', as only 'sharp' bifurcation will provide the basis for a viable one-party system (*ibid.*: 11–12). Huntington pointed to tropical Africa as an example of how this sharp bifurcation is unlikely to arise at an early stage of modernisation, and he concluded that, therefore, any one-party system created in tropical Africa was likely 'to be weak and fragile' (*ibid.*: 12). As several African one-party systems had already fallen victim to military coups, he had some justification for questioning their viability and suggesting that they were likely to be fragile.

Like Tucker, Huntington overemphasised the revolutionary origins of party regimes, contending that 'the largest number of one-party systems are produced by social revolutions' (*ibid.*). But most one-party systems had *not* been the product of social revolutions; most Third World one-party systems been the product of peaceful decolonisation or military coup, and the majority of communist one-party systems had been established with the assistance of the Soviet Union or through a war of liberation against foreign (fascist or colonial) occupation.

However, Huntington argued that the strength of a one-party system was affected by the intensity and duration of the struggle to acquire power. In many African cases 'the party came to power easily, without a major struggle' (that is, through a peaceful process of decolonising elections), and therefore the party 'withered in power' (*ibid.*: 14). As for Soviet-assisted cases of communist one-party systems, Huntington explained that these (seemingly easily established) party regimes had consolidated their power by intensifying class struggle in the initial, transformation phase of the regime.

In his analysis of the structure of one-party systems Huntington distinguished strong from weak systems by considering two questions relating to the role of the party (*ibid.*: 6–7). First, to what extent does the party monopolise (1) legitimation, (2) recruitment of leaders, and (3) policy-making and interest-aggregation? Even in a strong one-party system the party never completely monopolises these three functions, and in a weak system the party may be relegated to only a minor role. Second, there was the question of whether other political actors, apart from the party, may play a significant and perhaps dominant role in the one-party system. Huntington identified five other, non-party types of political actor:

1. personalistic, including a charismatic leader;
2. traditional, such as the church or monarchy (and presumably the tribe or ethnic group);
3. bureaucratic, such as the civil service, police and military;
4. parliamentary; and
5. functional socioeconomic, such as the working class, the peasantry, managers and intellectuals.

In weak one-party systems one or more of these actors eclipse the party's role. In other cases there may be a balance of power between the party and other actors. And in strong one-party systems the party plays the dominant role.

Brooker on Ideological One-Party States

After Tucker's and Huntington's classic theories and typologies there was a familiar tendency for later analysts to be less ambitious in their approach. For example, Brooker's (1995) work on ideological one-party states was content to emphasise the distinction between the 'party-state' and 'military-party' subtypes, and to examine from a new perspective the role played by the official party in these two types of one-party state.

He examined not only the extent to which the party performed the governing role of making policy and supervising its implementation, but also the extent to which the party performed political (electoral) and social (indoctrinating) roles. Moreover, he analysed in some depth the one-party or single-party nature of these regimes. The regime party's monopoly was seen as being

(a) either a legal or a *de facto* monopoly in 'literal' one-party states, or
(b) an effective monopoly in 'substantive' one-party states, in which other parties are allowed to exist but not to compete (successfully) with the official party.

But there was still no move to define the party type of non-democratic regime as including only specifically *party* dictatorships/regimes and excluding any military-party regimes.

The Military Type of Non-Democratic Regime

Finer on Military Regimes

The many analysts who have presented typologies of the military type of non-democratic regime have left little doubt that they were analysing specifically military dictatorships, as their typologies have tended to focus on the form or structure of military rule and its role or goal (see Table 2.1).

The tendency was evident even in such early works as Finer's 1962 *The Man on Horseback: The Role of the Military in Politics*, whose classic typology identified five different forms of military rule and regime: two direct, two indirect and one dual (1976 [1962]: 149–51, 245–6). The more standard of the two forms

TABLE 2.1

Typologies of military dictatorship

Finer Structural forms of military rule	*Perlmutter Goals/roles and structure*	*Nordlinger Goals/roles and structure*	*Huntington Goals/roles*
1. Indirect-limited 2. Indirect-complete 3. Dual 4. Direct 5. Direct: quasi-civilianised	1. Arbitrator 2. Ruler 3. Party-army (evolves from ruler)	1. Moderator (limited goals, indirect rule) 2. Guardian (limited goals, direct rule) 3. Ruler (ambitious goals, extensive rule)	1. Oligarchical (shift to radical) praetorian society with radical/reformer military 2. Middle-class radical praetorian society with arbiter/stabiliser military 3. Mass praetorian society with guardian/vetoer military

of direct rule involves openly military rule by a military junta or by a military government, with leading military officers installed as the country's president and/or government ministers. The 'quasi-civilianised' form of direct military rule differs by clothing itself in (supposed) evidence of civilian support, and/or in civilian garb and institutions (*ibid.*: 163). Its civilian features may even include a supportive political party, but all the regime's civilian institutions are only 'civilian trappings, emanating from and dependent on the military' (*ibid.*: 159). In contrast, the civilian component of the 'dual' type of military regime – a political party or some other organised civilian support – has been developed by a military dictator as reliable 'civilian forces' that can act as 'a counterpoise to the views and the influence of the army' (*ibid.*: 150, 158). As the head of both the military and this civilian organisation he can strengthen his personal position by establishing a balance of power between the dual, military and civilian bases of the regime.

Finer's typology also emphasised how military rule can take the indirect form of controlling a civilian government from behind the scenes (*ibid.*: 151–7). He identified two types of indirect military rule and regime:

1. the 'indirect-limited' type sees the military exerting control over the government only intermittently and to secure only limited objectives;
2. the 'indirect-complete' type sees the military continuously control all the activities of the civilian government.

In 1981 Finer returned to the issue of categorising military regimes and added some new features to his classic typology (1988: 255–72). Now he focused on the question of the extent to which the military 'as such' takes on a governing or policy-making role in a military regime. Here he seems to have been drawing the distinction between (a) rule by the military as an organisation, and (b) rule by military men operating as free agents or personal rulers. Surveying the whole field of then-existing military regimes, he looked in each case for the presence of a military junta and/or cabinet, as he assumed that this feature was an indication of rule by the military 'as such' – at least to the extent that supreme executive power is wielded by military men 'who in some sense or other command and/or represent the armed forces' (1988: 255). He noted that such regimes could be considered as belonging to the 'direct' or the 'direct: quasi-civilianised' categories of his long-established typology.

However, Finer did not suggest how to categorise the many regimes that lacked a military junta/cabinet but were ruled by a military president. He viewed them as possibly cases of the military (as such) playing only a supportive rather than a policy-making role – supporting personal-presidential government by a military man. As a number of these regimes have an official party, they seem quite similar to Finer's long-established 'dual' type. But he clearly created a new category of regime when he referred to the military playing a supportive and vital role in 'military-supportive' civilian regimes, which arise when a civilian government has to rely on active military support for its survival but is in no way a puppet of the military.

In his 1962 work, Finer had also made a pioneering distinction relating to the ruling military's role rather than structure.

He pointed to two quite different ways in which the ruling military may conceive of its duty of custodianship of the national interest:

1. as arbitrating or vetoing of civilian political affairs that threaten the national interest, or
2. as requiring 'overt rulership of the nation and the establishment of a more or less complete political programme under their [the military's] authority' (1976: 31).

Perlmutter on Military Regimes

A very similar distinction, between arbitrator and ruler types of ruling or 'praetorian' army, was made by Perlmutter (1974) and later included in his wide-ranging (1977) work on professional, praetorian and revolutionary armies, *The Military and Politics in Modern Times.* The main characteristics of Perlmutter's 'arbitrator' type are: '(1) acceptance of the existing social order; (2) willingness to return to the barracks after disputes are settled; (3) no independent political organization and a lack of desire to maximize army rule' (1977: 104–5). His 'ruler' type's main characteristics are: '(1) rejects the existing order and challenges its legitimacy; (2) lacks confidence in civilian rule and has no expectation of returning to the barracks; (3) has a political organization and tends to maximize army rule' (*ibid.*: 107–8). It has two subtypes that are again defined by the military's role or goal: the (radical or reforming) antitraditionalist subtype and the conservative antiradical subtype.

Perlmutter also identified and described another type of military regime – the 'party-army' regime – that would have to be added to his arbitrator/ruler typology (*ibid.*: 145–7). The obvious structural characteristic of this type is the presence of a political party, whether created or taken over by the military. (A ruler-type regime, too, may have a party, but may instead have a highly political kind of junta, such as a Revolutionary Command Council.) And in fact the party-army type differs from the other two – arbitrator and ruler – in being defined according to its structure rather than its goals. Evolving from a ruler-type regime, it sees a politically neutralised military return to the barracks and leave the regime in the hands of a military leader who has an official party at his disposal (in a situation reminiscent of Finer's dual-type regime).

Nordlinger on Military Regimes

Nordlinger's (1977) *Soldiers in Politics: Military Coups and Govern-ments* appeared in the same year as Perlmutter's work and presented a typology of 'praetorianism' that contained yet another example of the ruler(ship) category. In Nordlinger's typology the military's power reaches its greatest extent in this 'ruler' type of regime. Here the military 'not only control the govern-ment but dominate the regime, sometimes attempting to control large slices of political, economic and social life through the creation of mobilization structures' (1977: 24). This extensive control over state and society arises from the need to make far-reaching changes in order to attain the ruler type's ambi-tious political/economic goals. As these ambitious goals also require the military to stay in power for an indefinite period, Nordlinger's version of the ruler type of military regime seems very like Perlmutter's. However, Nordlinger also included the important point that ruler-type regimes were relatively rare – constituting 'roughly 10 percent of all cases of military inter-vention' (*ibid.*: 26).

Nordlinger's typology of praetorianism – the ruler, guardian and moderator types – was unusually systematic. His types were defined by a combination of two variables: (a) the extent of a regime's political/economic objectives or goals, and (b) the extent of the governmental power wielded by the military (*ibid.*: 22–6). The ruler type is distinguished from the other two types both by its more ambitious goals and by the extensiveness of the power wielded by the military. The other two types have quite limited goals, but the moderator type is distinguished from the guardian type by its preference for indirect rather than direct rule.

Although the goals of the guardian and moderator types were of an arbitrating/vetoing nature, they seem more reminiscent of Huntington's classic analysis of praetorian regimes than of Finer's work (see below and Table 2.1). The guardian type bears a marked resemblance to Huntington's conception of the ve-toing, guardian role performed by the military in a 'mass praetorian' situation, and of the arbiter/stabilising role per-formed by the military in a 'middle-class radical praetorian' situation.

Huntington on Military Regimes

Huntington's (1968) classic work on *Political Order in Changing Societies* included what has become the most famous account of the roles performed by military regimes. However, the book's theory and typology of 'praetorianism' actually referred to praetorian societies rather than regimes (see Exhibit 2.1). The three different types of praetorian society are each associated with a particular level of political participation: the oligarchical type is associated with a low level of political participation, the middle-class radical type with a medium level, and the mass type with a high level of participation (*ibid.*: 80). And in each type of praetorian society the military performs a distinctive and 'typical' role.

The oligarchical type of praetorian society is the oldest and least complex, predominating in nineteenth century Latin America and being common in the Middle East in the mid-twentieth century (*ibid.*: 199–201). It is associated with a low, traditional level of political participation that is limited largely to the dominant social forces – the big landowners, and the leading figures in the clergy and the military. The dominant political figure may well be a military man, but he is usually a highly personalist leader who is not the leader of the military as an institution – in fact the military lacks any autonomous existence.

However, the military plays an autonomous and also vital role in the shift from the oligarchical to the middle-class radical type of praetorian society, which arises from a 'breakthrough' or 'reform' coup by (usually) middle-ranking officers (*ibid.*: 201–5, 222, 214, 209). The officers who overthrow the oligarchical regime normally come to power with a programme of reforms aimed at achieving national integration and development, social and economic reform, and some extension of political participation. As it is the middle classes who benefit from the extension of participation, the middle-ranking officers leading the coup are depicted by Huntington as being the vanguard of the middle class, spearheading its 'breakthrough' into the political arena. (Huntington used a wide interpretation of middle-class that included union-organised industrial workers.) By the mid-twentieth century most praetorian societies in Asia, Africa and Latin America were of the middle-class radical type.

Exhibit 2.1   The Praetorian Society

The term 'praetorian' is derived from the historically famous Praetorian Guard units of the ancient Roman army, who exploited their position as guardians of the Emperor and capital city to put their favoured candidates on the Imperial throne. By analogy, the term 'praetorianism' has long been applied by political scientists to a situation of chronic military intervention in politics, or of the military exercising independent political power (Nordlinger, 1977: 2–3; Perlmutter, 1977: 90–3).

But in 1968 Huntington gave the term a much wider meaning by using it to describe a type of society or polity in which the military are only one of the groups resorting to such direct action as staging coups; where military intervention is only one particular manifestation of a general politicisation of social forces, groups and institutions (1968: 194–6). He argued that societies with a politicised military also have a politicised clergy and civil service and politicised universities, trade unions and business corporations. The political scene is plagued by a variety of forms of direct action as each social group uses its distinctive means of exerting direct political pressure: businesses bribe, workers strike, students riot and the military stage coups. It was presumably because military coups are 'more dramatic and effective' than other groups' means of direct action that Huntington felt justified in labelling ('for the sake of brevity') such societies as 'praetorian' (*ibid.*: 195–6).

Huntington also argued that modernising societies tend to be praetorian because their political institutions are too weak to handle the increasing levels of political participation that accompany modernisation (*ibid.*: 79–80). A praetorian society lacks 'effective' political institutions that are 'capable of mediating, refining, and moderating group political action' (*ibid.*: 196). And, if political institutions are to be effective, they must keep pace with increases in the level of political participation, which in turn increases as a society is modernised – from a low level of participation in traditional society to medium levels in transitional societies and, finally, to high levels in modern societies. Similarly, the failure of political institutions produces a different type of praetorian society according to the level of participation: oligarchical (low), middle-class radical (medium), and mass (high).

The military play a prominent but largely reactive, 'arbitral or stabilizing' role within a well-established middle-class radical praetorian society (*ibid.*: 216–18, 222). Military intervention is usually in response to escalating social conflict between other groups and 'serves to halt the rapid mobilization of social forces into politics and into the streets' (*ibid.*: 216). The military is the only social group or force that can take over the role of the increasingly ineffective government; only the military has some capacity to govern and to restore order – at least temporarily – by producing a rapid political demobilisation.

After the shift from the radical to the *mass* type of praetorian society the military's role still tends to be reactive and politically demobilising. But now it plays a 'guardian' role on behalf of the middle class, employing a 'veto' coup to protect the middle class's dominant position against the now politically participating lower classes (*ibid.*: 222–3). Mass praetorianism sees an extension of political participation to include the lower classes – such as urban unorganised labourers living in slums and shanty/squatter settlements – but the military seeks 'to block the lower classes from scaling the heights of political power' (*ibid.*: 222).

However, Huntington's depiction of the three types of praetorian society (and the political roles of the military) has not proved to be widely applicable. His account is clearly based on the experience of Latin America, and he himself recognised that other regions of the world have had a very different political history (*ibid.*: 199–200). For example, he acknowledged that the military-led breakthrough to radical praetorianism may involve the overthrow of a traditional monarchy (as in the Middle East) rather than the replacing of oligarchical praetorianism.

He also acknowledged that there were major differences between the Latin American and African situations (*ibid.*). The much more recent timing of decolonisation in Africa and the less stratified structure of society meant that African countries had not experienced oligarchical praetorianism. More importantly, in Africa it was civilian nationalists, not the military, who had led the middle-class's breakthrough to political participation (during the process of decolonisation). When the middle-ranking military officers took power in Africa, they were removing middle-class nationalist governments that Huntington could accuse only of lacking legitimacy and authority, not of failing to cope with escalating social conflict. Yet, despite its various failings and flaws, Huntington's concept and depiction of praetorianism remains one of the most striking and famous contributions to the study of military rule.

The Personalist Type of Non-Democratic Regime

Weber's Typology

The most influential typology of personalist rule has long been the historical-sociological analysis of types of legitimate rule that Weber had developed not long before his death in 1920. None of Weber's three types – the traditional, the charismatic and the legal-rational – was labelled 'personal' or 'personalist', but his typology was very concerned with the personalist aspect of rule. He pointed to how the *im*personal nature of the legal-rational type of legitimate rule contrasted with the personalist nature of the other two types. In the case of the patrimonial subtype of traditional legitimacy, 'obedience is owed to the person of the chief' or monarch, and in the case of charismatic legitimacy the leader is 'obeyed by virtue of personal trust in him' (Weber, 1964 [1922]: 328). Moreover, so many later analysts and researchers have applied these parts of Weber's typology to personalist dictatorships that his notions of 'charismatic' and 'patrimonial' rule have become two of the best-known terms used in the study of non-democratic regimes.

Weber viewed charisma as 'a certain quality of an individual personality by virtue of which he is set apart from ordinary men and treated as endowed with supernatural, superhuman, or at least specifically exceptional powers and qualities' (*ibid.*: 358). The charismatic type of rule is therefore highly personal (*ibid.*: 358–60, 364). A charismatic leader, such as a religious prophet or a heroic warrior, is the recipient of a wholly personal devotion from those who recognise his charismatic quality and mission, and after his death his successors have to 'routinise' this charismatic rule into the traditional or legal-rational type. (Even during his own lifetime the charismatic leader must continually provide proof, by means of miraculous successes, that he retains his charismatic quality; if success should for long desert him, then so will his followers.) Although Weber did

FIGURE 2.2
Weber's typology of legitimate rule (with modern adaptations)

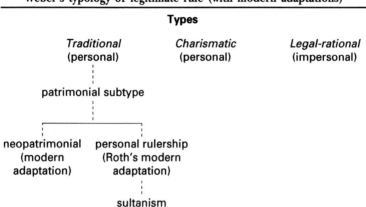

not envisage the rise of charismatic dictators, he confirmed
that charisma can appear within a modern political context,
mentioning demagogic intellectuals and charismatic party leaders.
Ideological 'prophets' and political 'heroes' are therefore perhaps
modern political equivalents of religious prophets and heroic
warrior leaders.

However, these are problems in applying the concept of charismatic legitimacy to modern dictatorships, despite the number
of cases where a dictator has been claimed by his propagan-
dists to possess exceptional personal qualities as political hero,
ideological prophet and so forth. This 'personality cult', as communist detractors of Stalin termed the glorification of a regime's
personal leader, has arisen in many party dictatorships and even
a few military regimes. But judging the extent to which the
claim has been *recognised* by the mass of purported 'followers'
is virtually impossible. For recognition of a claim to charisma
is a voluntary, internal acceptance which is impossible to judge
accurately in a regime where public expressions of personal
devotion to the leader are required on pain of dismissal, arrest,
torture, imprisonment and even death. There are cases where
the credibility of the claims and the apparent spontaneity of
seemingly unfeigned displays of devotion can lead outsiders to
confirm that charismatic legitimacy exists. But these judgements,

such as in the case of Egyptian leader Nasser's charisma, are still likely to be controversial and problematic (Dekmejian, 1971 and 1976; Bowie, 1976).

Weber viewed *patrimonialism* as only a subtype of the traditional type of legitimate rule. The two other subtypes, patriarchialism and gerontocracy, involve rule (by patriarch or elders) 'on behalf of the group as a whole' (Weber, 1964: 346). In contrast, the patrimonial chief rules over 'subjects' rather than fellow-members of the group – he exercises 'personal authority, which he appropriates in the same way as he would any ordinary object of possession' (*ibid.*: 347). Tradition limits as well as legitimates the use of these personally appropriated public powers, but the patrimonial ruler is allowed a degree or sphere of arbitrariness that in some societies reaches an absolutist extreme which Weber terms 'Sultanism' (*ibid.*).

Modern Applications of the Concept of Patrimonialism

Tradition and patrimonialism   Weber's classification of patrimonialism as a type of traditional rule has complicated attempts to apply the concept to modern regimes. For example, at the close of his study of West African one-party states, Zolberg (1966) argued that they approximated Weber's patrimonial type in some important respects, but questioned whether it was possible to speak of first-generation regimes being based on traditional legitimacy. He therefore loosened and expanded the concept of traditional legitimacy to mean a legitimacy based either on the notion 'this is how things have always been', or on what he termed a 'past-orientation' – such as the official party's past glories (*ibid.*: 143–5).

Patrimonial 'personal rule'   Instead of revamping the notion of traditional legitimacy, Roth (1968) separated the notion of patrimonialism from that of traditional legitimacy and emphasised the personalist aspect of patrimonialism. This 'detraditionalized, personalized patrimonialism' was (somewhat confusingly) labelled 'personal rulership' and was said to be based on personal loyalties 'linked to material incentives and rewards' (1968: 195–6). But Roth still referred to Weber's archaic term 'sultanism' when describing the 'highly centralized variant of personal governance' that allows the ruler 'maximum discretion' (*ibid.*: 203). The influence of Weber was also evident when Roth contended that the concept of (patrimonial) personal rule was best applied to the new states of the Third World – some of which 'may not be states at all but merely private governments of those powerful enough to rule' (*ibid.*: 198, 196).

A virtual typology of Roth's concept of (patrimonial) personal rule was later developed by Linz (1975) to categorise some non-democratic regimes that seemed quite distinct from totalitarian and authoritarian regimes (*ibid.*: 253, 259–64). Adopting Roth's notion that personal rule is based on personal loyalty linked to material rewards, Linz identified four different systems of personal rule: modern sultanism, oligarchic democracy, *caudillismo* (rule by military chieftains), and *caciquismo* (rule by local political bosses). Modern sultanism was the most obviously personalist of these four types of personal rule, and Linz's conception of modern sultanism could be used to describe a type of personalist dictatorship that did not readily fit into other categories. For example, the dictatorship established by 'Papa Doc' Duvalier in Haiti in the late 1950s had been based upon neither the military nor a party but instead on a paramilitary/political organisation, the Volunteers for National Security or 'Tontons Macoutes' (bogey men), which provided him with a body of local political loyalists and terroristic political police (Ferguson, 1988).

Linz considered the modern sultanist system to be relatively rare and most likely to be found in small countries with largely agrarian economies and few urban centres, such as Duvalier's Haiti, Trujillo's Dominican Republic and other Central American countries (Linz, 1975: 253, 259–62). He followed Roth and Weber in viewing this sultanistic rule as the most centralised and most arbitrary or discretionary form of personal rule. Other important similarities with traditional patrimonialism are the private use of public power (as exemplified by corruption), and the personal nature of the ruler's staff – which tends to include his family, friends, cronies and even business associates.

Linz acknowledged that sultanist personal rule was based on the extensive use of fear as well as on personal loyalty linked to material rewards. The army and the police 'play a prominent role' in the sultanist regime, and 'men directly involved in the use of violence to sustain the regime' are members of the ruler's personal staff (*ibid.*: 260). But, unlike in totalitarian regimes, the use of terror is not ideologically motivated or justified, and the regime's lack of any ideological commitment is also evident in the lack of a mass party, the absence of mass mobilisation, and the ruler's enriching of himself, his family and other members of the ruling group (*ibid.*: 217, 260, 189, 262).

Neopatrimonialism and patrimonialism   The term 'neopatrimonial' (Eisenstadt, 1973) was to prove more popular than Roth's notion of 'personal rule' in drawing the distinction between traditional and modern patrimonialism. The concept of neopatrimonialism seemed particularly applicable to African states, and was further developed for this purpose in the 1980s and 1990s (Medard, 1982; Van de Walle, 1994), but it was also applied to such non-African regimes as Pinochet's military dictatorship in Chile (Remmer, 1989).

Other researchers preferred to apply the concept of traditional patrimonialism to a modern regime rather than use some concept of neopatrimonialism. For example, Crouch (1979) viewed the patrimonial features of Suharto's Indonesia in terms of the persistence or reemergence of traditional features dating back to the precolonial Javanese kingdoms. The common element in these various uses of the older or newer concept was that characteristic features of patrimonialism (recast in suitably modern form) were viewed as important features of a contemporary regime that was based upon modern organisations and, officially or publicly, upon modern bureaucratic and legal norms.

Other Conceptions of Personal Rule

Not all conceptions of personal rule have been derived from Weber's typology. Jackson and Rosberg's (1982a) *Personal Rule in Black Africa* was influenced by Weber but was based on the older distinction between government (a) by individuals, and (b) by laws and institutions (*ibid.*: 9–10). In their conception of personal rule, the absence of effective political institutions results in the predominance of a personal authority and power that is limited more by countervailing power than by institutions; personal rule is a system of personal relations centred on the ruler's relations with his associates, clients, supporters and rivals (*ibid.*: 12–19). Such personal rule is also 'inherently authoritarian' in its monopolising of power (denying political rights and opportunities to competitors), and it can arise in military as well as party regimes (*ibid.*: 23, 37–8).

Jackson and Rosberg's descriptive theory of African personal rule included a typology comprising the prophetic, the princely, the autocratic and the tyrannical types (*ibid.*: 77–81). Prophetic personal rulers are visionaries who place great emphasis upon ideology and seek to shape society to fit the principles and goals of the ideology – usually a form of African socialism. In contrast, the princely type of personal ruler tends to base his rule on patron–client relations and manipulation rather than ideology and to rule in alliance with other oligarchs. The autocratic type of personal ruler, though, tends not to share power with other leaders. His unlimited discretionary power is reminiscent of absolute monarchy and of Weber's notion of traditional sultanist patrimonial rule. The tyrannical type of personal ruler is similar to Linz's notion of modern sultanist personal rule, as the tyrannical personal ruler exercises a wholly arbitrary power that is based upon both instilling fear in his subjects and rewarding his collaborators, who are kept personally dependent upon him.

This typology could also be applied to many non-African regimes. Jackson and Rosberg noted that personal authoritarianism had existed in modern non-African states, such as Mussolini's Italy and Franco's Spain, and that 'marked features' of personal rule had been exhibited by Hitler's Germany and Tito's communist Yugoslavia (*ibid.*: 21). Moreover, the typology could also be applied in a supplementary fashion – to distinguish between different types of military or party dictatorship – and, used in this way, it highlights important differences between not only personal and non-personal but also different *types* of personal military or party dictatorship.

Assessing the *degree* of personal rule is another important way in which the concept can be used in analyses of party or military dictatorships. The existence of varying degrees of personal rule was implied in Jackson and Rosberg's reference to 'marked features' of personal rule being present in some non-African states. The existence of degrees of personal rule was more explicitly recognised in Brooker's description of the degeneration from 'organisational' (party or military) to personal dictatorship (1995: 9–10, 18). He suggested that in cases of highly personal rule, the initial principal–agent relationship between ruling organisation and regime leader may be actually reversed, with the organisation now only an agent of the personal ruler. Although this organisation–individual, principal–agent approach to personal rule lacked the depth and breadth of Jackson and Rosberg's theory, it enabled him to include an assessment of (the degree of) personal rule in his analysis of one-party states.

3

The Emergence of Military Dictatorships

The military dictatorship has been the most common form of dictatorship in modern times. Between the end of the Second World War and the onset of the 1970s–90s wave of democratisation, the military had 'intervened in approximately two-thirds of the more than one hundred non-Western states', and in the later 1970s 'controlled the government in about one-third of these countries' (Nordlinger, 1977: 6). It is not surprising, therefore, that many attempts have been made to explain or analyse why and how military dictatorships emerge. Yet the framework developed by Finer in the early 1960s still offers the most comprehensive approach to analysing the military intervention in politics which results in the emergence of military regimes.

Finer argued that the military's intervention in politics, such as when a military coup overthrows the civilian government, is best explained by examining both subjective and objective factors – what he termed the *disposition* and the *opportunity* to intervene in politics (1976 [1962]: 74). He presented the relationship between disposition and opportunity as a 'calculus of intervention'. This calculus does not resemble the differential or integral calculus of mathematics, but rather is a form of political calculation (in the sense of a 'calculating' politician) which may be very similar to the calculations of officers contemplating a military coup. The calculus of intervention is derived by combining the two variables, disposition and opportunity, to produce four possible combinations and four inferences about the likelihood and fate of military intervention. Finer's four inferences were:

1. no intervention because there is neither disposition nor opportunity;
2. intervention because there is both disposition and opportunity;
3. 'on the whole' no intervention because there is no disposition although there is an opportunity; and
4. unsuccessful intervention because although there is disposition, there is no opportunity (*ibid.*: 74–5).

The calculus of intervention can also be used to analyse past coups to determine why and how they were attempted and succeeded (or failed). It therefore offers a framework for analysing the emergence of past or present military regimes as well as for assessing the likelihood that a new military regime will emerge in any particular country.

A similar approach to Finer's was adopted many years later by Nordlinger, who based his analysis of military coups on the 'dual' question of 'why' and 'when' do the military intervene in politics (1977: 63–4). He differed from Finer in including only motives, not motives and mood, in the 'why' part of this dual question, but Finer's framework would lose little if its disposition aspect was simplified by excluding mood and concentrating on motives. Moreover, his calculus of intervention would then replicate the forensic formula for determining who committed a crime ('the accused had the motive and the opportunity to commit the crime') even if in the case of military intervention, the question or issue is not 'whodunit' but rather (1) what is the likelihood that a suspect *will* actually commit the crime, or (2) why and how was the crime committed?

The forensic analogy is striking and has such useful implications as highlighting the question of whether to include another element commonly added to the forensic formula – the question of what *means* were or will be employed to perpetrate the crime. As will be seen in a later section of the chapter, there is good reason to include a separate heading of 'means' to incorporate important features noted by Janowitz and by Finer himself. The resulting motive/means/opportunity framework

TABLE 3.1

The (Finer-based) calculus of military intervention/usurpation

Motive	Means	Opportunity
1. National interest 2. Corporate self-interest 3. Individual self-interest 4. Social (especially ethnic or class) self-interest	1. Coup method (seizure of power) 2. Coup-threat method (seizure of power)	1. Civilian government's lack of legitimacy (Finer and Nordlinger) 2. Civilian government dependent on military 3. Civilian government discredited – e.g. corruption, economic failings (O'Kane)
Inhibiting motives	*Capacity-reducing factors*	*Negative factors (reducing opportunity)*

1. Belief in civil supremacy (national interest?)
2. Fear of coup failure (corporate and individual self-interest)
3. Fear of politicisation of military (corporate self-interest)
4. Fear of repeat of past failures of military rule (corporate self-interest and national interest)
	Various factors weaken internal cohesion = factional instead of corporate coups and less credible coup threat (Janowitz)	1. Civilian government has legitimacy (Finer and Nordlinger)
		2. Obstacles (O'Kane)
		  (a) absence of previous coups
		  (b) newly independent state
		  (c) presence of foreign troops
		3. Operational obstacles (Decalo) e.g. elite or paramilitary units

for analysing military intervention provides a comprehensive check-list that takes all factors into account. Moreover, the framework readily allows two or more theories/explanations of intervention to be used in combination and in an integrated and coherent fashion. This feature also enables any detailed description of the framework and calculus to readily supplement and even replace Finer's ideas and examples with those of other theorists and researchers (see Table 3.1).

However, before beginning such a detailed exposition of this framework and calculus of intervention, it is best to narrow the focus to include only those forms of military intervention that lead to the emergence of clear-cut military dictatorships. For Finer defined military 'intervention' quite widely, as being 'the constrained substitution' of the military's policies *and/or* persons 'for those of the recognized civilian authorities' (*ibid.*: 20). And the constrained substitution of only the military's *policies*, not military persons, for those of the recognised civilian government may involve situations of indirect rule by the military from behind the scenes (see Chapter 2).

This is far from the popular image of military dictatorship as a uniformed General residing in the presidential palace and ruling by decree – in fact it does not fit any common conception of a military regime. The problem of how to categorise such less-than-military dictatorships will be discussed more fully at the end of the chapter. Until then, the problem will be avoided by narrowing the focus of the calculus of intervention and concentrating upon the form of intervention from which emerges (direct) rule by military men – the seizure of public offices and powers by the military.

Motive

Finer pointed out that the military, or rather the officer corps that leads it into politics as well as into battle, is affected by a variety and often a varying *mixture* of motives for seizing power (1976: 52). This is no different from the standard assumption that civilian politicians have 'a multiplicity of motivations (some altruistic, others crassly self-serving) in their quest for political power' (Decalo, 1990: 7). The principal types of motives that Finer identified were:

1. the self-proclaimed 'manifest destiny of the soldiers';
2. the national interest;
3. the sectional interest, which in turn includes class interest, particularist interests (regional, ethnic and religious), and corporate self-interest; and
4. individual self-interest (1976, ch. 4 and p. 230).

As he acknowledged, this is only a convenient check-list which can be reduced or expanded according to whether it is thought too elaborate and complicated or too economical and not sufficiently systematic. It can therefore be restructured and reduced to four main types of motive: national interest, corporate self-interest, social self-interest (notably class, ethnic or religious), and individual self-interest. These motives can be derived from four aspects of the officers' world-view – those of citizen, soldier, member of a social group, and individual.

The citizen's concern for the national interest is often depicted both inside and outside the military as being particularly evident within the officer corps. But, as was described earlier (see Chapter 2), Finer argued that the military's view of its political duties as custodian of the national interest may take the form of either an arbitrating/vetoing role or a more ambitious role as the ruler of the country and implementor of a sometimes comprehensive policy programme (*ibid.*: 31).

Moreover, the second, ruler type of military 'have no uniform notion of what constitutes the "national interest"' (*ibid.*: 33). For example, although the military are conventionally perceived as having a right-wing conception of the national interest, some ruler-type military regimes have displayed leftist tendencies. Several purportedly Marxist–Leninist military regimes arose in Africa in the 1960s–70s, such as in Ethiopia and Somalia, while the Burmese military regime pursued in 1962–88 a 'Burmese way to socialism' that was no less radical than the socialist practices of most Marxist–Leninist military regimes. Moreover, three other military regimes, Kemal Ataturk's in Turkey, Nasser's in Egypt and Velasco's in Peru, have been classified as examples of 'revolutions from above', which 'destroy the economic and political base of the aristocracy or upper class' by means of an alliance with a rising capitalist or landed class rather than by mobilising the working class and the peasantry (Trimberger, 1978: 3, 10).

The national interest is not the real or primary motivation of many coups, and is often used to disguise one or more self-interested motives. Individual self-interest may motivate not only the military's leaders, but also the officer corps collectively in the sense of a desire for better pay, easier promotion, and even opportunities for attractive jobs in civilian organisations (Finer, 1976: 50–1). But here the motive of individual self-interest begins to merge into that of *corporate self-interest*, as for example when new promotion or career opportunities are opened up by an expansion or technological development of the military that meets the professional aspirations of the officer corps.

The distinction between the corporate and the individual form of self-interest can be drawn in terms of the officers' professional role as soldiers as distinct from their personal aspirations as individuals (see Exhibit 3.1). The *self*-interestedness of the corporate motive may not be apparent to the officer corps because their concerns will be framed, even privately, in terms of national security or other national interests. Cuts in the military budget or a lack of (what are viewed by officers as) 'necessary' increases in military expenditure can readily be denounced in these national-interest terms, especially as the military has a remarkable ability to discern real or potential threats to the nation. Like other professions, military officers also have a corporate self-interested desire to protect professional autonomy and monopoly (*ibid.*: 41). But the crucial aspects of autonomy are the military's control over appointments and over disciplinary matters; decisions in these areas must conform to internal professional criteria and not be influenced by political or other extraneous factors.

Nordlinger went even further than Finer in emphasising the military's corporate interests, declaring that 'the great majority of coups are partly, primarily, or entirely motivated by the defense or enhancement of the military's corporate interests' (1977: 78). However, Thompson's research into coup-makers' grievances did not support this emphasis on the corporate-interest motive. As Thompson (1980) soon pointed out, he had identified corporate-interest grievances as being present (often along with other grievances) in less than half of the 1946–70 coups. He also noted that there was a lack of circumstantial evidence indicating a corporate-interest motive for military seizures of power; evidence was emerging that military governments actually did not seem to be more committed to the military's corporate welfare, in terms of size and expenditure, than were non-military governments!

In a later survey of 1970s research into this issue, Zuk and Thompson (1982) discovered that, although there had been at least 11 cases of cross-national research into the issue of whether there is a 'relationship between military governments and their

Exhibit 3.1 Old and New Military Professionalism

The distinguishing characteristic of the modern military officer corps is its professionalism, in the sense of being a profession such as medicine or law (Huntington, 1967 [1957]: 7, 10). Like any other profession, the military officer's has the characteristics of (1) expertise, (2) social responsibility, and (3) corporateness, in the sense of its members forming a corporate body distinct from 'laymen'. The military officer's professional expertise is the 'management of violence', specifically the 'direction, operation, and control of a human organization whose primary function is the application of violence' (*ibid.*: 11). The social responsibility of the officer's profession is the 'military security' of society, but in practice this responsibility is primarily owed to the state (*ibid.*: 15–16). Yet, although the officer is therefore the servant of the state, he or she is 'the servant only of the legitimately constituted authorities of the state', which in practice means those authorities whom the officers deem to have the legal right to command the military (*ibid.*: 77–8). Huntington also argued that with the professionalisation of the officer corps had come the opportunity for a new, 'objective' form of civilian control of the military, because professionalising the military renders it 'politically sterile and neutral' (*ibid.*: 84).

However, Stepan's theory (1973) of the 'new professionalism' argued that in some countries the officer corps had developed a new interpretation of its professional expertise and responsibility – focused on the internal rather than military security of society – that could motivate the military to intervene in politics for professional reasons. For by the late 1950s and early 1960s, some Third World armies were turning their attention to devising political as well as military strategies to prevent as well as combat the internal, revolutionary warfare which had proved so successful in China, Vietnam, Algeria and Cuba. In both Brazil and Peru, military officers 'politicised' by academic study of the political/social conditions conducive to revolutionary movements came to the conclusion that their civilian governments were unwilling or unable to implement the social and economic changes needed for national development and internal security. Therefore the military coups in Brazil in 1964 and Peru in 1968 were 'one of the logical consequences of the "new" professionalism' (Stepan, 1973: 48), even though the resulting military regimes differed markedly in the specific policies that they introduced to deal with their society's particular internal-security-threatening problems. (For a critique see Markoff and Baretta, 1985.)

military spending propensities', the results had been contradictory or inconclusive. Their own seemingly definitive
cross-national statistical study of the 1967–76 period 'found no
support for the hypothesis that military coups accelerate the
growth rate of military expenditures', but found 'some evidence'
that military takeovers *may* have played 'a minor role' in re-
tarding a decline in the proportional size of military budgets
that was occurring in all types of regime during these years
(1982: 71).

Nevertheless, the military clearly has strong corporate concerns that may overshadow its *social* self-interested motives for
seizing power. By social self-interest is meant the officers' concern for the interests of the particular social group to which
they belong – be it class, ethnic or religious. But the military's
highly corporate nature, socially as well as professionally, means
that the officers are likely to be more detached from their role
as members of a wider social group – from class, ethnic or
religious loyalties – than are any other professional group.

Therefore Finer contended that the class origins or status of
the officer corps are usually less important than the 'narrower
corporate interests' that arise from the 'selective induction,
professional training and social code, along with the organiza-
tional and often the social self-sufficiency of the military
establishment' (1976: 234). He argued that the seemingly class-
motivated anti-leftist coups that sprang up in Latin America in
the 1960s and early 1970s were at least partially prompted by
the officer corps's corporate fear for its own survival if there
were a communist takeover like that in Cuba (*ibid.*: 236–7).

But Finer acknowledged the importance of ethnic forms of
social self-interest. He introduced the new category of an ethnic
motive for coups in the 1976 edition of his work, and pointed
out that the Nigerian coups of 1966 and many other African
coups had strong ethnic overtones (*ibid.*: 230). The Nigerian
cases were particularly significant because they had led to the
attempted secession by Eastern-Nigeria/Biafra and one of the
most costly civil wars in history (Luckham, 1971).

Motives Inhibiting the Seizure of Power

The military may also have motives for *not* seizing power, and
Finer examined various motives that could *inhibit* the military
from intervention in politics (1976: 26–7). He contended that

the military's belief in the principle of civil supremacy was a truly effective restraint on its intervention in politics. But he acknowledged that more self-interested motives could also inhibit military intervention, and identified several factors that could deter intervention by raising self-interested fears of the consequences of failure. There is the corporate and individual fear that if the coup fails, not only will the individual officers face drastic retribution but also the military as an organisation may face serious repercussions, as when a failed coup in Costa Rica in 1948 led to the army's being replaced by a police force. There is also the corporate fear that if only part of the military attempts a coup, fighting may break out between pro- and anti-coup sections of the military.

Finally, even a successful coup may endanger some of the military's corporate interests, as when a resulting politicisation of the military seriously undermines its corporate cohesion and military effectiveness. For the politicised military may become more like a political party than a highly centralised and disciplined fighting organisation. The many coups that have been launched by groups of middle-ranking officers are evidence of how 'politics' undermines the military's centralised and disciplined structure. Perhaps even more striking evidence of the dangers of politicisation is the fact that the majority of attempted coups in the 1940s–70s were actually aimed at military governments, and in the 'vast majority' of successful cases involved the replacement of one military government by another (Nordlinger, 1977: 140).

An extreme example of the 'partyfying' of the military arose in Syria in 1961 when the army's officer corps responded to potentially violent political conflicts among its members by convening a Military Congress. Comprising representatives of all the military regions and major units, the Congress discussed and voted on such weighty political matters as whether to restore civilian rule and whether to attempt another unification of Syria with Egypt (Rabinovich, 1972: 32–3).

To the fear of politicisation can often be added a more general concern that a new bout of military rule will only lead to a repeat of past failures – with all their negative effects upon the military and the nation. Many South American officers, for instance, have preferred to dissociate themselves from the legacy of 1960s–80s military rule. For the 'incompetence, self-aggrandizement, and repression' that the military displayed while in office led to a decline in 'military stature, unity and self-confidence', and to armies so anxious to protect themselves from the effects of holding public office that they were practising 'coup avoidance' (Pion-Berlin, 1992: 86).

Considering the number and significance of the possible motives inhibiting the military from seizing power, any assessment of whether there is a motive to stage a coup is clearly no simple matter! Indeed, the assessment of motive bears some resemblance to preparing a balance sheet of motives, some favouring and some inhibiting, in order to determine whether 'on balance' there is motivation for the military to seize power.

Means

An important step in the further development of Finer's calculus of intervention and overall framework is the inclusion of the separate factor or variable of *means* of intervention. Though it could be included under the heading of opportunity, the means factor deserves separate consideration as a variable of comparable significance to motive and opportunity. Without the means of doing so, the military could not intervene in politics. Means can be viewed again from a forensic perspective as including (1) the *modus operandi* or 'method', and (2) the capacity to use that method.

Although the coup is the obvious method of the military's seizing power (see Exhibit 3.2 examples), Finer emphasised that it is not the only method available to the military. In particular, the military may be able to achieve the same effect as a coup by simply *threatening* to stage a coup – what Finer terms 'blackmail' – to remove a government from power (1976: 134–8). Such threats may be largely implicit. The 1966 'disguised coup' in Indonesia (which saw the President confer sweeping governmental powers upon army commander General Suharto) involved the deployment of soldiers outside the presidential palace – and the military has always maintained that it did not exert any pressure on the President (Crouch, 1978: ch. 7). Finer even identified two different methods of carrying out a coup. He adopted the Latin American distinction between the *golpe de estado*, aimed at the head of state, and the *cuatelazo*, the 'barracks coup', in which a single barracks or unit revolts against

Exhibit 3.2   The Military Coup in Action

The 1952 factional coup in Egypt was aimed at the corrupt and incompetent monarchical regime and carried out by the secret 'Free Officers' movement of middle-ranking and junior officers within the army and air force (Stephens, 1971: 103–8). The movement's executive committee, headed by Major Nasser, led the military units that carried out the coup on the night of 22 July. The factional nature of the coup was displayed by the priority given to securing control of the military as a whole by seizing its general headquarters and the senior commanders who were meeting there on that evening. The coup forces also seized control of other key points in the capital city, such as government buildings, the radio station and telephone exchanges. In addition to putting tanks in the streets and having warplanes swoop low over the city, the coup-makers made their presence felt the following morning by a radio-broadcast proclamation justifying their actions. The prime minister quickly resigned, the royal palaces were later surrounded and seized by coup forces, and the King formally abdicated on 26 July.

The 1973 corporate coup in Chile was aimed at democratically elected President Allende and his leftist supporters (Sigmund, 1977: 239–53). The heads of the three armed services (and, later, the head of the national police) had actually agreed in writing to stage the coup on 11 September. Early that morning the navy took over the port city of Valparaiso, while in the capital city the army shut down radio stations, broadcast a proclamation justifying the coup, and by mid-morning had deployed tanks in front of the presidential palace. The siege of the palace and incumbent President included a rocket attack by the air force's planes. President Allende refused the offer of safe passage into exile and committed suicide before the presidential palace was surrendered early in the afternoon. The new, self-declared government was a military junta declared to be the Supreme Command of the Nation, exercising legislative power by means of numbered decree-laws, which had already decreed a 'state of siege' allowing summary arrest and detention. By mid-afternoon thousands of civilians were being rounded up and indeed several thousand died in the coup and its immediate aftermath. That night the four-man junta, comprising army commander Pinochet and the heads of the navy, air force and national police, appeared on television to justify their action and describe their policies.

the government in the expectation that other units will join it in a march on the capital or in other forms of pressure that will topple the government (Finer, 1976: 139–42).

A more important distinction between types of coup (see Exhibit 3.2) is that between:

1. the 'corporate' coup, in which the military acts as a unified, corporate body; and
2. the 'factional' coup, in which only a part of the military attempts to stage a coup. Often a factional coup is aimed at the military's corporate/professional leaders – its highest-ranking, commanding officers – as well as against the civilian government.

Therefore another difference between these types of coup is that while the corporate coup is led by generals, the factional coup is usually led by such middle-ranking officers as colonels and majors.

But the difference between the corporate and factional types of coup is more a matter of capacity than method. Although a united military is 'virtually certain to succeed' in staging a (corporate) coup, the great majority of attempted coups – some 80 per cent – have not been corporate and less than half of them have succeeded (Nordlinger, 1977: 101–2). In recent times the odds against a non-corporate, factional coup succeeding have become even worse. In 1990–92 less than a third of the 38 attempted coups (mostly factional) were successful (Kebschull, 1994). The factional coup is inherently less likely to be successful than the corporate coup because it may run into opposition from other sections of the military or lack the force and credibility to overcome civilian opposition. Moreover, any attempt at 'blackmailing' a government with the threat of a coup would have little credibility unless it appeared likely that the blackmailers could deliver a corporate coup. Therefore, the factional coup is not so much a different method of seizing power as a case of a divided military using the coup method at much less than full capacity and thereby running a much greater risk that the method will fail.

In fact the non-corporate, factional coup is a sign of weakness in a key and distinctive aspect of the military's capacity to seize power – its highly centralised and disciplined organisational structure. In his analysis of the political strengths of the military, Finer emphasised not only its possession of highly lethal weapons but also its organisational capacity to use those weapons to carry out a particular mission – its centralised command, hierarchy of ranks/posts, strict discipline and emotional solidarity (1976: 10, 5–8). Janowitz's (1964) pioneering work on the political role of the military in 'new nations' explicitly argued that a reason for the military's greater capacity than civilian groups to intervene (unconstitutionally) in politics is its distinctive organisational format (*ibid.*: 27–8, 31–2). He emphasised the importance of the military's control over the 'instruments of violence' but also pointed to the military's organisational unity and internal cohesion as another characteristic of its distinctive organisational format.

Moreover, Janowitz identified the factional coup as a symptom of weaknesses in a military's internal social cohesion which reduce its capacity to intervene effectively in politics. While one of the political expressions of a socially cohesive military is intervention directed by its senior commanders, a lack of internal social cohesion leads to coups being attempted by only a part of the military – by 'a powerful faction acting without the "legitimate" authority of the top commander'(*ibid.*: 68). The internal social cohesion of the officer corps can be weakened by differences in the officers' social background, such as their ethnic or religious background, and also by differences in career experiences, particularly those associated with intergenerational differences between younger and older officers (*ibid.*: 70–1).

Later, Finer pointed to two other important threats to the military's internal social cohesion – organisational divisions and political differences (1976: 226). Different branches or services (army, navy and air force), and even particular units or garrisons, may develop a separate solidarity that reduces the overall cohesion of the military. Secondly, the military may be infected by political divisions within civilian society, and see its own cohesion undermined by differences in officers' ideological, party or factional loyalties.

Therefore, just as there are motives which inhibit the military from seeking power, so there are also factors that reduce the military's capacity to seize power – reducing its capability to the level of only factional rather than corporate coups. The success or failure of factional coups comes down to such operational factors as the tactics or techniques used and to relatively contingent factors, including simply good or bad luck (Kebschull, 1994). In addition to Nordlinger's analysis of coup-making techniques (1977: 102–6), there are specialised works devoted to analysing the preparation and implementation of coups, such as Luttwak's (1968) classic handbook, and Farcau's (1994) more recent, Latin-American-focused book. But these issues go well beyond any general investigation of the military's capacity to successfully stage or threaten a coup.

Such an assessment of the military's means of seizing power is clearly an important part of a comprehensive 'calculus' of the likelihood of successful military intervention or of the reasons for an earlier success or failure. However, the assessment of the military's opportunity to intervene is an even more important 'objective' aspect of this calculus and the motive/means/opportunity framework for analysing seizures of power.

Opportunity

Finer and several other analysts of military rule have identified a range of factors that affect the opportunity for the military to seize power. Some of them are actually 'negative' opportunity factors in the sense of reducing rather than increasing the opportunity to seize power (just as internal divisions reduce the military's capacity to seize power). Other opportunity factors have both a positive and a negative aspect depending upon their strength or the particular situation.

The Legitimacy Factor

Finer's theory of political culture identified a legitimacy factor which has both negative and positive aspects for the prospects of a military seizure of power (1976: 79–80). On the one hand, societies with a mature or developed political culture could be expected to reject or resist any claims that military rule was legitimate and to strongly resist military intervention in politics – clearly reducing the opportunity for any intervention. On the other hand, legitimation of military rule is possible or simply unimportant in societies with lower levels of political culture and they would not strongly resist military intervention – clearly *increasing* the opportunity for the military to seize power.

The legitimacy opportunity factor was also identified by Nordlinger, and he, too, saw it as having negative as well as positive aspects for the military's prospects of seizing power. For he emphasised that civilian moral condemnation of illegitimate military intervention in politics is expressed in direct action, such as 'mass protests, general strikes, riots, sporadic violence, and possibly armed resistance', and that the prospect of having to deal with this active resistance *deters* the military from intervening in politics (1977: 94–5). On the other hand, the level of resistance to military intervention is likely to be proportional to the degree of legitimacy enjoyed by the civilian government. Therefore, the 'absence or loss of governmental legitimacy' by the civilian authorities substantially *increases* – more than any other factor – the military's opportunity to seize power (*ibid.*: 93).

Nordlinger also argued that the legitimacy of a government can be eroded by failures in its performance. Such 'performance failures' (see Exhibit 5.1) as illegal actions, economic downturns and disorder and violence can therefore be seen as indirectly increasing the opportunity to seize power (*ibid.*: 64, 85–92). But his most significant difference from Finer's approach was his extension of the legitimacy factor to cover the military as well as civilian society. By pointing out that some or most officers would refuse to support a coup attempt against a legitimate government, he highlighted the effect of legitimacy upon the motive and capacity as well as the opportunity for military intervention (*ibid.*: 95).

Political and Operational Factors

In addition to his theory of political culture and the legitimacy factor, Finer identified a very opportune political situation for military intervention. He contended that the opportunity for the military to intervene is maximised when both (1) the civilian authorities are abnormally dependent upon the military, and (2) the military's popularity is enhanced while that of the civilian authorities is depressed (1976: 64). The civilian authorities' dependence on the military is most likely to occur when they are having to use the military for internal security purposes, either because of violence between rival political forces or because of strong opposition from the masses to the rule of the political elite or dominant social class (*ibid.*: 64–6, 69). As for the military's enhanced popularity, this arises largely from the civilian authorities being discredited by inefficiency, corruption or political intrigue – in such circumstances the military may even be seen as a 'deliverer' by the civilian population (*ibid.*: 72–3).

What might be viewed as a case of civilian governments being discredited by economic inefficiency was later identified and statistically validated by O'Kane. She used cross-national statistical evidence to support her argument that instability in export prices (in poor countries dependent upon exporting primary products) 'is conducive to coups because it generates problems for both the economy and society that can be directly blamed on the government' (1981: 291–2). However, her statistical test of the relationship between these economic factors and military coups also took into account three 'obstacles' that 'reduced the likely success of a coup', namely:

1. the recent independence of the state;
2. the lack of any previous coups; and
3. the presence of foreign troops (*ibid.*: 294–5).

These obstacles are therefore typical negative opportunity factors, with the first and second being opportunity-reducing political factors, and the third, the presence of foreign troops, being an operational factor that reduces the opportunity for a militarily successful coup.

Various other operational obstacles to coups can also be included as negative opportunity factors. Several were unearthed by Decalo (1989) when examining the military-controlling strategies that had been used by the 16 African states – little more than a quarter of all African countries – which had managed to escape military rule. (These coup-free states were almost equally divided between democracies and one-party states.) Among the negative opportunity factors that he identified were the familiar external ones of foreign (French) military support, and the use of expatriate, foreign officers to hold key posts.

However, two new factors are the use of family members to hold key military posts and of ethnically loyal military recruits.

They can also be found outside the African region, especially in the Middle East, though some South American armies would have viewed such measures as a blow to their professional/ corporate integrity and as possible grounds for political intervention! The same could be said of another factor identified by Decalo – using totally (often ethnically) loyal elite or paramilitary units to counterbalance the regular military forces. For he acknowledged that these units often provoke military jealousies that may become a corporate-interest motive for a coup. Therefore, the creation of such units as elite presidential guards needs to be 'properly rationalised and executed, and without simultaneously diminishing the corporate status of the regular armed forces' (Decalo, 1989: 562).

When properly developed and used, though, elite and/or paramilitary units seem to have been quite successful in defeating and deterring coups within Africa, and they have been widely used in other parts of the world. The most famous example is Saddam Hussein's Republican Guard, which was originally an elite presidential guard (recruited from his home-region of Tikrit) and apparently still retains a special loyalty to the President. Even much less powerful units than the Republican Guard can markedly reduce the opportunity for a successful factional coup and make a corporate coup more risky and potentially bloody.

But there is a conceptual ambiguity about the nature and role of elite units that can lead to serious misunderstandings when discussing the political stance of the military in such countries as Iraq. Such elite units as the Republican Guard are military professionals employed by the state and could be classified as being a different branch/service *of* the military rather than an armed force *separate from* the military. Assessments of the political reliability of the Iraqi military might come to quite different conclusions depending upon whether the elite units are regarded as part of or separate from 'the military'. If they are viewed as a part of the military, they should be included as (negative) 'means' rather than 'opportunity' factors – as being an important internal division within the military that markedly reduces its capacity to seize power.

A similar problem can arise when considering the effect of another important obstacle to military seizures of power, namely 'intelligence-gathering units' and 'informal networks of political spies' (Decalo, 1989: 562). Although these covert controls on the military usually take the form of a political police or other civilian security organ (see Chapter 5), they may also include military intelligence/police units spying on their fellow officers. They are presumably seeking to preempt and deter factional coups but, when the prospect of a corporate coup looms, the question of whether these control units are truly 'in' and 'of' the military becomes more than just an academic problem. The complexities of assessing the opportunity aspect of a military seizure of power only reflect the complexities of the real world of military interventions in politics.

Clearly the opportunity aspect, like the means aspect, of the calculus of military intervention is actually a matter of degree rather than a simple yes/no question. Even the assessment of motive can be seen as a matter of assessing whether, on balance, there is a strong or weak motive for seizing power. So applying the calculus of intervention could involve cases of very strong or very weak motive, means and opportunity, and in between these two extremes there could be many much less straightforward combinations. But at least the range of *outcomes* is apparently only (1) no attempt, (2) a failed attempt, and (3) a successful attempt to seize power.

The Emergence of Less-than-Military Regimes

As was noted at the outset, the focus of this chapter has been upon military interventions in politics that lead to the emergence of what are clearly military dictatorships. These are the military seizures of public office and powers that lead to military men becoming the official governors of their countries. However, there are other forms of intervention and other types of military regime. In fact the various types of 'less-than-military' regime – those which are less than clearly or fully military – are too important a category of dictatorship to be ignored.

From Indirect Military Rule to Military-Supported Regimes

Finer identified types of *indirect* military regime and rule, in which the military intervened from behind the scenes to exercise some control over a civilian government's policies (see

Chapter 2). To maintain this control the military normally uses the discreet methods of threatening a coup or such other forms of 'blackmail' as threatening not to defend the government against its foes (1976: 134–8).

The extreme cases of indirect rule, in which civilian government is only a puppet or agent of the military, could well be classified as military dictatorship. (Often such a regime has arisen from a military seizure of power that has been transformed into indirect rule through a civilian puppet/agent.) Finer categorised such puppet–master rule as an 'indirect-complete' type of military regime, in which complete and continuous control is exercised over the civilian government (*ibid.*: 151, 156–7). To his example of Batista's 1933–40 indirect rule in Cuba could be added Calles's indirect rule in Mexico in the early 1930s, and the much more recent cases of Noriega's rule in Panama in the 1980s and Cedras's rule in Haiti in the lead-up to the 1994 US intervention. This type of indirect rule is not solely a Caribbean and Central American phenomenon, though, nor is it associated only with personalist military rulers. The highly corporate military regime in Uruguay operated behind two successive civilian presidents in the 1970s.

But beyond such cases lies a spectrum of civilian/military regimes with a decreasingly military content. It ranges from what Finer termed 'indirect-limited' military rule, to mild versions of what Nordlinger termed 'moderator' forms of indirect rule, and finally to what Finer termed 'military-supportive' civilian regimes (see Chapter 2). These distinctly less-than-military regimes are often better viewed in relation to democracy or party dictatorship than to military dictatorship. For example, indirect-limited rule (in which the military intervenes only intermittently to exercise control over a limited range of policies) seems more like a flawed democracy than any form of military regime – as more like a less-than-democratic than a less-than-military regime (see Chapter 9).

So, too, do some mild versions of the moderator form of indirect rule. For in such cases as 1950s' Brazil the moderator military intervenes only on rare occasions to remove a civilian government, hand power over to a civilian caretaker government, and allow the voters to choose a new government. The most dramatic case of such intervention occurred in Brazil in 1954 when the democratically elected President Vargas responded to the military's ultimatum by refusing to resign and instead committing suicide. The military had once before, in 1945, forced him to resign from the presidency and he was not willing to suffer that fate again. But on the previous occasion the Brazilian military had been seeking to hasten the country's democratisation by putting an end to Vargas's military-dependent civilian dictatorship.

The dictatorship established by Vargas in 1937 was an example of the 'military-supportive' *civilian* regime, whose only military feature is that the civilian government is wholly reliant on military support for its survival (see Chapter 2). President Vargas had avoided the constitutional prohibition on his serving a second, successive term in office by dissolving Congress, presenting the country with a new (but never ratified) Constitution, and ruling through state-of-emergency decree powers (Schneider, 1991: ch. 4). The military was 'largely responsible for permitting Vargas to establish this dictatorial regime', whose inception has even been described as a military coup in civilian guise (*ibid.*: 138). Nevertheless, this was not the military's, but Vargas's (personal) dictatorship – he was by no means a puppet or an agent of the military. Finer's example of such a military-supported civilian dictatorship was Marcos's regime in the Philippines. The elected President Marcos 'introduced martial law in 1972 and used it to suspend Congress, arrest opponents, censor the press and then introduce a totally new constitution' (Finer, 1988: 256). The President's attempt to set up this new regime would have been abortive if the military had refused to support him, if only by refusing to administer martial law, but instead Marcos went on to rule the Philippines until 1986.

The Autogolpe or Self-Coup

Both the Marcos and Vargas military-supported regimes were also examples of an unusual form of coup known as the *autogolpe*. This Latin American term, literally a 'self-coup', describes 'a coup launched by the chief executive himself in order to extend his control over the political system in some extra-constitutional way' (Farcau, 1994: 2). The *autogolpe* is usually associated with the creation of a military-supported civilian personalist dictatorship or the extension of a military dictatorship. Only rarely, as in the case of Prime Minister Gandhi's state-of-emergency rule of India in 1975–77, has such a regime not been based on the public office of president.

A 1990s example of a civilian *autogolpe* leading to a military-supported regime is provided by elected President Fujimori of Peru. In 1992 he suspended the constitution, dissolved Congress, and introduced a new constitution (ratified by referendum) that removed the prohibition on his being reelected for a second term. Even before his coup, President Fujimori had been preparing a 'marriage of convenience' with the army by exploiting not only some senior officers' individual self-interest in career advancement, but also the army's corporate self-interest in acquiring a free hand to prosecute its counter-insurgency campaign against the leftist Shining Path guerrillas (Obando, 1996). This mutually supportive relationship was confirmed when the military backed his coup and received extensive new powers to prosecute its counter-insurgency war. The key relationship was actually the personal alliance between President Fujimori and his chosen army commander General Hermoza Rios, who stayed in his post even after Fujimori's comfortable victory in the 1995 presidential election reduced the President's dependence on the military.

The military's support for a civilian president's *autogolpe* – and for his resulting dictatorship – could be viewed in similar forensic fashion to the military's seizure of power. For the military seems to be acting as an accomplice ('before and after the fact') in the president's misappropriation of his public office and powers. The misappropriation is evident in the president's misuse of public powers to (1) extend his decree powers and/or remove the law-making powers embodied in the Congress or parliament, and (2) remove the constitutional prohibition on his serving a second term and/or ensure that he will be reelected. But misappropriation is most evident in the improper hold on public office that results from this misuse of powers – he has in practice taken personal possession of the public office of president.

Yet there is too little military involvement and influence to classify such a regime as a military dictatorship. It is no more than a military-supported civilian dictatorship which in these *autogolpe* examples has taken a personalist presidential form. In other circumstances it might well have taken the form of a weak party dictatorship becoming wholly reliant on the military for its survival – a military-supported party dictatorship rather than military-supported personalist dictatorship.

However, the problem of how to categorise cases of misappropriation arises again when considering the case of an *autogolpe* carried out by a military rather than civilian president. An excellent example was provided by President Park of South Korea in the early 1970s. After seizing power by coup in 1961, he had constructed an elaborate multiparty democratic disguise but eventually he resorted to an *autogolpe*. In 1972 he declared martial law, suspended the constitution, dissolved the National Assembly, and introduced a new constitution that entitled him to appoint a third of the Assembly and to be elected president indirectly instead of by popular vote. Although Park's public office and powers had originally been acquired by military coup, his 'self-coup' was a separate, quite distinct measure – a misappropriation of presidential public office/powers comparable to that perpetrated by Vargas, Marcos and Fujimori.

The calculus of military intervention can be modified to accommodate misappropriations as well as seizures of power. But the main reason for this modification is that it will provide a better basis for making comparisons with the emergence of party dictatorships, which have often arisen through the misappropriation rather than seizure of power. Therefore the notion of 'usurping' power will be used to describe both a seizure or a misappropriation of power, and 'usurpation' will refer to the usurping of public office and powers by either seizure or misappropriation. The motive/means/opportunity framework and calculus of intervention will become the framework and calculus of usurpation. And in this form it will also be able to analyse the emergence of party dictatorships.

4

The Emergence of Party Dictatorships

When compared to the many attempts to analyse and generalise about military intervention in politics, the analysis of when, why and how party dictatorships emerge has received scant attention. The issue is usually covered only in respect to a particular variety of party dictatorship, such as the communist or fascist, rather than the whole type. This lack of interest in analysing the emergence of party-type dictatorships may be due to their apparent rarity when compared to the much more numerous examples of the military type. But when the various categories of party dictatorship are added together, the total number of historical examples of this type of dictatorship is surprisingly high.

The most numerous category appears at first glance to be the communist party dictatorships, those that espouse and seek to implement Marxism–Leninism. At their numerical peak in the 1980s there were no fewer than 23 avowed communist regimes but only 16 of these were classified by Holmes as 'core' examples and, with the possible exception of Cuba, were party rather than military dictatorships (1986: viii). The other ideologically defined category of party dictatorship, the fascist regimes, provides only two examples: the Fascists in Italy and the Nazis in Germany. Similarly, the geographical rather than ideologically defined categories of Latin American and Middle Eastern regimes provide only a few examples. In Latin America there have been the party dictatorships of the PRI in Mexico, the Sandinistas in Nicaragua and the MNR in Bolivia. In the Middle East, including North Africa, there have been Saddam Hussein's Baathist regime in Iraq, Bourguiba's regime in Tunisia and Ben Bella's short-lived regime in Algeria.

But the geographically defined category of African party dictatorships provides a large number of examples and is in fact the most numerous category. McKown and Kauffman's (1973) estimate covering the 1963–68 period identified 17 examples of one-party states, existing or defunct, in sub-Saharan Africa (1973: 55–6, 55 table 1). Similarly, Finer estimated that at least 20 examples of single-party regimes had been seen in continental Africa in the 1960s (1974: 527). When boosted by a few later examples, such as Zambia and Marxist–Leninist Mozambique, the African one-party states therefore make up the majority of cases of party dictatorship.

A total of more than 30 cases of the emergence of party dictatorship would seem to be more than enough for conceptual analysis and generalisation. However, nearly half of the 16 communist cases were established with the aid of external military forces, namely the occupying forces that the Soviet Union deployed in 1921 in Outer Mongolia, and in 1944–48 in countries formerly held by or allied with Nazi Germany or Imperial Japan. The Soviet forces have been credited with the actual 'installation' of communist regimes in Mongolia, Poland, East Germany, Hungary, Bulgaria, Romania and North Korea (Hammond, 1975a). With these regimes, along with Cuba, consigned to the 'awkward cases' (see Exhibit 4.1), only eight examples remain to be included in the total number of party takeovers. Moreover, the Mexican Latin American case of party dictatorship and the Iraqi Middle Eastern case both arose from gradual transformation of a military regime into a party dictatorship and they, too, will have to be examined separately as 'awkward cases'.

Yet even without these cases there would still seem to be a sufficient number of examples available – more than 20 – to develop an analytical framework of similar comprehensiveness to Finer's calculus for analysing the military's intervention in politics and seizure of public offices and powers. Indeed, the obvious place to begin is to seek to apply the same Finer-based framework (the motive/means/opportunity calculus of usurpation) that was used in the previous chapter on the

Exhibit 4.1 'Awkward Cases' of the Emergence of Party Dictatorship

There is a group of seven communist party dictatorships – Mongolia, Poland, East Germany, Hungary, Romania, Bulgaria and North Korea – which were said to have come to power, not through their parties' efforts, but through having been installed by the Soviet Union's occupying military forces (Hammond, 1975a). Bulgaria may be better categorised with Yugoslavia and Albania rather than as a case of installation, and the Hungarian case has some similarities with events in Czechoslovakia (Swain and Swain, 1993). But this does not detract from the general point that some communist party dictatorships emerged only because the country was under the military occupation of a communist foreign power.

The installed communist dictatorships appear to have followed a rough blueprint aimed at disguising and smoothing their takeover, which may have helped to reduce local and international opposition to their installation (Hammond, 1975b). As manifested in 1944–49, this strategy of 'creeping communism' emphasised camouflage and gradualism that employed (a) 'salami tactics' to eliminate one foe or rival at a time, and (b) the popular-unity Front tactic of forming a coalition Front with other parties and mass organisations that were or would soon become communist-controlled puppets (Hammond, 1975b).

Another group of dictatorships that are difficult to include in the motive–means–opportunity framework are those where a party dictatorship has emerged out of a military regime. In Cuba, the Castro-led guerrilla army that overthrew Batista's dictatorship in 1959 eventually established a military-dominated communist regime that has been gradually transformed into virtually a party dictatorship. The Mexican regime completed the transition as long ago as the 1940s when the military leaders ensured a smooth transition to party dictatorship by the official party that had been created after the 1911–17 Mexican Revolution by leaders of the revolutionary armies and their civilian allies. The Iraqi Baathist regime completed a similar transition in 1979 when the civilian Saddam Hussein formally succeeded to the leadership (see Chapter 6). And in Taiwan the 1970s transition from rule by General Chiang Kai-shek to dictatorship by his official party, the Kuomintang, was accompanied by the beginnings of a gradual transition to democracy (see Chapter 8).

emergence of military dictatorships. It is true that party dictatorships often emerge through misappropriating rather than
seizing public office and powers, but as was pointed out at the
end of the previous chapter, the concept of *usurping* power
refers to both its seizure or misappropriation. Moreover, there
are major advantages in applying the same analytical framework (calculus) to the emergence of both types of dictatorship,
party as well as military. In particular, it would assist comparisons and contrasts between examples of these two quite different
types of modern non-democratic regime.

Motive

The Finer-based check-list of (mixed) motives for military usurpation of power that was developed in the previous chapter is
readily applicable to usurpation of public offices and powers
by a party. But this check-list

- national interest,
- corporate self-interest,
- social self-interest in various forms, and
- individual self-interest

requires some addition and shifts in emphasis.

For example, the national-interest motive is insufficient to
cover those cases where members of a party are motivated by a
wider concern or loyalty than their citizenship of a particular
country. Several of the ideologies espoused by parties are committed to an international class, race or nation. The most obvious
example is the communists' Marxist–Leninist focus on the working class as an international social class and on the international
class-loyalty expressed in the notion of 'proletarian internation-
alism'. The Nazis' focus on the international Aryan race is
another famous example; and the Baathists' focus on pan-Arab
nationalism is a classic example of international (Arab) nationalism. It is difficult to determine the extent to which these
international concerns and loyalties have replaced or subsumed
the citizen's concern for the national interests of his/her country.
But any comprehensive check-list of motives has to provide for

the possibility that these wider concerns can be one of the motives for a party's attempt to usurp power.

Therefore a new motive will be added to the check-list, that of *ideological interest*, based upon a party member's (possibly) being a 'believer' in an ideology. As well as addressing the issue of international loyalties, adding an ideological motive means that national interest will no longer be the only altruistic motive in the check-list. The altruistic aspect of ideological interest helps to distinguish class- or ethnic-focused ideological motives from the self-interested and parochial motives derived from membership in a *particular society*'s class or ethnic social group.

Like the military, parties usually present their usurpations of power as having been altruistically motivated. And there is some reason to believe that usurping parties may be less influenced by corporate self-interested motives than are officer corps. In fact, it seems more accurate to refer to *organisational* rather than corporate self-interest where parties are concerned, for they are so far removed from the military's corporate nature as a socially segregated and self-sufficient body that it seems a misnomer to describe them as corporate. Members of a non-ruling party are usually not even employed by it, let alone wear its uniform, live in its accommodation and obey its legally enforceable code of discipline. Some parties, notably the fascist and communist parties, do espouse a near-corporate ideal in their emphasis on commitment and discipline, such as with the fascists' party uniform and the communists' use of 'comrade' to describe fellow members. Yet it is unlikely that the role of party member is as significant to a fascist or communist as the role of soldier is to an officer.

Moreover, there seems to be no party equivalent of the manner in which the military's corporate self-interest motive is aroused by threats to its budget, its autonomy, or its professional monopoly. A party might be motivated to seize power because it is threatened with destruction or loss of independence. But it seems more likely that a party threatened with repression would be seeking to open, rather than monopolise, the political arena (unless the party was already motivated, by ideological and/or other motives, to seize power).

Similarly, a party already holding public offices might be motivated to misappropriate them in order to prevent the loss of party privileges that would result from loss of office. But, again, it seems more likely that significant party privileges would be acquired after, not before, usurpation and that it is the actual acquisition of these privileges which would motivate usurpation. Indeed it is because a party would seem to have so much to gain by becoming the official party that it seems safe to assume that organisational self-interest does often help motivate a party's usurpation of power – even if seldom as an important or strong motive.

The motive of individual self-interest is another case of a shift in emphasis being needed when applying the check-list of motives to parties. But in this case the motive has to be given greater, rather than lesser, emphasis. As the leaders of the party have focused their career ambitions on acquiring public office, they presumably have a greater individual self-interest in usurping public offices than do the leaders of the military, whose career ambitions have been focused on the military ranks and posts they have pursued since adolescence. Furthermore, middle- and lower-ranking party leaders can expect to enjoy greater and more secure political (and often material) rewards if their party usurps public offices/powers and becomes the official, privileged party.

The motive of social self-interest, particularly that of class self-interest, also needs greater emphasis than when the check-list of motives was applied to the military. As party members are much less separated from society than is the corporately organised soldier, they are presumably more affected by their membership of a social group, whether class, ethnic, religious or regional. Such social self-interest is evident in the ideologies or programmes and the social composition of the membership of many parties that have established a dictatorship.

Most commonly it has been a class type of social self-interest, concerned for the interests of the working class and/or peasantry. This motivation has been found in the communist and, to varying degrees, in the Baathist and the Latin American party dictatorships – the Mexican, Bolivian and Nicaraguan. Often the leaders of these parties have *not* been members of the working class or peasantry – by birth, let alone by occupation – and so can hardly be depicted as motivated by social self-interest. The prevalence of middle-class intellectuals in the leadership of communist parties was so great that Kautsky categorised communism as 'totalitarianism of the intellectuals' (1962: 109, 59–60). But it is not just the senior leaders' motives which are crucial in a party's usurpation of power; so, too, are those of the lower-ranking leaders and the ordinary membership of the party – and in a communist party these are drawn largely from the working class and peasantry.

As for ethnic, religious and regional types of social self-interest, they have been no more prominent as motives for party usurpation than for military seizures of power. There have been several parties in Asia based on these social interests but, with the possible exception of UMNO in Malaysia (see Chapter 9), they have not usurped public office and powers. And few of the many African cases of party usurpation appear to have been motivated by social self-interest. The many African parties which misappropriated power had won their election victories by presenting themselves as mass nationalist parties, and it was their electoral rivals who had tended to resort to parochial ethnic/ kinship appeals (Zolberg, 1966: 22).

The Middle East provides many examples of religious-motivated parties, but these Islamic parties seem to be motivated more by altruistic religious belief comparable to ideological belief rather than by self-interested concern for their religious social group. More importantly, only one such party has actually usurped power: the Islamic Republican Party in 1980s Iran. Even the case of the IRP is problematical because this party was basically a vehicle used by politicised clergy to take charge of the purportedly democratic Islamic Republic established after the 1978–79 revolution – and the party was dissolved in 1987 after having served its purpose (Brooker, 1997: 146–8).

Finally, as with the military, there are motives that inhibit parties from usurping power. For example, presumably some political parties believe that democracy is in the national interest and perhaps even have an ideological belief in democracy. Also it is possible that some political parties share the military's concern that usurping power will have serious implications for organisational integrity and effectiveness. (For many parties have discovered that a lack of political competition can eventually have negative side-effects on morale, unity and political persuasiveness.) Certainly most parties share the officer corps's corporate and individual self-interested concern about the consequences of a failed bid to take power – few parties have been

allowed to survive a botched attempt at usurping power. Therefore, as in the case of the military's calculus of intervention/
usurpation, a balance-sheet approach must be taken when assessing whether there is motive for usurpation.

Means

Analysing parties' means of usurping power, their methods and
capacities, is more complex than analysing the military's means.
For parties have used two very different methods to usurp power
– the electoral and the revolutionary. The revolution method
involves a seizure of power and is comparable to the military's
method of staging a coup. But the electoral method involves a
misappropriation of power that has been preceded by a legal,
electoral acquisition of public office and powers. Assessing
whether any particular party has the means to usurp power
therefore requires assessing two very different types of capacity:
(1) the capacity to stage a revolutionary seizure of power, and
(2) the capacity to achieve an electoral misappropriation of
power. And this dual assessment must in turn be based on an
understanding of the characteristics and historical 'track record'
of the two methods.

Electoral Misappropriation of Power

The *electoral* method of usurpation exploits the party's inherent
capacity as a misappropriator of power, just as the military's
coup method exploits its inherent capacity to seize power.
For the party's vote-winning capacity enables it to peacefully
accomplish, through success in democratic elections, the first
step on the way to misappropriation of power – acquiring a
hold on the public offices and powers that it will misappropriate.
   Obviously the success of the electoral method requires that
a particular party has the capacity for electoral success (and
the basic 'opportunity' of operating in a democratic rather than
a monarchical or dictatorial environment)! And on occasions
electoral success has been insufficient to provide a clear-cut
claim to hold the governing public offices, as in the cases of
the Nazis in Germany and the communists in Czechoslovakia
requiring coalition governments and support from an 'above-

parties' presidential head of state. But the electoral method of usurpation always has the advantage of allowing a party to acquire a hold on public offices and powers in a legal, democratic fashion that disguises and protects its move to establish a dictatorship.

Having acquired a hold on these public offices, the party can then misuse its newly acquired public powers to misappropriate public offices, specifically by ensuring that it will not be defeated in future elections. The misappropriation is therefore similar to that of a president staging an *autogolpe*, but in this case public office is being converted into the party's (not the officeholder's personal) 'property'. Moreover, misappropriation by a party seldom takes the dramatic form of a self-coup; it tends to use a more gradual and less blatant approach. For example, often a party has established a form of one-party state by using more subtle measures than simply the passing of a law prohibiting all other parties.

Yet whatever variations there may be in this stage of the misappropriation, in each case the party has the advantage of employing public powers that have been acquired by legal and democratic means, not by a blatantly illegal and undemocratic coup or threatened coup. Furthermore, the party is able to deploy its established expertise and resources in the field of political persuasion in its attempt to win the people's support for, or at least acquiescence in, this misappropriation of power. Considering the advantages of the electoral method, it is not surprising that this has been the most common way in which party dictatorships have been established.

The great majority of the incidences of electoral misappropriation were associated with the emergence of African party dictatorships. Only one of the many communist party dictatorships, the Czechoslovakian, came to power in this fashion and even this case involved a degree of latent or threatened armed insurrection (Tigrid, 1975). Like the notorious Nazi case of electoral misappropriation, it had been based upon a less than clear-cut election victory that had required the party to use measures not normally associated with the electoral method.

In contrast, most African party dictatorships had used the electoral method to usurp power and these misappropriations had been based upon massive election victories. During the decolonising 1954 and 1956 elections in Ghana, for example,

Nkrumah's CPP won two-thirds of the seats in the colony's legislative assembly, while the decolonising 1957 elections in Guinea saw Touré's PDG win nearly all the seats in the colonial assembly. With public office securely in the party's hands when the country finally became independent, the misappropriation of power involved only the removal of any democratic form of threat to the party's continued hold on these public offices.

In the African cases, the removal of political competitors often involved the use of the carrot rather than the stick (Carter, 1962; Coleman and Rosberg, 1964: 666–7; Zolberg, 1966: 87). In addition to absorbing other parties there was a willingness to coopt individual opponents – party leaders, members of parliament and even trade-union leaders. Although these coopted individuals and parties may have been motivated by the national interest, there was a self-interested, patronage aspect to their willingness to be coopted. (As will be seen in later chapters, the manipulation of patronage opportunities often directly or indirectly involves a misuse of public powers.) The patronage factor was particularly potent in these Third World countries, where (1) the allocation of scarce public amenities and services was of great social and political significance, and (2) public/state office was the prime source of economic welfare as well as social status.

Nevertheless, the African regimes used the stick as well as the carrot, often in a surprisingly open misuse of public powers. Quite frequently the governing party's monopoly was secured by a law declaring it to be the country's sole party, as in Ghana and Tanzania. It is true that there were a number of cases, as in Guinea and the Ivory Coast, where a *de facto* rather than legal one-party state was preferred, and there were even a few cases of the semi-dictatorship (see Chapter 9) or substantive form of one-party state – in which minority parties have no chance of competing effectively against the official party (Bienen, 1970a: 111–12).

But even when a *de facto* or substantive rather than legal form of one-party state was preferred, public powers were often misused to eliminate or weaken other parties. To prevent the official party's competitors being represented in parliament, most of the former French colonies in sub-Saharan Africa adopted an electoral law which gave *all* the seats to the winning party (Carter,

1962). Another common legal ploy was to ban 'the formation of any organization devoted to ethnic or other forms of "particularistic" propaganda' – a prohibition which could be interpreted to make most opposition groups 'illegal by definition' (Zolberg, 1966: 82). When combined with the use of various forms of (often quite mild) repression against individual political opponents, the result was to secure virtually as strong a hold on public offices as the legally recognised form of one-party state.

However, the electoral method also has several weaknesses:

- First, any particular party seeking to use this method must compete electorally with other parties that are likely to highlight any indication of its dictatorial ambitions.
- Secondly, the state apparatus, and especially the military, may refuse to acquiesce in the party's misappropriation of power.
- Thirdly, the public may refuse to acquiesce in being politically expropriated by the governing party. In fact, doubtless one of the reasons why misappropriation has been attempted so rarely by Western governing parties is because they have anticipated the likely negative reaction of the state apparatus and people to such a move.

Revolutionary Seizure of Power

The party's *revolution* method of usurping power involves the seizure rather than misappropriation of public offices and powers. They are acquired by the party's leading a successful uprising against the regime in power (Calvert, 1990: 2–4). This revolutionary uprising usually takes the form of an armed insurrection (such as a coup or guerrilla war) rather than of crowds of people taking to the streets – and even when relatively non-violent, it is an illegal process relying on force or the threat of force. A constitutional, electoral or popular gloss may be given to the completion of the revolutionary seizure of power, but this is little different from the military formally adhering to the constitutional proprieties when removing a government by the threat of a coup.

Although a political party is a form of organisation developed specifically for the purpose of acquiring public office, it would seem to have much less capacity than the military for seizing public offices and powers. A party's power is based not upon the use or threat of military force, but upon the use of political *persuasion* – persuading people to vote for the party's candidates and/or in other ways to identify with the party and assist its activities. Organisationally, the party differs markedly from the military. The modern political party was originally developed as a loosely knit private association of voluntary, dues-paying members engaged (usually as very much a part-time or leisure activity) in legally regulated political competition with other parties.

Nevertheless, the political party has sometimes been organisationally adapted to operate in a non-democratic context and to seize power by leading a revolutionary uprising. In fact the introduction in the early 1900s of the now familiar communist or Leninist notion of a revolutionary vanguard party, with its principles of elitist membership and (democratic) centralism, represented a move towards the selective recruitment and centralised discipline found in professional military organisations. As Holmes has pointed out, the introduction of this new organisational format was initially justified by Lenin as a response to the repressive conditions that his Bolshevik (Communist) Party faced under Russia's Tsarist autocracy (1986: 9). But his party's self-proclaimed role of leader of the proletarian revolution also seemed to require such organisational changes. If the party was to lead a revolutionary uprising rather than use the electoral method being adopted (ultimately unsuccessfully) by Marxist parties in Western Europe, then clearly some features of a normal, democratic party would have to be sacrificed to improve its military-like effectiveness.

The two fascist parties went several steps further than the communists in militarising their organisational format to suit the needs of the revolution method (Brooker, 1995: 28, 41). The formally democratic internal procedures retained by communist parties were replaced by unadorned centralisation, with overall command exercised by an individual leader figure, and there was even an explicitly hierarchical structure of party leaders and sub-leaders. However, the most striking evidence of militarisation was the use of party uniforms, emblems and salutes (though the fascists did not adopt the principle of selective recruitment until after they had usurped power).

The fascists' militarisation of their parties was not in response to the difficulties of operating in a repressive political environment – they were legal parties operating in a democracy – and was largely due to the violent activities and ambitions of these parties in their founding years in the early 1920s. The Italian Fascists had originated after the First World War as a paramilitary movement, not a party, which used organised violence to smash leftist parties and trade unions. Although the movement was formed into a party (and took part in elections) in 1921, the Fascists came to power the following year through the 'March on Rome' by their militia forces. The Nazi Party, too, was oriented towards a violent seizure of power until the failed attempt at a coup – the failed Munich 'Beer Hall' putsch of 1923 – showed the Nazis that they would have to use a more legal method of acquiring power. And they would go on to show the world a decade later that a militarised party may also be able to successfully use the electoral method – to use persuasion rather than violence to achieve its ambitions.

However, even the use of the revolutionary method is in a sense dependent upon a party's capacity to persuade. In attempting to lead a revolution a party is inspiring as well as organising people to engage in a political activity that is much more dangerous than supporting the party at the ballot box. The party may be seeking support at the barricades or seeking to use its supporters as 'human bullets', in the sense of a sheer mass of people filling the streets and public spaces and forcing its way into public buildings. Or the party may be recruiting and inspiring supporters who will use real bullets and attempt an operation that is very similar to a military coup.

Most party-led revolutions have in fact been the result of party coups and/or civil wars between the party and its opponents. The argument that 'armed force was the determinant of victory in *all* cases in which Communists have not only seized power but have managed to retain it' could be applied to other parties that have sought to use the revolutionary method of establishing dictatorship (Hammond, 1975a: 640). However, the role of armed force can be more psychological and political than military, as in the case of the Italian Fascist Party's successful coup, the March on Rome of October 1922. Initiated by the party's poorly armed and poorly trained militia, the coup has been termed a 'colossal bluff' and 'psychological warfare' aimed at building pressure on the government and King 'to take a positive initiative to restore order' or to hand over power constitutionally to the Fascists (Lyttelton, 1973: 85–87). Instead of using the army to put down the attempted coup, the government resigned and left the King with the responsibility of appointing the Fascists' leader, Mussolini, to the post of prime minister. Although this constitutional and 'voluntary' aspect to the acquisition of public office would lead to the Fascist usurpation being as much a misappropriation as a seizure, the Fascists' psychologically and politically successful coup was the crucial event in the emergence of the world's first fascist regime.

The amount of armed force used by a party to carry out its coup may be surprisingly small if the targeted government or regime lacks reliable defenders. The classic example is the October 1917 coup in Russia that led to the emergence of the world's first communist regime. The Bolsheviks carried out their coup against the Provisional Government in the capital city, Petrograd, by using worker-militia Red Guards, several thousand Bolshevik-supporting sailors from the naval base, and a small minority of the 245 000-strong Petrograd garrison – the rest of which remained neutral (Pipes, 1991: 478).

A party coup may also be based largely on the armed force contributed by a military faction belonging or allied to the party. An extreme example is the July 1968 coup in Iraq which was carried out largely by the military wing of the Baathist Party and which resulted in a military Baathist regime that was gradually transformed into a civilian, truly party dictatorship now ruled by Saddam Hussein (see Chapter 6). But the unreliability of military allies was displayed in the Bolivian revolution of 1952. The National Revolutionary Movement (MNR) coup against the country's military rulers was jeopardised when MNR allies in the police and military abandoned the coup; victory was won only after armed workers, particularly miners, came to the aid of the middle-class MNR fighters embroiled in armed combat with army units in the capital and a number of other cities (Malloy, 1971: 111–12).

As has occasionally occurred with partially failed military coups, a partially failed party coup can develop into a civil war. The 1918–20 Civil War in Russia was a result of the failure of the October 1917 coup by the Bolshevik (soon to be renamed Communist) Party to win control of the countryside, where most of the population lived, and of the peripheral regions of the former Russian Empire, including Siberia, the Caucasus, the Ukraine, Poland, the Baltic states and Finland. Not until 1920 did the communists' Red Army finally destroy the counter-revolutionary 'White' armies. With the conquest of the Caucasus completed in 1921 and eastern Siberia occupied in 1922, the communists ended up by 'recovering' most of the territory of the old Russian Empire; only Poland, Finland and (temporarily) the Baltic states had been 'lost'.

But a party-led revolution may from the outset take the form of a civil war, as in the famous case of the Chinese communists' military defeat of the Kuomintang regime in 1947–49 (see Eastman, 1984: 161–5; Dreyer, 1995: 315–33). By 1947 the communists controlled extensive rural areas in northern China but they were far away from the country's capital city (Nanking) and urbanised heartland. Instead of attempting a revolutionary coup, the communists therefore had to fight their way into the rest of China by defeating the Kuomintang army. They inflicted a series of devastating military defeats upon the Kuomintang by using a burgeoning army organised and equipped in similar fashion to the Kuomintang state's military forces. The party's regular or conventional armed forces (as distinct from guerrilla or militia forces) grew from some 90 000 in 1937 to some 475 000 in mid-1945, had reached nearly two million by 1947 and attained actual numerical parity with the Kuomintang forces in 1948.

A more recent example of party-led revolutionary civil war was the Nicaraguan revolution of 1978–79 that routed the Somoza family's long-standing military regime. The Sandinista movement's fight against the Somoza regime seemed to have suffered a major setback in 1978 when its attempted five-city coup was crushed, but this failure actually increased support for the movement, and the flow of recruits and resources was converted in 1979 into a victorious military campaign using conventional as well as guerrilla forces (Gilbert, 1988: 10–12, 110).

The fundamental *weakness* of the revolutionary method is the difficulty a party has in acquiring either the masses of unarmed people or the units of armed supporters that are needed for an effective attempt at revolution. In a democracy it is difficult to persuade people of the need to go to such extremes, whether it is a mass of people taking to the streets or a smaller number taking up arms. In a non-democratic country the degree of repression makes it more dangerous to inspire people to revolt and more difficult to organise them. Consequently, unarmed revolutions by the masses tend to be spontaneous, as with the February 1917 revolution in Russia, or to be led by some more-established institution than a party, as with the clergy-led revolution in Iran.

Another, only slightly less fundamental, weakness is the difficulty in overcoming the police and military power of the state. If a government is prepared to use the force available to it, and if the armed forces obey these orders to suppress the attempted revolution, then any successful revolution will usually require a formidable armed force – probably including a conventional as well as guerrilla army. It is not often that a party will be able to deploy armed forces that are more effective than the armed forces of the regime it is seeking to replace. Therefore it is not surprising that so few party dictatorships have been established through the revolution method – and that one of the opportunities for usurpation arises from a weakening of state power.

Opportunity

There is not the space to offer more than a cursory glance at the question of when does an opportunity arise for usurpation of power by a party. However, opportune situations for parties' electoral misappropriation of power and/or for party-led revolution can be identified by looking back at the historical circumstances in which party dictatorships have emerged. Three such opportune situations are:

1. a weakening of the state power of the incumbent regime;
2. a war of liberation; and
3. a process of decolonisation.

A leading theorist of revolution has used historical evidence from the French, Russian and Chinese revolutions to argue that the weakening of the old regime's state power, especially its military power, provided an opportunity for revolution (Skocpol, 1979). She contended that a revolution occurred only after the way had been opened by the disintegration of the old regime's

TABLE 4.1

The calculus of party usurpation of power

Motive	Means	Opportunity
1. National interest	1. Electoral method	1. Weakening of state
2. Ideological interest	(*misappropriation* of	power
3. Social (especially	power)	2. War of liberation
class) self-interest	2. Revolution method	3. Decolonisation
4. Individual	(*seizure* of power)	
self-interest		
5. Organisational		
self-interest		

Inhibiting motives

1. Belief in democracy
   (national interest or
   ideological interest)
2. Fear of failure
   (organisational and
   individual self-
   interest)

administrative machinery and armies (*ibid.*: 47). Therefore the disintegration of the Russian army in the second half of the First World War was 'a necessary cause' of (1) the demise of the Tsarist monarchical regime at the hands of the spontaneous February 1917 revolution, and (2) of the revolutionary seizure of power by the Bolsheviks in October – a 'military coup' which faced 'no immediate military opposition that could not be overcome in brief struggles' (*ibid.*: 94, 213). Similarly, in the case of the Chinese communist revolution against the Kuomintang regime, the 1937–45 war with Japan had had a devastating effect upon the Kuomintang army, seriously weakening its ability to fight the 1947–49 civil war with the communist army (Eastman, 1984: 219).

The communist seizures of power in Russia and China seem, therefore, to be examples of exploiting a state-weakening opportunity provided by the state's military defeats at the hands of a foreign foe. That a war can provide the opportunity for party usurpation of power may seem somewhat paradoxical, but it has long been recognised by practitioners and analysts of politics. 'Almost all Communist takeovers have occurred either during international wars or in the aftermath of such wars', as they 'undermined the old political, economic and social order' (Hammond, 1975a: 641).

A special case of the opportunity that war provides for party usurpations of power is the 'war of liberation'. An opportunity that can be exploited by either the revolution or the electoral method arises when a party has led a successful war of liberation against either (a) an intransigent colonial power, or (b) a conquering power's occupying military forces. With the foreign forces expelled, there is no state power available to contest a revolutionary seizure of power; and if democratic elections are held, the party which has led the war of liberation is in a strong position not only to win an election victory but also subsequently to misappropriate these public offices and powers. Three communist regimes – Yugoslavia, Albania and North Vietnam – exploited the war-of-liberation opportunity, as did the party dictatorships established in (ex-French) Algeria and (ex-Portuguese) Mozambique, Angola and Guinea-Bissau.

The most fruitful opportunity to use the electoral method was provided by decolonisation. Most of the African examples of party dictatorship benefited from this opportunity, as the party which inherited power from the colonial rulers in the 1950s–60s – thanks to its election victory in the transitional period of decolonisation – went on to misappropriate the public offices and powers of the new state. After the Second World War the British and French colonial empires had begun to allow their African subjects to participate in the governing of their territories (and to prepare for eventual self-government) through electing representatives to colonial assemblies and governments. With these colonial and eventually decolonising elections came the development of mass political parties, which seized the opportunity to win the support of a voting public that was still untouched by political parties and partisan loyalties. The first mass parties to be established in each of the African colonial territories were able to exploit the great advantage of being the first political organisation to establish a link with the mass public, with a further advantage arising from the 'bandwagon effect' as the franchise was extended by the colonial rulers to successively wider sections of the public (Zolberg, 1966: 14–15, 19–21).

However, this electoral opportunity was less important than

the party's subsequent opportunity to misappropriate its demo-cratically acquired public offices. For the state apparatus, particularly the military, clearly could have blocked or over-turned the party's misappropriation of power, as would be confirmed when eight party dictatorships were overthrown by their armies during the 1960s (Finer, 1974: 527).

There were some *decolonisation*-linked factors, though, which helped to ensure the state's as well as the public's acquiesence in misappropriation of public office. It is commonly argued that the new, elected rulers were able to step into the shoes of the dictatorial colonial rulers, who recognised the electorally victorious parties and party leaders as their legitimate successors (Coleman and Rosberg, 1964: 655, 659). Therefore the public's and the state officials' residual respect for dictatorial colonial authority 'was transferred to the Africans who assumed the roles hitherto filled by Europeans', with a prime minister or presi-dent being seen as comparable to a colonial Governor (Zolberg, 1966: 17–18). Furthermore, not only was the counterbalancing influence of democratic institutions, processes and norms both novel and weak but also the new governing parties and leaders enjoyed the prestige of being the founding fathers of their newly independent states (Zolberg, 1966: 90).

The decolonising opportunity to use the electoral method of usurping power may appear to have been a historically unique 'window of opportunity' in the 1950s–70s that would never re-occur. But a similar situation seems to have arisen in Central Asia in the early 1990s as the former republics of the disinte-grating Soviet Union became independent states (see Exhibit 8.2 and Chapter 9). The five new states in Central Asia went through a transition that in at least the case of Tajikistan 'bore a resemblance to the decolonization of Western states' empires a generation earlier' (Atkin, 1997: 621).

5

Consolidation, Legitimacy and Control

Following its seizure or misappropriation of power the usurping party or military is faced with the problem of consolidating its hold on power. Where power has actually been seized rather than misappropriated, it is difficult to avoid the appearance of having stolen the country's public offices and powers. In the case of party-led revolutionary seizures of power, though, there is a 'popular-will' aspect to the image of revolution which can be emphasised to present an appearance of the people's rightfully laying claim to 'their' public offices and powers. But military coups lack such 'popular' connotations, and military regimes have had difficulty in presenting a credible claim to have a right to hold public office – to be 'legitimate'.

When a regime's claim to legitimacy – to have a right to rule – is accepted by its subjects or citizens, they feel duty-bound to obey the regime's rules and commands. The importance of legitimacy has been recognised academically ever since Weber's classic analysis of legitimate rule, in which he argued that the dutiful obedience produced by legitimacy is a more stable basis for rule than is obedience based on habit or on 'expediency' – which presumably means greed and fear (Weber, 1964 [1922]: 124–5). However, Weber acknowledged that legitimacy does not always produce the expected obedience. He mentioned the problems of not only deliberate disobedience and evasion, but also partial (self-justified) deviations and honest misinterpretations (*ibid.*: 125).

Therefore, even if a regime's claim to legitimacy is accepted by its society, it still has to rely on its state machinery of administrators, police and military to make its public powers effective. These state organisations use coercion as well as legitimacy and other means to enforce the government's policies, and without that coercive element (which elicits obedience based on 'expediency') in the state's control over society, the policies could not be effectively implemented. It is vital, therefore, for even a legitimate regime to maintain, through its legitimacy and other means, the obedience of its state machinery.

Consequently, a new dictatorship usually adopts a two-pronged approach to the consolidation of its hold on power. On the one hand, the new regime claims to be legitimate and seeks to have its claims to legitimacy accepted by state and society. On the other hand, it also deploys a range of organisations, organs or administrative devices that strengthen its (at least partially coercive) control over state and society – so that even if the claims to legitimacy are unsuccessful, the regime may still be able to hold and effectively use the public offices/powers it has seized or misappropriated.

Seeking Legitimacy

At first glance the acquiring of legitimacy seems much less important than strengthening control. In fact Przeworski (1991) has argued that a dictatorship's hold on power is not threatened or endangered by a lack of popular legitimacy – by members of society not considering it to be a legitimate regime. 'Some authoritarian regimes have been illegitimate since their inception, and they have been around for forty years' (*ibid.*: 54 n. 2). Yet the actual rulers themselves seem to have little doubt about the importance of legitimacy. 'It is generally agreed that all regimes, from naked tyrannies to pluralistic democracies, seek to legitimate themselves' (White, 1986: 463). Not only do rulers expend time and effort seeking to legitimate their rule, but also the search for legitimacy often seems to have shaped or influenced their regimes' official principles or goals, policy objectives and even political structure.

This is no less true of military rulers, despite the military's apparently having sufficient force or 'might' to be able to ignore the question of its right to rule. In the case of Latin American military regimes, Rouquié (1986) has argued that the dominance of liberal-democratic ideology in Latin America has had a marked influence on the region's military regimes. They

> must invoke it [democracy] for their own legitimation and in their own policy objectives, while at the same time proposing to improve, reinforce, amend, and even protect it. (*ibid.*: 111)

He pointed to the transitoriness in Latin America of (undisguised) military rulers, who can be legitimised only by their promises of an eventual return to democracy (*ibid.*: 110, 113). The only alternative was to establish a democratic disguise by allowing multiparty elections in which the regime's party had to face a degree of competition from other parties (see Chapter 9).

A similar situation prevailed in the region with the most military regimes: Africa. Although liberal (multiparty) democracy lacked the ideological dominance that it enjoyed in Latin America, the principle of civil supremacy 'remained a remarkably powerful notion in post-independent Africa', and military regimes 'dealt with this problem of legitimacy deficit' in similar fashion to their Latin American counterparts (Wiseman, 1996: 32 n. 4). Either there was the familiar promise of a return to democracy, such as was constantly heard in Nigeria and Ghana, or there was the use of civilian disguise to conceal the military nature of the regime. But in Africa the civilian disguise took the form of a supposed one-party state rather than a supposed multiparty democracy. In a number of countries the military's leader became a party leader by establishing some sort of monopolistic party and then having himself chosen by this official party to be its nominee for the country's one-candidate presidential election (*ibid.*: p. 17).

Why then are military regimes so concerned with legitimacy, with right rather than might, if it is so unnecessary? Finer suggested two reasons:

1. the need to establish some form of protection against countercoups by factions within the military (who can then be depicted as rebels or mutineers rather than competitors); and

2. the need to establish a more efficient or economical means
   of securing civilian obedience than simply relying on force
   (Finer, 1976: 14–19).

The need to secure civilian obedience is all the more pressing
in economically advanced societies because the military lacks
the technical skills to administer such societies; it is dependent upon civilian collaboration simply to keep things running,
let alone to implement any new policies. Indeed, Finer argued
that the reason why such societies are seldom ruled by the
military is that they are usually highly resistant to military claims
to legitimacy and therefore would require the military to use a
very costly amount of force to secure the extensive civilian
collaboration required to administer an economically advanced
society.

It is true that Finer foreshadowed Przeworski in arguing that
the legitimacy issue is not a serious handicap for military regimes
in societies with an unsophisticated economy and/or political
culture. But since then an assessment of African states' control
over their societies has indicated that the failure to achieve
popular legitimacy reduces *any* regime's capacity to administer
its rural hinterland (Forrest, 1988). So although in some societies a dictatorship may be able to survive without popular
legitimacy, in any society a dictatorship's lack of legitimacy will
require it to make more use of comparatively costly means of
securing the obedience of state and society.

Dictatorships have sought legitimacy in several different ways,
most obviously through ideological and electoral/democratic
means which will be described in some detail below. But two
other common bases for claims to legitimacy have been (1)
legality and (2) national-interest or patriotism. Claiming a legal right to rule usually involves the dictatorship's promulgating
a new constitution or passing a constitutional amendment (or
similarly significant law). However, most constitutions promulgated by the military have not explicitly legitimised military
rule – they are usually democratic in form. The constitutions
of communist and African party dictatorships have been much
more likely to include a reference to the leading or monopoly
role of the party, but even these will in other respects usually
take a democratic form and recognise only an electoral/demo-
cratic basis for holding public office.

In contrast, a dictatorship's national-interest or patriotic claim to legitimacy is more explicit and less formal. It has commonly been voiced by military regimes and is often best described as a public-interest or public-safety claim to legitimacy. For often it involves a claim that rule by the military is the necessary response to a crisis threatening the public with such drastic consequences as anarchy, social revolution, civil war or secession. The national-interest or patriotism claim to legitimacy can also be difficult to distinguish from what is commonly termed 'performance' legitimacy (see Exhibit 5.1). Although performance legitimacy has frequently been claimed by dictatorships, it is a conceptually problematic type of legitimacy that does not clearly establish the right to rule and duty to obey that are the crux of legitimacy and are found in electoral/democratic and ideological claims to legitimacy.

Electoral Means of Legitimation

That dictatorships so often use an electoral/democratic facade is in a sense their recognition that public offices should indeed be owned by the public, or (to use familiar arguments) that a legitimate government must be based upon the people's choice, the popular will, or some other democratic basis. It is significant that even parties espousing an apparently anti-democratic ideology have been reluctant to oppose all forms of democracy. Nazi Germany saw itself as embodying 'German democracy' and Fascist Italy was said by Mussolini to be an 'authoritative' as well as 'organised' and 'centralised' democracy (Brooker, 1995: 40, 26).

African one-party states rejected multiparty democracy but supported one-party elections and 'African democracy' (see Exhibit 5.2). The communist regimes, too, attacked only 'bourgeois' democracy and espoused their 'proletarian' or 'people's' democracy as the true form of democracy. Indeed, communist regimes lauded their elections as 'channels for expressing popular sovereignty and socialist democracy', with the absence of electoral choice supposedly being due to the lack of political conflict in a socialist society (Pravda, 1978: 170).

The official commitment to (some form of) democracy is also evident among military regimes (Nordlinger, 1977: 133–4; Finer,

Exhibit 5.1 Performance Legitimacy

The concept of performance legitimacy was probably first expressed in Lipset's comment: 'Prolonged effectiveness which lasts over a number of generations may give legitimacy to a political system; in the modern world, such effectiveness mainly means constant economic development' (1959: 91). Since then the concept of performance legitimacy has lost his proviso of 'a number of generations', and has incorporated several other forms of governmental performance such as a military regime's restoration of law and order (Alagappa, 1995: 61) or a communist regime's delivery of a package of socioeconomic benefits to its workers: 'comprehensive social security, full employment, stable prices, easygoing industrial discipline and steadily rising living standards' (White, 1986: 468).

But the notion of performance legitimacy has continued to beg the question of whether performance produces actual legitimacy, the right to rule and duty to obey, or whether it produces only what Weber described as obedience based on 'expediency' – on a self-interested desire to secure the benefits flowing from a high-performing regime. Recently Alagappa argued that moral authority can be generated by effective performance because the 'enormous concentration of power in the state cannot be justified except in terms of its use in pursuit of the collective interests of the political community' (1995: 22). However, this argument (like other conceptions of performance legitimacy) seems similar to the national-interest claim to legitimacy, and it also seems more suited to explaining the negative dimension or implication of performance legitimacy – namely, that a regime's legitimacy, of whatever type, will be lost if it fails to perform.

Finally, as he and other analysts have pointed out, there are several inherent problems involved in using performance as a basis for claiming a right to rule:

1. vulnerability to challengers offering greater benefits;
2. vulnerability of performance to external factors outside the regime's control;
3. rising expectations demand greater performance;
4. claims of high economic performance need several years of success to be credible; and
5. success in restoring public order may seem to reduce the need for the military regime, while success in economic development may give rise to new social/economic groups that generate new political demands and tensions (Alagappa, 1995: 41; Nordlinger, 1977: 137 n. 21; Huntington, 1991: 50, 55).

1976: 164). After a coup the military normally declares that its intention is to institute democracy once it has cured the polity's ills, such as corruption or leftist extremism. Sooner or later the regime honours this commitment to democratise or it institutes a (multiparty, one-party or even no-party) pseudo-democratisation, establishing a democratic facade or disguise through the use of elections of varying degrees of credibility. Finer pointed out that Latin America's long historical experience with such civilianising measures has produced a specialised vocabulary, such as the *candidato unico* election (1976: 164).

The one-candidate, plebiscitary form of election for presidency or for parliament (one proportional-representation list or one candidate per constituency) has been the preferred method of establishing a claim to electoral/democratic legitimacy. The one-candidate election has the flexibility to be employed in a multiparty fashion, as was shown by many of the new communist regimes established in the later 1940s. They maintained a multiparty facade through the use of puppet parties and a coalition Front organ controlled by the Communist Party. In theory the Front supervised the nominating of a single list of candidates for parliamentary office. But in practice the Communist Party predetermined that all the candidates were 'reliable', whether they were members of the Communist Party, of puppet parties, of mass organisations controlled by the Communist Party or of social groups given symbolic representation in parliament (Holmes, 1986: 166; Pravda, 1978). All communist regimes also used elected (in similar fashion) representative assemblies or councils at regional and local levels of government.

The communist regimes in Hungary, Poland, China and Vietnam eventually adopted a different system of elections that allowed the voter a limited choice among the candidates standing for public office. The voter's choice was limited by the fact that all candidates stood for the same 'party line' of policies and were selected in similar fashion to those for one-candidate elections (Pravda, 1978). Furthermore, either (a) only some of the parliamentary seats had more than one candidate, or (b) the list of candidates still fell short of providing even twice as many candidates as seats.

A few African party dictatorships, too, introduced limited-choice parliamentary elections. The most famous case is the Tanzanian regime's introduction in the 1970s of a degree of choice by providing two official candidates for each parliamentary constituency (Martin, 1978). These candidates campaigned together, but competed with each other in showing how the party's election manifesto could best be adapted to local needs. However, the Kenyan case was more impressive than the Tanzanian in terms of numbers of candidates and of incumbents defeated (Barkan and Okumu, 1978). In Kenya the official party, KANU, was a loose coalition of local political forces and as early as the 1960s adopted preliminary, primary elections as a means of allowing rival local politicians to compete for parliamentary office, with political debate focused on local issues and on which candidate could do the most for his constituency.

The most sophisticated type of undemocratic election is the semi-competitive (see Chapter 9), which has been most commonly found in Latin America. It goes beyond non-competitive multiparty elections and limited-choice elections by allowing other parties 'to retain a degree of autonomy and to compete with the official party in supposedly democratic elections' which are biased in favour of the official party and against its competitors (Brooker, 1995: 16). However, the user of semi-competitive elections may eventually face the problem of having to find a not too blatantly undemocratic way to hobble a party that is competing too successfully with the official party.

Semi-competitive elections offer a dictatorship the most credible claim to electoral/democratic legitimacy. In comparison, the limited-choice elections lack the credibility provided by a competing party and policy programme. And plebiscitary, one-candidate elections provide only a yes/no, reject/approve or valid/spoiled voting 'choice'. The plebiscitary form of choice is usually further devalued by the various pressures placed on the voter, notably the lack in practice of a truly secret ballot (Holmes, 1986: 168). To these pressures can be added the simple device of vote-rigging, which is much less likely to be challenged than in a semi-competitive system. Vote-rigging and/or various forms of pressure are evident in the characteristically 90–100 per cent totals and turnouts associated with such elections. Occasionally party dictatorships have lost all credibility by opting for the ultimate victory, as with Guinea's 100 per cent support for President Touré, or North Korea's 100 per cent turnout as well as 'yes' vote in parliamentary elections (Brooker, 1995: 119–20; 1997: 66).

Ideological Legitimation

An ideological claim to have a right to rule has not been as common as the electoral-democratic claim. This is largely because military regimes have seldom brought an ideology with them into power and have normally shown little inclination to develop one after having seized power. In its *narrower* sense, ideological legitimation is focused on the issue of the military's or party's right to rule, but in its *broader* sense it involves a less direct legitimation of the regime in terms of the goals and principles enshrined in the ideology.

The narrower sense of ideological legitimation is very rarely claimed by military dictatorships. The classic example is Nasser's notion of the Egyptian military's acting as the 'vanguard of the revolution' by carrying out its 1952 coup and continuing to lead the ongoing Egyptian Revolution (Brooker, 1995: 149). However, these military revolutionaries also promised the Egyptian people that military rule would be only temporary – or 'transitional' – and indeed made an elaborate pretence of civilianisation in 1956. In contrast, the Indonesian military's 'dual function' doctrine, formulated in 1965, has not claimed actual leadership for the military, but has been used to claim a permanent and open role for the armed forces in Indonesian politics and society. For the dual-function doctrine contends that in addition to their military function, the Indonesian armed forces have a social-political function that covers ideological, political, social, economic, cultural and even religious matters (*ibid.*: 183–4).

As for ideological justifications of party dictatorship, the oldest and most widely adopted is the Marxist–Leninist theory of 'leadership' (rule) by the Communist Party. It was developed by Lenin from his 1902 doctrine of the need for a 'vanguard party' of dedicated Marxist revolutionaries to lead the 'proletariat' (working class) in a Marxist revolution against capitalist society. In 1921 he added the new notion (presented as if it were Marxist orthodoxy) that party leadership of the proletariat would continue *after* the revolution. As Marxist doctrine envisaged a temporary post-revolutionary 'dictatorship of the proletariat', Lenin's doctrine of continued party leadership of the proletariat implied that the Communist Party would exercise a post-revolutionary dictatorship on its behalf.

The Leninist legitimation of party dictatorship was adopted explicitly by all later communist regimes as part of their avowed commitment to Marxism–Leninism. Suitably modified versions were also adopted by some non-communist parties and regimes, such as the Kuomintang (KMT) in China and Taiwan, the Arab-nationalist Baathists in Syria and Iraq, and the Sandinistas in Nicaragua. However, the two fascist party dictatorships showed little Leninist influence and did not develop any significant ideological justifications of party dictatorship.

The many African party dictatorships that arose in the 1960s brought forth a new ideological basis for party dictatorship, with the emphasis upon one-partyism rather than party leadership (see Exhibit 5.2). In the early 1960s, leaders of African party dictatorships 'put forward a theoretical defense', a new ideology, that sought to 'rationalize and legitimate' the postcolonial one-party states (Coleman and Rosberg, 1964: 668). The new ideology had a defensive tone, responding to Western criticisms of African one-partyism, and may have been partly an exercise in self-justification. It was most rapidly and extensively adopted in West Africa, where almost every regime leader developed his own version of this ideological justification of one-partyism (Zolberg, 1966: 48).

A broader and less direct form of ideological legitimation than these justifications for party or military rule may be derived from a dictatorship's ultimate ideological principles or goals, such as Nasser's Egyptian military regime's Arab nationalism and Arab socialism. Most military regimes, though, have not employed this broad form of ideological legitimation (except in claiming to favour democracy as principle or goal). Only a minority of even twentieth-century military regimes either developed or borrowed an official ideology, with its abstract commitment to sacred ideas, principles or goals.

The party dictatorships are much more ideology-prone and in fact it is rare to find one that does *not* espouse an ideology of some description. However, often a party dictatorship has espoused a version of Marxism–Leninism or African socialism rather than an ideology of its own devising, and the prevalence of Marxism–Leninism has been particularly striking. In addition to its espousal by all clear-cut communist regimes, there have been other regimes which explicitly espoused Marxism–Leninism but which are not normally classified as communist,

Exhibit 5.2   The African One-Party-State Ideology

The one-party ideology consisted of various strands of argument that were often interwoven and occasionally even contradictory (Nursey-Bray, 1983; Coleman and Rosberg, 1964: 668-70; Zolberg, 1966, ch. 2; Shaw, 1986). The traditional/communal argument, sometimes described as the theory of African one-party democracy or of African democracy, argued that the 'community democracy' of precolonial traditional African society, which had emphasised consultation, discussion and consensus, was best given modern form through the one-party system. The popular-will argument pointed to the overwhelming electoral victories of the decolonising period and its aftermath as proof that the people were content with a one-party system. The lack-of-classes argument contended that the lack of socioeconomic classes in modern as well as precolonial African society rendered competing (class-based) parties unnecessary. The nation-building argument maintained that the one-party system was needed to unite the various ethnic and tribal groups within African states into a new, national community. The development argument emphasised the need for unity of effort – presumably encouraged by one-partyism – in the pressing task of economic and social development. The democratic-party argument claimed that party leaders were sensitive to and would submit to majority opinion within the party (which was not seen as contra-dicting a traditional/communal-style emphasis on the African heritage of strong chiefly leadership).

There were also several negative arguments attacking multi-partyism. The traditional/communal argument denounced the un-Africanness of a system of competing parties opposing one another. The nation-building argument charged that competing politicians would play up ethnic and tribal divisions in the new African states. And the development argument contended that na-tional energies would be dissipated in the political wrangling and obstructionism encouraged by a multiparty system.

such as several party (and military) dictatorships established in Africa in the 1970s. And there were also regimes whose ideologies were strongly influenced by Marxism–Leninism but which preferred not to say so, such as the Nicaraguan Sandinista regime of the 1980s. Marxism–Leninism has also proved to be quite amenable to reinterpretation and modification to fit a particular movement's or regime's requirements, as when Mao Zedong shifted Chinese communism's emphasis from the working class to the peasantry, and when Castro's Cuban communism argued that a guerrilla band can fulfil the role usually performed by a party.

African socialism has shown an even stronger tendency than Marxism–Leninism towards local interpretations, and can be viewed as not so much a distinct ideology as a general approach that has been 'fine-tuned' by a number of particular leader-ideologists. It was so prevalent an ideology in 1960s Africa that nearly every leader seemed to have 'at one time or the other paid lip service to some form of African Socialism' (Grundy, 1964: 175). Although such sophisticated variants as Nkrumah's 'Consciencism' included other topics, the common core of African-socialist thought was the notion that the communal-socialist features of precolonial traditional African society could be used as a guide and justification for the development of modern socialist societies in Africa (Andrain, 1964; Brooker, 1995: 102).

Some regimes have found, though, that their ideological claim to legitimacy increases the pressure on them to 'perform' (in a manner similar to performance legitimacy), as was very evident in the case of communist regimes. The ideological pressure on such regimes arose from the Marxist–Leninist doctrine that socialism is only a transitional stage of economic restructuring and development which establishes the material abundance that is required for a truly communist society. The ever-extending length of this transitional stage led ideologists in the Soviet Union to identify stages within the socialist transition (thereby supporting the image that progress was being made in the transition to communism): 'building socialism' in 1917–36, then actual socialism until the early 1960s, and finally 'developed' or 'mature' socialism (Holmes, 1986: 103).

But in Eastern Europe this whole future-oriented approach lost so much credibility that the regimes' ideologists shifted their emphasis to a more present-oriented, pragmatic form of socialism – to the present achievements of 'real', 'realistic' or 'actually existing' socialism (*ibid.*: 100). However, this more mundane ideological/legitimacy emphasis only created new credibility problems thanks to not only rising (and frustrated) expectations, but also unfavourable comparisons with the prosperity of neighbouring Western countries.

Strengthening Control

A dictatorship's most effective means of strengthening control over state and society has been to deploy a (competent) security/ intelligence organ or organisation – typically a form of political or 'secret' police. This may have been inherited from the previous regime, but 'revolutionary' dictatorships usually establish their own form of political police. In military regimes the civilian political police are often augmented and sometimes overshadowed by military police or military intelligence units, but only rarely, as in Nazi Germany and Baathist Iraq, has there been a similarly powerful party security/intelligence unit.

The political police exercise the most coercive form of control over state and society. Highly repressive dictatorships allow their political police to inflict torture, detention in prison or labour/concentration camps, and even execution or 'disappearance'. In less repressive regimes the political police may be restricted by the formal legal system's procedures and punishments when it comes to using such physical forms of coercion, but they will probably be allowed arbitrary/discretionary use of such prosaic sanctions as having a state employee disciplined or dismissed. Coercion based on these prosaic sanctions is often little more than a negative form of patronage, in the sense of denial rather than bestowal of jobs, career advancement, business opportunities and other sought-after benefits that are in the regime's power to give and take away.

The degree and extent of repression during consolidation may be very high if the new regime is seeking to eliminate, not just deter, a large number of opponents or potential opponents. While even physical coercion usually involves only the *threat* of physical force, in these situations of preemptive or proactive repression there is an extensive *use* of force and a 'disproportionate' resort to execution rather than some form of imprisonment. Not only are large numbers of people detained, tortured and imprisoned, but also many of them are killed or sent to labour/concentration 'death' camps in which many inmates can be expected to succumb to the harsh physical conditions and treatment. However, a regime's repression may reach its peak not during consolidation, but instead:

1. during or immediately after a revolutionary or military-coup seizure of power, as in the 1973 Chilean coup;
2. in dealing with any second wave of opposition later in the regime's life, as in Brazil in the early 1970s or Syria in the early 1980s;
3. in dealing with opposition to such policies as land reform or collectivisation of agriculture; and
4. in dealing with internal opposition within the regime itself, as when Stalin and Saddam Hussein secured their personal positions by instigating bloody purges within the party.

In these peak periods of repression the political police are likely to be so concerned with potential as well as actual opponents that the 'terror' inspired in the population is as much fear of the repression's arbitrariness and incompetence as of its extensive use of physical force.

Even when not engaged in intense repression and the widespread use of torture, the political police are able to gather information on hidden opponents and potential opponents through such means as informers and the use of modern technology. Informers can be either (a) 'regulars' recruited by the police to act as its part-time secret agents, or (b) simply 'amateurs' providing malicious or good-citizen denunciations of disloyal talk or behaviour. For example, the communist regime in East Germany deployed no fewer than 110 000 regular informers (out of a population of 17 million), but the preceding Nazi regime had been able 'to rely much more on voluntary denunciations' (Ash, 1997: 74). The use of modern technology has gone beyond phone-tapping to include 'bugging' and video surveillance. For example, the Iraqi political police established surveillance centres in Baghdad which in some cases were able to monitor their allotted area visually through 'video cameras concealed on rooftops or built into statues and public monuments' (al-Khalil, 1989: 3).

Other controlling organs and organisations exercise a less physical and/or less directly coercive form of control than that of the political police. For example, members of a dictatorship's official party exercise an indirectly coercive control by providing the political police and other authorities with information about opponents and recalcitrants. Such a weak, 'monitoring' form of control by party members and grassroots party officials can occur in the workplace, in public places and even in the home. (As will be seen in a later section, though, some parties have also performed a more direct supervisory role in state workplaces and have held appointment powers over state posts.) A classic example of monitoring 'in the home' is provided by the Nazi party's many thousands of block leaders (Unger, 1974: 100–1). Each was responsible for 40 to 60 households in his neighbourhood, and through regular pastoral visits and other forms of surveillance was able to keep comprehensive files recording political and other information about each household. In fact it has been argued that the neighbourhood supervision by block leaders contributed more than the Gestapo to strengthening the Nazi regime (Unger, 1974: 102 n. 59).

These party officials also exercised a form of indirectly coercive control in their efforts to politically mobilise their neighbours. Such mobilisation included organising crowds to greet visiting party bigwigs and to attend public meetings (*ibid.*: 102–3), and generally attempting to 'activate' the people in support of the regime's various norms and goals (see Exhibit 1.1).

In many dictatorships the people were also mobilised by political-social mass organisations that recruited them into the organisation's mass-membership – sometimes by legally drafting them into the organisation but often by using more subtle means of compulsion. The most common forms of these controlling, mass-mobilising organisations have been youth organisations seeking to indoctrinate the new generation in the regime's ideology, and labour unions seeking to boost labour productivity and discipline as well as ideological commitment. Such mass organisations were most extensively or comprehensively used in Nazi Germany and Fascist Italy. In their attempt to instill a new national or racial solidarity in society, the two fascist regimes deployed a comprehensive array of ideology-indoctrinating organisations aimed at specific sectors of society, such as youth, women and labour, and at specific social activities, such as leisure and social welfare.

Some regimes have also expanded their control over society through using their state machinery to implement massive socioeconomic changes. The communist regimes, especially, greatly increased the size and social control of their state machinery by transforming their economies into state-owned/controlled economic systems aimed at rapid industrialisation (see Chapter 7). The African-socialist party dictatorships, too, expanded the state sector of the economy but to a lesser extent, usually refraining from a state-controlled collectivisation of agriculture. The fascist regimes' economic concerns were limited to ensuring, through largely *ad hoc* state intervention in the economy, that their political and military needs were met.

Such a high level of control through mass-mobilising organisations and the state's administration of the economy would seem to be required not so much to consolidate the regime's hold on power as to implement ambitious policies that involve massive social and/or economic changes. However, a more cynical interpretation would argue that such a massive expansion of control over society has in fact been more a matter of survival, of consolidation, than of pursuing ambitious social goals. For not only does ideological indoctrination support the regime's ideological claims to legitimacy, but also the extension of state ownership and control of the economy increases opportunities for building patronage support and for using the less physical forms of coercion.

Moreover, this interpretation can account for the fact that military dictatorships have been much less inclined than party dictatorships to pursue such ambitious policies as transforming the nature of social solidarity or rapidly industrialising a largely agricultural society (see Chapter 7). For it can be argued that as the military has a far greater capacity than a party for (direct) physically coercive control, a consolidating military regime does not feel the same need to expand its control over society through such 'revolutionary' policy programmes.

Although this argument takes a too cynical or 'self-interested' view of dictatorships' motivation, it is true that the military has a substantial capacity for physically coercive control. In addition to possessing its own police/intelligence apparatus, it can

deploy a host of soldiers on the streets to enforce the imposition of martial law or other means of social control. As was
noted in earlier chapters, the military's coercive capacity is so
formidable that it may rule 'indirectly', from behind the scenes,
by 'blackmailing' a reluctant or servile civilian government. Such
indirect forms of military rule will not be examined in this
chapter but there will be a detailed examination of the direct
or open military regime's strengthening of control over civilian
state and society.

Military Dictatorships' Strengthening of Control

During or immediately after its seizure of power the military
normally introduces the characteristically 'military' forms of
strengthening control – establishing a junta and imposing martial
law. The declaration of martial law is meant to ensure at least
a law-and-order level of control of society, as the soldiers take
on a policing and judicial role that is aimed primarily at crushing
and deterring any opposition to the seizure of power. Some
military regimes prefer to use a more civilianised, state-of-
emergency or state-of-siege justification and format for the imposition of such blatant military control over society. Similarly, a
new military regime may soon reduce the scope of the martial-
law system, restricting it to only political 'crimes' or disorder.

The Junta

While martial law is a means of controlling the streets, the
military 'junta' (the Spanish word for 'council') is a means of
controlling the government. The military is often not satisfied
with just a 'hands on' control over government through individual officers taking over the public office of president or prime
minister and some of the other government posts, such as
minister/secretary of the interior. Instead, and in addition, a
military junta is often established to exercise a degree of institutional control over the activities of the 'military' government.
Either the junta is formally converted into the country's ultimate governing body (complete with absolutist decree powers),
or it exercises an informally binding control over the government's activities.

The military junta is an *ad hoc* political committee formed by the military's leaders, whether leaders in the corporate/professional sense of being senior commanders or in the more political sense of being officers that enjoy wide support within the military. The junta is a political organ that is intended to represent the military in a Burkean 'virtual' sense, where 'there is a communion of interests and sympathy of feeling' between the representative and those represented (Finer, 1988: 260 n. 62). But it is formed only when the military is seeking to establish and control a military regime; it is not a standard part of the military's organisational structure! Although the military junta is of Spanish-American origin (the Junta Militar), it has been regularly employed in Latin America only since the 1920s and reflects the growth of the 'group identification that has accompanied the greater institutionalization of the services' (Johnson, 1964: 114). An institutionalised, highly corporate/professional junta became the norm in Latin America, with the core membership being the heads of the three armed services – army, navy and air force. The three service commanders may be joined by the equivalent of a service commander (in the Chilean case the head of the national police) or by an officer who has been given the public office of president but is not one of the three service commanders.

Military juntas outside Latin America have adopted more imaginative and purposeful self-descriptions: the title of Revolutionary Command Council has been popular in the Middle East; a reference to 'revolutionary' was also included in some African juntas; the 'nation' has figured in such titles as Turkey's National Security Council and Poland's Military Council of National Salvation; and Burma's junta coined the unimaginative but purposeful title of State Law and Order Restoration Council. Often these juntas have also been much larger than their Latin American counterparts, and indeed by the 1980s the average (median) junta had 11 members rather than the three or four usually found in Latin America (Finer, 1988: 260). Whereas the small junta is indicative of the military's seizing power through a corporate coup, the large junta is quite often the product of a factional coup by a group of middle-ranking officers. They are the military's (self-proclaimed) political leaders rather than its hierarchical commanders.

The junta is a control organ that faces inwards as well as

outwards, controlling members of the regime as well as 'outsiders'. It is an important means of counterbalancing the civilian influence upon military governments – especially civilian technocratic influence on policy-making – that can escalate into a surreptitious civilian takeover within the regime and virtually 'indirect civilian rule'. For, as was mentioned earlier in the chapter, the military's lack of skills and experience in the running of civilian society means that military regimes are (to varying degree) dependent upon civilian collaborators, some of whom are usually included in the government as ministers of finance, health and other technical branches of the administration. Indeed, by the 1980s civilians predominated (holding two-thirds or more of the ministerial posts) in the governments of the majority of junta-headed military regimes (Finer, 1988: 260).

The most pervasive civilian influence upon a military government is exerted by the state's administrative officials, the civil service. Not only are some civil servants often included in the government but also the military members of the government are likely to be strongly influenced by the advice of their ministry's civil servants. In O'Donnell's concept of a bureaucratic-authoritarian regime the description 'bureaucratic' refers to civilian and military technocrats sharing a common policy agenda (see Chapter 1). But when First (1970) used the term 'military-bureaucratic' rule to describe the many 1960s African military regimes that lacked a reformist agenda, she was referring to an informal or practical civilian dominance of the regime's policy-making. For this type of military rule embodied 'a civil service–military axis in which armies have the physical power to conserve the regime, while the civil service wields effective executive power in the state' (*ibid.*: 432–3).

Some military regimes have strengthened their control (and counterbalanced civilian policy-making influence) by placing military officers in important civilian posts, such as in the civil service and in regional or local government. For example, while Pakistan's first military regime (under General Ayub Khan) saw rule by a 'military-bureaucratic axis' that gave the civil service an important role, a later military regime (under General Zia) was 'plainly military in character' and saw the civil service

> reduced to a wholly subordinate role by the regime's policy of grafting military officers to key jobs in the central and

provincial administrations, public sector industries as well as other semi-government and autonomous organizations (Jalal, 1995; 55, 103, 105).

This military 'colonising', as Finer described it, of civilian state and society has tended to occur in regimes with an ideology or well-defined agenda (Finer, 1988: 273). Among the best examples of the practice are the socialist regimes of Nasser in Egypt and Ne Win in Burma, the right-wing regimes of Franco in Spain and Pinochet in Chile, and Suharto's ideological regime in Indonesia.

The most extensive and intensive system of colonising civilian state and society was developed by the Indonesian regime (Brooker, 1995: 189–90). Its extensive use of military personnel included deploying officers in the state apparatus, from ministry to mayoral level, in the military's political party and in other social organisations. (Other examples of the extensive militarisation of the regime are that a fifth of the parliament's seats were reserved for military men, and a soldier was stationed in each of the country's thousands of villages as the military's local representative.) Moreover, there were mechanisms for maintaining control over military colonisers. A Karyawan (Civic Mission) Management Board attached to the military's General Staff maintained regular contact with the eventually no fewer than 16 000 soldiers on detachment to civilian posts, receiving quarterly reports from them and sending them official policy statements and other information. Such administrative devices went some way towards reducing the possibility that any civilian-deployed military man 'might consider his primary duty to lie in his membership in the new organization in which he worked full-time' (Stepan, 1978: 169–70).

Civilianisation of Control

But such blatantly military means of control as colonisation, juntas and martial law may be difficult to reconcile with the regime's claims to legitimacy, and therefore may have to be avoided or relinquished. For example, if the Indonesian military regime had added a junta to its system of control, this would have blatantly contradicted its declared commitment to the constitution and to the Pancasila (Five Principles) ideology's

TABLE 5.1

Military dictatorships' strengthening of control

Seizure of power →	Military controls (very common)	→ Civilianisation of control (likely in long-term regimes)
	1. Martial law, junta	1. End of martial law and junta
	2. Possible colonisation of state and society	2. Wearing of civilian garb and possibly use of ex-officers for government and colonisation
	3. Possible party and/or mass organisations	3. Probable use of party and/or mass organisations

principle of democracy. In Iraq a junta already existed but was transformed into a more appropriate form of governing organ for a self-proclaimed Baathist party dictatorship. The Baathist (military and party) leader brought to power by the 1968 coup soon civilianised the RCC junta by stacking it with civilian party members, such as Saddam Hussein, and also gave it constitutional status as the state's supreme executive and legislative organ. But the usual approach has been a more drastic, overall civilianisation of control that sees the regime dissolve the junta, end martial law and rely on less blatantly military means of control. Whether from the outset or because of a later civilianisation, more than a third of military regimes were *not* using a junta in the 1980s (Finer, 1988: 260).

The civilianisation of military regimes' means of control can be seen as virtually a second stage of consolidation, in which the regime is reshaped into a pseudo-civilian form. Many military regimes never embarked on this stage, while others instituted a less drastic civilianisation that fitted their particular 'profile' of control-strengthening measures and legitimacy claims, such as the Indonesian regime's lack of a junta yet 'dual function' justification for permanent military colonisation. But a second, civilianising stage of consolidation (often also including 'elections') is always likely if a regime aspires to long-term military rule behind a facade of pseudo-civilianisation.

Although the civilianisation stage of consolidation may appear to involve a serious weakening of control, military regimes have developed means of relinquishing the form but retaining much of the substance of military rule. The purely cosmetic device of having military men in government and colonising posts wear civilian suits rather than military uniforms is common but presumably lacks credibility in the eyes of most civilians. (Similarly, Stalin's and Saddam Hussein's acquisition of military rank and uniforms presumably did not convert them into military leaders in the eyes of their 'fellow' officers.) However, having these officers formally *end* their military careers produces a more credible civilianisation without too great a loss of control. For example, when the earlier-mentioned Egyptian and Burmese regimes instituted dramatic 'civilianisations' (which saw an end to juntas, martial law and other obvious means of military control), the many officers in the government or holding colonising posts resigned or retired from the military. But the evidence of the Egyptian case of colonisation suggests that such ex-officers retain a high degree of corporate solidarity even when scattered among the state's administrative machinery (Brooker, 1995: 154). Moreover, in Egypt pseudo-civilianisation of the regime added a new weapon to the regime's armoury of control – the deploying of an official party.

The use of a political party as a controlling organisation is one of the least blatant means of strengthening military control. By deploying a party in this fashion, the military can acquire indirectly some of the opportunities for control that party dictatorships enjoy and do so in a relatively civilianised fashion. In fact some regimes have used a party at the initial, militarised stage of consolidation before or without proceeding to civilianisation (and occasionally these still-militarised regimes have even used mass organisations to strengthen social control). But the most extreme use of the party as a control organisation arose from the pseudo-civilianisation of the Burmese regime in the early 1970s. Years earlier it had established a military-colonised official party, the Burma Socialist Programme Party, and the regime's supposed civilianisation involved its metamorphosis into an apparent party dictatorship ruled by the (still military-dominated) BSPP. Military men, in the form of retired/resigned officers, continued to dominate the central organs of a party which seemed to control not only the country's parliament, government, regional/local government and civil service, but also an array of mass organisations aimed at youth, workers and peasants (Brooker, 1995: 163–6).

Other military regimes, though, have been wary of such a wholehearted adoption of civilianised forms of strengthening control. In Spain the large FET party was given less control over state and society than the BSPP in Burma and was formally headed by General Franco, who retained his military post as supreme commander. In Egypt the larger and more civilianised ASU party was at least led by ex-officers, but it was allowed little control over state and society.

Although by the 1980s a (largely African) majority of military regimes had an official party (Finer, 1988: 262–70), few of these parties would have added much strength to the regime's control of state and society. Few were strong and controlling organisations, such as the Syrian Baathist Party. Many of them, especially in Africa, were weak or sketchy organisations that were used primarily as channels for distributing patronage and/ or as token victors of 'one-party state' elections. Moreover, several of the stronger official parties were used primarily to bolster an image of multi-party democratisation and were therefore focused on contesting and winning semi-competitive elections rather than acting as control organisations. For example, the Indonesian military regime's quite impressive official party, Golkar, and in the 1970s virtually went into hibernation between elections (Rogers, 1988: 259–60). In fact it could be argued that the differences between these various forms of military-party regime are as great as the difference between them and the standard, party-less military regime.

The shift to a military-party type of regime is a clear example of how strengthening/transforming control can be associated with developments or changes in the actual type of military regime. (See Table 5.2 and Chapter 2 on the many types of military regime that have been identified by analysts of military rule, such as Finer's quasi-civilianised type.) In fact a shift to a form of military-party regime indicates a development or change in the goal/role type of regime as well as in the structural type. For the fact that it has made the effort to create or take over a party confirms that the military has developed a commitment to goals that will require a long-term hold on power. (Although analysts of the ruler type of regime have viewed these

TABLE 5.2

Changes or developments in type of military regime

Internal (structural) types	Structural types	Goal/role types
1. Military 'representatives' determine or co-determine (with civilians) the policy agendas; *or*	1. (a) Militarised, *or* (b) 'Quasi-civilianised' type (Finer, 1976); *and*	1. 'Arbitrator' type (Finer, 1976; Perlmutter, 1977) or 'guardian' type (Nordlinger, 1977) with temporary political role; *or*
2. 'Military-bureaucratic' type (First, 1970) with internal, hidden takeover by policy-making civilians (civil service); *or*	2. (a) Party-less, *or* (b) 'Military-party' type: (i) party as auxiliary arm of military regime, *or*	2. 'Ruler' type (Finer, 1976; Nordlinger, 1977, and Perlmutter, 1977) with long-term or permanent political and social/ economic role
3. 'Personalist ruler' type with degeneration into personalist rule by military leader – likely to take form of 'dual' type (Finer, 1976) with ruler heading party or other organised civilian support	(ii) supposed one-party state, *or* (iii) supposed multiparty democracy	

goals as being relatively altruistic, a more cynical view would also point to cases where the military regime's goals seem distinctly self-interested and even parasitical.) Of the at least nine military regimes which have met Nordlinger's 20-year survival criterion for stability, only the Thai case had lacked an official party; those in Indonesia, Burma, South Korea, Brazil, Paraguay, Zaire, Syria and Egypt were all military-party regimes (Nordlinger, 1977: 138–9).

These issues of permanence and control are also related to the type of *internal* structure that a regime has developed, specifically whether it has developed into a personalist dictatorship by an individual military leader (see Table 5.2). Of the nine stable military regimes mentioned above, seven had been *personalist*-ruler as well as ruler-type regimes for much or part of their existence. Only the Brazilian and Thai regimes had avoided being ruled by an individual military dictator enjoying a degree of personal rule. It is true that in some personalist regimes the military as an organisation has been independently committed to permanent or long-term military rule, even if only personal rule by a military man. But the fact that so many personalist military regimes have been of the military-party type raises the issue of whether the apparent strengthening of military control (by use of a party) may have also strengthened the personal position of the military regime's leader and thereby assisted his achievement of personal rule. Has the establishment of an official party been used by him to control or counterbalance the military, as in Finer's 'dual' type of military rule? (See Table 5.2 and Chapter 2.) Have even colonisation and the political police been used to strengthen the leader's personal control?

The junta may in fact be the only control device that protects a military regime from being taken over internally by an individual military leader and transformed into a personalist-ruler type of military regime. Yet, as in the case of Pinochet in Chile, even a junta may fail to prevent a degeneration into personalist rule (see Chapter 6). And it will be seen in the next chapter that not only the military but also party dictatorships have frequently failed to prevent this degeneration – despite the party dictatorships' often extensive efforts to strengthen party control over state and society.

Party Dictatorships' Strengthening of Control

Party dictatorships have both a greater need and a greater capacity for control than military dictatorships. Their greater need arises from parties' tendency to have less capacity for (direct) physically coercive control than the military but to have more ambitious social goals and/or greater commitment to long-term rule. Their greater capacity arises from the several advantages that parties have over the military when it comes to developing longer-term and less physically or directly coercive forms of control. This is reflected, for example, in the party dictatorships' superiority as developers and controllers of mass-mobilising social organisations.

Parties' most important control advantage is that a party can readily expand its membership to incorporate the military officer corps, the civil service and a significant proportion of society. Even the elitist, 'vanguard' communist parties eventually incorporated in some cases more than 10 per cent of the population, and the Soviet Union's 6–7 per cent was about the (median) average for ruling communist parties (Holmes, 1986: 142). Although such a huge expansion brings many opportunists into party ranks, the party can at least exert some discipline over members through the threat of expulsion or of lesser penalties that will have similarly negative effects upon career prospects.

However, there are marked variations in the degree of control that party dictatorships have sought to achieve through the use of the party. The strongest and most extensive party control over state and society has been sought by the communist party dictatorships. Their Leninist model of exercising party 'leadership' control was developed by the Lenin-led Communist Party in 1918–23 as it sought to consolidate its hold on Russia after the October 1917 revolution. The party's equivalent of a junta was the Central Committee and its Political Bureau (Politburo) subcommittee, which was founded in 1919. They became the *de facto* government of the country, making the key policy decisions and giving instructions to the constitutionally recognised government, the Council of People's Commissars (ministers). Unlike a military junta, the party Central Committee and its Politburo were not *ad hoc* organs but rather an integral part of the party's organisational structure. The members of the Central Committee had been elected by the delegates to the Party Congress to be the party's executive committee, and the Politburo had been established as a standing political/policy subcommittee that could quickly decide pressing issues. The Politburo contained the party's collective leadership, some of whom also held key posts in the legal government, and it gradually took over the role of *de facto* government from the increasingly large and unwieldy Central Committee.

To ensure that the party's policy decisions would be properly implemented – and that the party would remain in power – the new communist regime also established a series of party-based devices to control state and society (Brooker, 1995: 62–5, 71–2). The military was controlled by a complex system that went beyond the use of the numerous party members and 'cell' units within the Red Army. In addition there were (a) political departments established within major units of the Red Army, and (b) political commissars (who were attached to all sizeable military units) with the power to veto the unit commander's orders. Civilian state and society were controlled through party officials receiving information from and issuing directives to the many party members and workplace party units to be found within the Commissariats (ministries), regional/local government, and such social organisations as the labour unions. Finally, the party's *nomenklatura* appointment powers provided the means of ensuring that only 'reliable' people were appointed to party posts, public offices, state offices and leadership posts in social organisations.

Later, under Stalin's leadership, the party expanded its control over society through the first Five-Year Plan's massive expansion of party-controlled state ownership and control of the economy. But this was only an extension of the basic Leninist model into new areas, through the expansion of the state apparatus into the economy, and in the military there was actually a weakening of Leninist control methods, with the political commissars being transformed into less powerful and more militarised 'political officers'.

The Leninist model of strong and extensive party control over state and society would be adopted by all later communist regimes and some other party dictatorships, such as the earlier mentioned cases of the Kuomintang, Baathists and Sandinistas. But it is surprising that the powerful Leninist model was not copied by *more* party dictatorships, especially the African one-party states of the 1960s. The PDG in Guinea was one of the few that did so, but it also waived the elitist-membership aspect of a Leninist party in favour of a 'party-nation' approach that saw every citizen automatically enrolled in the party.

The two fascist regimes did not adopt the Leninist model of strong party control (Brooker, 1995: 30–3, 43–6). In fact the Italian Fascist regime's 'model' was perhaps the polar extreme to the Leninist, as it transformed the party in theory and practice into an *auxiliary* arm of the Fascist state. The party's leader, Mussolini, based his power on the public office of Chief of the Government, not on his party office. The party's Politburo-like Grand Council of Fascism was transformed into a (seldom-convened) state organ, headed *ex officio* by the Chief of Government and stacked with his personal appointees and state officials rather than with party figures. The party's key regional officials, the provincial secretaries, were subordinated to their civil-service counterparts, the Prefects, and the party's Fascist militia was reconstituted as a public rather than party organisation. Although party membership was made compulsory for all civil servants (and was available to military officers on request), they were subject to no more than a monitoring, not vetoing or directing, form of control by party officials.

The Nazi Party enjoyed a more favourable position *vis-à-vis* the state, but still fell well short of Leninist-style control. Its party leader, Hitler, based his power primarily on his public offices of head of state and government; the relatively few party members in the senior ranks of the civil service were subject to only a monitoring form of control by party officials; the party's Gauleiter regional officials exercised a varying degree of control over state and municipal officials; and the party was denied any presence in the military – serving soldiers were actually prohibited from being active party members.

Later Declines in Party Control

A party dictatorship may well experience a post-consolidation decline in the strength of party control. For example, Saddam Hussein's Baathist regime shifted power from the party to the ministries in the 1980s, with civil servants being publicly instructed to obey their state rather than party superior (Brooker, 1997: 118). A few communist regimes have experienced a less public but marked decline in party control that has gone far beyond allowing more autonomy to reliable state technocrats. The most famous cases arose from Stalin's Great Terror purge in the Soviet Union and from Mao's Cultural Revolution in China (see Chapters 6 and 7). However, in both cases party control was eventually revived, and such dramatic fluctuations or declines have become more the exception than the rule for communist regimes.

Among the African party dictatorships there was a marked tendency for the party to decline and become informally subordinated to the state (Tordoff, 1993: 97). By the end of the 1960s it already seemed that the party was being used largely 'as an auxiliary task force', indeed 'as a sort of public relations agency', and some analysts went so far as 'to argue that one-party states can perhaps better be described as no-party states'

(Zolberg, 1966: 126, Bienen 1970b: 109). Even in cases where the party was officially supreme, its role could be severely curtailed by organisational weaknesses. In Tanzania the central officials of the purportedly supreme party were incapable of controlling even the party, let alone the state and society; the tiny National Headquarters staff enjoyed only intermittent communication with, let alone control over, the party officials in the regions (Bienen, 1970a: ch. 5 and p. 456). Although this organisational weakness was partly due to a lack of human and material resources, there were also political factors involved in the party's lack of enthusiasm for strengthening its central administrative staff (*ibid.*: 197–8).

A political factor was also emphasised in a 1990s assessment of the decline of the party in African one-party states. Tordoff argued that one reason for this decline was the emergence of 'presidential rule' after the party leader became the country's president and became the focus of a 'personalisation' of power (1993: 97, 94). In other parts of the world, too, the emergence of (usually presidential) personalist rule by the party leader has produced a decline in the party's position. As will be described in the next chapter, a major threat to these parties' hold on power has been the regime's degeneration into personalist rule – into a party equivalent of the military's personalist-ruler type of regime.

6

Degeneration into Personal Rule

The Nature of Personalist Rule

A key issue in the government of modern non-democratic regimes is whether the military or party regime degenerates into personal rule by an individual dictator (see Chapter 2). With this degeneration into 'monarchical' personal rule by an individual, the regime loses some of its modern structure and some of the credibility of its distinctively modern claim to favour democracy.

The most blatant shift to personal dictatorship occurs when an elected civilian president stages an *autogolpe* and uses this self-coup to misappropriate the public office and powers he has acquired by democratic, constitutional means (see Chapter 3). But the much more common and historically significant form of personal dictatorship arises from degeneration *within* an existing dictatorship – *after* public office and powers have already been seized/misappropriated by a party or military. (It often emerges at the outset when a leader of the military or party becomes the new regime's leader and acquires some personal control over the public offices and powers that his organisation has seized or misappropriated.) In this situation the personal misappropriation of public office and powers will not be as blatant and abrupt as a presidential self-coup. Moreover, the dictator's conversion of public office/powers into his own personal 'property' will be a misappropriating of his usurping party's or military's 'property' – the expropriator of public office/powers will have itself been expropriated.

Degeneration into personal rule is common among dictatorships, particularly among party regimes, but it is far from being inevitable. Many military regimes and some Communist party regimes have not succumbed to it, and some personalist military dictators have been removed from power by the military. Parties have proved less able to remove or rein in a personal ruler and usually they have had to wait until his death to regain power. Yet even when the degeneration into personal rule has been prevented, reversed or outlived, the continuing possibility of personal rule remains a central issue in the regime's internal development.

Degrees of Personal Rule

There are *degrees* of personal rule and often it is better described as personal*ist* rule (see Chapter 2). This notion is by no means new and can be found in not only analyses of personal rule but also descriptions of military and party regimes and in relation to political development, political structure and political economy (Huntington, 1968: 201; Rigby, 1972: 453; Haggard and Kaufman, 1995: 56). However, the notion of degrees of personal(ist) rule is more complex than it first appears, and has to be used with some precision.

Some of the degrees of personalist rule actually fall short of personal misappropriation of power, while others in fact go beyond it by involving an increasingly arbitrary/discretionary or absolutist use of the powers that have been usurped. The notion of absolutist personal rule can be traced back to Weber's observation that although there are traditional limits on a chief's or monarch's arbitrary use of his powers, these limits vary from one society to another and are virtually non-existent in cases of Sultanism (see Chapter 2). In fact Weber used the term 'Sultanism' to refer to situations where 'absolute authority is maximized' (1964: 347). The Sultans of the Turkish Ottoman Empire (1308–1922) offer a classic example of formally absolutist monarchy and, in some cases, of the adage that absolute power corrupts absolutely. The decline of this huge empire from a virtual superpower in the seventeenth century to the 'sick man of Europe' in the nineteenth century also illustrates that even the absolutist use of public powers is inherently limited by the capacity of the state's administrative/military machinery to implement public policy (see Chapter 7).

The variations in degree of personalist rule can be viewed as constituting a range, scale or continuum. It begins with a weak personalism in which the regime leader is allowed a deal of autonomy by his party or military colleagues and acts as virtually a 'free agent'. The most institutionalised example is provided by the Mexican presidency since the 1940s, with each president being allowed a degree of personalist rule during his single, six-year term of office as president of the country and leader of the ruling party, the PRI. Such 'free agent' personalism is also found in a form of democracy known as 'delegative democracy', in which the people (rather than a ruling military or party) allow the winner of a democratic presidential election to govern as he sees fit during his term of office (O'Donnell, 1994).

At the other end of the range or scale is the highly personalist rule of a dictator who has relegated his party or military to being only an instrument of his personal rule. (To use more technical language, the increasing degrees of personalist rule involve the increasing autonomy of the agent from his principal and then an increasing reversal of the original principal–agent relationship.) Some historical cases that have been marked by a rapid degeneration into highly personal rule have reached the end of this range or scale within only a few years, as in the case of Hitler in Nazi Germany. But there has been great variation among personalist leaders in the amount, speed and even direction of movement along the scale.

It is often difficult to judge whether a personalist regime leader has gone on to actually misappropriate power and quietly expropriate his party or military. However, a good indication that public office and powers have been converted from the 'property' of the party or military to that of the personalist ruler is whether he appears to have acquired a permanent hold on his public office and is using its powers for his own ends rather than on behalf of party or military. Further increases in the degree of personalist rule, beyond the point of misappropriation of power, involve the increasing lack of political limits on the personal ruler's use of this power. While in traditional societies it is tradition that limits (to varying degrees) the chief or monarch's use of his public powers, in modern societies it is not tradition, or even usually law, but powerful autonomous organisations that politically restrain (to varying degrees) a dictator's use of the powers he has personally misappropriated. The most powerful organisation is likely to be the military or party that the regime leader has quietly expropriated. Although it has lost its hold on public office/powers, it is still a sufficiently powerful organisation to act as a political restraint (whose strength varies from one regime to another) on the personalist ruler's use of power. Therefore, only if the ruler removes this organisation's autonomy by transforming it into an instrument of his personal rule, can he acquire a virtually 'unlimited', truly absolutist, use of the public powers he has misappropriated.

However, the transformation of his military or party colleagues into an instrument of his rule does not guarantee that the dictator will reach the high end of the scale of personalist rule – it is necessary but not sufficient. For if the military or party has not acquired much control over state and society, there may be other organisations with the autonomy and power to politically restrain the ruler's discretionary use of his powers. For example, the Fascist Party's lack of control over Italy meant that Mussolini still had to deal with such autonomous and powerful organisations as the military, police and civil service even after he had transformed his party into an instrument of personal rule. As (unlike Hitler) he never secured personal control over organisations not controlled by his party, Mussolini was also unable to acquire a high degree of personal rule.

Personal and Structural Factors

Degeneration into a personal misappropriation of power can be analysed by applying the same motive/means/opportunity framework that was applied earlier to party misappropriation (see Chapter 4). But the key aspect is the *means* employed to personally misappropriate power, for they also form the background to the regime's personalist government and politics. The means of personal misappropriation involve a variety and combination of methods exploiting capacities that are best viewed in general terms as the ruler's: 1) personal calibre; 2) personal prestige; and 3) personal position in the regime. His calibre is based in turn on personal attributes that are found in varying degrees and combinations: self-confidence, political shrewdness, ruthlessness, ideological dexterity, oratorical brilliance, administrative ability and effort, military or party leadership skills – and luck.

His prestige is based on his celebrated attributes. These attributes may be 'celebrated' because of their contribution to celebrated events in the history of country or regime, party or military, such as a victorious war, revolution or struggle for national independence. But the attributes may also be celebrated in the sense of being glorified by the regime's propaganda – which is likely to present exaggerated or even fictitious accounts of attributes and contributions, often advertised and promoted by the glorifying *personality cult.* This term became prominent when Stalin's successor denounced his development of a 'cult of personality' that flagrantly contravened the Leninist principle of collective leadership; Stalin had been publicly acknowledged to be the regime's individual leader (*vozhd'*) and had received extravagant public praise from the party, including attributing every successful initiative and policy to the Great Teacher and naming a multitude of factories, schools and villages after him (Brooker, 1995: 71–3).

The term 'personality cult' is now commonly used to describe a propaganda/indoctrination campaign glorifying the regime's leader and making extravagant claims about his personal attributes and the manner in which they have contributed to the successes of the regime and country. In some cases the propaganda is building upon actual attributes and successes – or at least attributes and successes that the public readily believes to be genuine – and the personality cult is therefore seeking only to enlarge rather than establish personal prestige. For example, the 'Hitler cult' in Nazi Germany was a particularly successful personality cult because it could build upon Hitler's apparently remarkable successes in economic, social and foreign affairs (Kershaw, 1987: ch. 2). The more artificial personality cults are unlikely to have much of an impact upon the public but a massive propaganda/indoctrinating effort will at least bring the leader to the public's attention. In Mussolini's Italy, for instance, it seemed that the extravagant cult of the Duce (leader) had led to *mussolinismo* actually replacing Fascism (Brooker, 1995: 34). Therefore even the relatively artificial personality cults can potentially provide some legitimation for personalist rule and misappropriation of power.

However, a more important source of capacity for personal

misappropriation are the 'structural' attributes that strengthen the leader's personal position within the regime – such as control over public powers that are legally absolutist or very extensive. For example, this legal absolutism will protect the leader from being removed by legal means. As will be described later, while Mussolini could be removed from power constitutionally in 1943, the only way that war-weary Germans could have removed the legally absolutist Hitler was by such violent means as the July 1944 assassination plot.

Such extensive public powers may be only *indirectly* controlled by the regime leader; instead of holding the public office that has these powers, he controls all the party members who hold public offices. The standard case of such indirect use of public powers is provided by the communist regimes' system of party control of public offices/powers by the party Politburo and Central Committee, which enables a party leader to exercise public power even if he lacks a public office, as for example when Stalin used the state's (NKVD) political police to devastating effect in the 1930s.

Another structural attribute that strengthens the regime leader's personal position is that almost invariably he is also the leader of the military and/or official party. Leadership of the military helps to safeguard him from all civilian as well as military attempts to overthrow him. Leadership of the party provides him with some kind of control organisation which may also have (1) a coup-deterring role, by potentially mobilising civilian opposition to military intervention, and/or (2) a significant electoral role if his public office formally requires an occasional electoral charade. Therefore the strength of this leadership position over the military or party can be crucial. A military commander who is also the personal or political leader of the military can rely all the more surely on their loyalty, and a party leader who is formally absolutist and permanent is in a stronger position (other things being equal) than a party leader who can be removed from power by the Politburo or Central Committee.

Moreover, the strength of a leadership position over military, party and regime can be greatly enhanced by supplementary structural attributes. Hitler's powerful SS security and military organisation is a famous but unique case. A more common form of supplementary structural attribute, often found in Africa and the Middle East, is the regime leader's use of family members and people from his locality, tribe, sect, or other minority group to fill high-security posts.

Three 'Classic' Cases: Hitler, Stalin and Mussolini

History's most famous dictators, Hitler and Stalin, provide the two classic examples of structural attributes being used to build a very powerful personal position – the basis of highly personalist rule. Although both were party leaders, there were some striking differences between the two cases. Hitler led his party to power and soon after dramatically strengthened his personal position, but Stalin was a second-generation regime leader who gradually secured the position of party and regime leader after Lenin's death and then moved on to establish an increasingly personal rule. Moreover, Hitler had already established an absolutist leadership position over his party before he led it to power, and he would strengthen his personal position as regime leader largely by establishing an absolutist public office and securing personal control over state organisations. In contrast, Stalin had 'only' to secure a strong leadership position over the all-powerful Communist Party, the controller of state and society, and he would thereby almost automatically acquire a very powerful personal position.

Hitler

Hitler's rule over Nazi Germany is the most obvious and complete case of formally personal rule that has occurred in modern times. Within two years of being appointed head of government (Chancellor) by President Hindenburg in January 1933, Hitler had acquired the most absolutist public office possessed by any modern dictator (Brooker, 1995: 47–50). His powers as head of government were greatly increased by the Enabling Law of March 1933, which transferred legislative power from the parliament to his government.

But the key development was his acquisition of the powers of head of state after President Hindenburg's death in August 1934. Under a new law the title of President was abolished and the office and powers of head of state were conferred upon

Hitler with the new, combined title of 'Fuehrer and Reich Chancellor'. This not only removed any possibility of Hitler's dismissal from office by higher authority, but also gave him the former presidency's extensive decree powers (now known as 'Fuehrer decrees') and its titular command of the armed forces. He quickly capitalised on his new position by having the military, his ministers, the civil service, and even the judiciary swear an oath of loyalty to him as Fuehrer of the country – thereby securing his personal control over state organs and organisations. His legally recognised absolutist autocracy, termed a *Fuehrerstaat* (leader state) by Hitler and his legal theorists, was a unique modern version of a formally absolutist monarchy.

Hitler not only quickly established a uniquely powerful legal position but also developed a unique personal security/military force, the notorious SS (*ibid.*: 46–7). Originally founded as the Nazi Party's bodyguard/security force, the SS (Schutzstaffel or 'protection units') became a Hitler rather than party organisation and underwent a huge expansion in power and size after he came to power. It became the regime's leading control organisation, with a membership of more than 160 000 by 1938. The SS had soon taken over the regime's powerful new political police organ, the Gestapo, thanks to SS-leader Himmler's successful struggle in 1933 to win control of all the political police in Germany. And in 1936 Hitler's bestowal upon Himmler of the specially created post of Chief of the German Police had given the SS the opportunity to take over the ordinary police. In fact the police force was in theory 'fused' with the SS, with police officers being pressured into joining this neither state nor party organisation. The SS retained and institutionalised the personal bond with Hitler that had been established in the 1920s when it had been primarily a bodyguard unit. (The personal bond with the Fuehrer was proclaimed in the SS induction oath of personal loyalty to Hitler and in the SS motto of 'my honour is loyalty'.) The personal rather than state or national basis of SS loyalty was also retained in the organisation's military units, the Waffen-SS, despite the massive wartime expansion of this supposedly volunteer military force, which may have eventually numbered as many as 900 000 men.

In contrast to the new role acquired by the SS (and to Hitler's desire to secure an absolutist public office), the Nazi Party was given a relatively minor role in strengthening Hitler's personal position (*ibid.*: 40–5, 50). The party as an organisation, as distinct from individual party officials, was relegated by Hitler to a largely indoctrinating role. Instead of allowing the party to control state and society, he gave it only a legal monopoly – all other parties being banned by law – and a formally prestigious yet vague 'separate but equal' status *vis-à-vis* the state apparatus. He could be confident that the party would not balk at being confined to a secondary role (and seeing him misappropriate power), as he had already established his absolutist leadership over this very hierarchical party before 1933 and had various means of blocking any attempt by the party to remove him from power. (For example, in 1934 the SS had been used to carry out a bloody purge of the leadership of the Nazi paramilitary movement, the SA or 'Storm Troopers'.) As Hitler also established some personal control over such powerful state organisations as the military, his highly personalist rule would be ended only by the Allies' 1945 invasion of Germany and his suicide in a Berlin bunker.

Stalin

As was noted earlier, Stalin's rise to personalist rule differed markedly from Hitler's (Brooker, 1995: 69–72). Stalin had been preceded by Lenin as the first leader of the communist regime established in the former Russian empire, later renamed the Soviet Union. Moreover, he had not been Lenin's heir apparent nor even the most prominent figure in the collective leadership that headed the regime after Lenin's death in 1924. Stalin took several years to defeat and politically destroy – one individual or group at a time – the other leading figures within the post-Lenin collective leadership.

In the 1930s the party and regime's new leader went on to establish a highly personalist rule but his powerful personal position, unlike Hitler's, was not bolstered by a personal security/military force or even by important public offices (which he would not acquire until the 1940s). Instead, he was able to exploit the Communist Party's control of state and society that had been established under Lenin (see Chapter 5). As the party had become the ultimate controlling organisation, any regime leader who established a strong leadership position over the party had also gone a long way towards establishing a powerful personal position within the regime.

In the 1920s Stalin had laid the foundations for a strong leadership position over the party by exploiting the opportunities for power that came to him as head of the party's increasingly powerful administrative apparatus (*ibid.*). His expertise in matters of party organisation and routine administration led in 1922 to his acquisition of the new post of party General Secretary. As head of the Secretariat of the party's Central Committee he became the boss of not only the central party administrators but also the apparatus of party secretaries that extended out into the regions and down to the local and workplace secretaries. At all levels of the party beneath the Central Committee the secretaries had come to dominate the party units they 'served', and by 1925 no less than two-thirds of the delegates to the Party Congress were members of the party's administrative apparatus. Moreover, by 1926 his central Secretariat wielded personnel powers (*nomenklatura* appointment-making and vetoing powers) over some 5000 top posts in the party apparatus as well as in state and society.

Although this administratively based control of the party was not the only reason for his succession to the party and regime leadership, it was clearly the main factor in his rise to power and enabled him to go on in the 1930s to establish a strong leadership position over the party. Furthermore, a Secretariat department that operated informally as Stalin's personal secretariat was officially responsible for liaising with the political police on behalf of the party. And in the later 1930s Stalin would use the party-controlled political police to transform the party into an instrument of his personal rule.

Stalin did not establish a highly personalist rule until after he launched the political police on the massive political/ideological witch-hunt that became known as the Great Terror (or Purge) of 1937–38 (*ibid.*: 73–5). The NKVD political police arrested some five million people, executed over 800 000 of them, and incarcerated most of the remainder in prisons or labour camps. From a purely political perspective the nature of the victims was more significant than their number. The NKVD had arrested leading communists in the military, the state departments, the social organisations and even the party's administrative apparatus (in the regions). Among the victims were a large majority of the party's Central Committee and more than half of the delegates to the most recent Party Congress. The Terror destroyed the party as an independent political entity – it was now officially described as a party of Lenin–Stalin followers – and the once all-powerful Communist Party was relegated to being only one of several instruments of Stalin's personal rule, including the political police and the state's administrative apparatus (*ibid.*: 76).

In the 1940s Stalin went on to occupy several major public offices, state posts and military ranks. He took on the public office of Premier (head of government) in May 1941. And after the German invasion of the Soviet Union in June 1941 he added the offices and posts of Commissar (Minister) for Defence, Chairman of the emergency State Committee of Defence, and Supreme Commander-in-Chief. He also took the military rank of Marshal and later the newly created rank of Generalissimo of the Soviet Union. But in the 1940s he was only further strengthening an already very powerful personal position, pushing his already highly personalist rule towards the end of the scale. Not surprisingly, his rule remained unchallenged by the party or any other organisations until his death in 1953.

Mussolini

Mussolini's Fascist regime in Italy, another 'classic' dictatorship, offers a striking example of how an apparently powerful personal position can conceal important structural deficiencies, which eventually contributed to the collapse of Mussolini's personalist rule. After being appointed Prime Minister by the King of Italy in 1922 (see Chapter 4), Mussolini waited several years before substantially strengthening his personal position by (1) transforming the prime ministership in 1925 into the more powerful and 'presidential' public office of Chief of the Government, and then (2) strengthening his leadership position over the Fascist Party by making it a truly hierarchical party headed by its formally recognised Duce (leader). But although in the later 1920s the personally powerful Mussolini was able to misappropriate power, his flamboyant personalist rule was built upon weak foundations that prevented him from establishing a highly personalist regime in the 1930s and which contributed to his removal from power in the 1940s.

The two key structural deficiencies in Mussolini's personal

position were (1) his inability to secure the office of head of state, and (2) his subordination of the party to the state. During his misappropriation of power in the later 1920s, Mussolini had seriously downplayed the Fascist Party's role in his regime, to the extent of formally subordinating the party to the state (see Chapter 5). This had ensured that the party could not prevent or reverse his personal misappropriation of power, and it also helped Mussolini to transform the party into an instrument of his personalist rule in the 1930s. But the Fascist Party was a weak instrument, which did not exercise any significant control over such powerful state organisations as the military, police and civil service. Moreover, the subordination of party to state had also created a potential weakness in his leadership position over the party. For in 1928 the Grand Council of Fascism was made the ultimate source of authority over the Fascist regime, including the Fascist Party, even though (a) the great majority of the Council's largely *ex officio* membership were public and state officials rather than party officials and leaders, and (b) the Grand Council was headed by Mussolini only by right of his being the Chief of the Government – if he lost that public office, he also lost the Chairmanship of the Fascist Grand Council.

What made this subordination of party to state so dangerous to Mussolini's personal position was that he could not acquire the office of head of state, which in Italy was held by a hereditary monarch and was also legally more powerful than Mussolini's own public office of head of government. The Chief of the Government was legally subordinate to and dependent upon Italy's constitutional head of state, the King. The monarch had the constitutional authority to dismiss Mussolini from public office and to appoint someone else to be Chief of the Government. Therefore even in the 1930s Mussolini was hardly in a position to remove the crucial obstacle to acquiring personal control over the military, police and civil service – their oath of loyalty to the King as Italy's constitutional head of state.

In fact Mussolini was removed from power in July 1943 (following the Allies' invasion of Sicily) by a combination of the Fascist Grand Council's and the King's authority over party and state organisations. After receiving an implicit vote of no confidence from the Grand Council, Mussolini was dismissed as Chief of Government by the King – who replaced him with a military man – and was taken into police custody. Mussolini was later rescued by German troops, not by the docile Fascist Party, and went on to head a German puppet state in northern Italy. In April 1945 he tried to flee to Germany but was captured and executed by anti-fascist guerrillas.

Three Military Cases and the Awkward Case of Saddam Hussein

Franco

The only *military* personalist regime in twentieth-century history which is anywhere near as famous as the dictatorships of Hitler, Stalin and Mussolini is General Franco's long-lasting and highly personalist rule over Spain (Brooker, 1995: 139–47). His regime emerged from the Spanish Civil War of 1936–39, in which Franco had been the military and political leader of the victorious Nationalist rebels. During the war he had already secured a very powerful personal position by acquiring:

1. the military post of Supreme Commander and the rank of Generalissimo,
2. the public offices of Chief of State and Chief of the Government, and
3. formally absolutist leadership over a new official party, the FET, which had merged the radically rightist, if not fascist, Falangist movement with the monarchist-Catholic Traditionalist movement.

After the Civil War Franco could rely on not only his status as supreme commander and highest ranking officer, but also his personal leadership of the military (as its victorious commander in the Civil War) to ensure that the military became an instrument of his personal rule. Moreover, he used the military to secure his hold over state and society; military men held about a third of the provincial governorships, of the senior posts in the civil service, and of the senior positions in the FET. Franco's permanent tenure of the public offices of head of state and government was confirmed in a 1939 law which also bestowed legislative powers upon him. (A few years later, though, he set up an appointative parliament that acted as a rubber-stamp legislature and enhanced the regime's image of being a supposed Organic Democracy.) In 1947 Franco's legal status was further regularised by the Law of Succession, which restored Spain to the status of a hereditary monarchy (which it had been until 1930) but gave Franco the title of Regent for life and the responsibility for preparing the way for one of the branches of the former royal family to reassume the throne.

During the 1950s Franco continued to shift the ideological basis of his regime to monarchist-Catholic conservatism rather than the fascist-style Falangism that had seemed to dominate the regime in the early 1940s. But he would have no difficulty controlling the Falangists within the FET, and he remained this hierarchical party's undisputed and absolutist leader – officially responsible solely to God and History – until his death in 1975.

Pinochet and Stroessner

Although no other military regimes have become as famous as Franco's, two other more recent examples of personalist military regime – Pinochet's in Chile and Stroessner's in Paraguay – form an interesting pair of cases. They arose in neighbouring countries and came to an end in the late 1980s, but they represent two quite different approaches to building a powerful personal position in a military regime. Both these generals took over their countries' key public office of President and strengthened their leadership position over the military, but Pinochet did not set up or take over a political party – the Chilean military regime would never have an official party. He 'solved' the problem of democratic legitimacy by resorting to the time-honoured method of promising an eventual return to democracy (and enshrining this commitment in the new, 1980 Constitution's provision that in eight years' time a plebiscitary, one-candidate presidential election would act as a binding referendum on rapid democratisation).

When Stroessner took power in the mid-1950s, he preferred a potentially more permanent 'solution' to the problem of democratic legitimacy, and sought to conceal his dictatorship behind a democratic guise, complete with presidential and legislative elections (see Chapter 9). As this solution required an official party, it gave his regime some of the appearance of Franco's military-party regime. However, Stroessner's pseudo-democratic form of military-party regime involved a looser political situation in which a few other parties were allowed to exist and the official party was allowed a less hierarchical and leader-dominated structure than Franco's fascist-style party – a difference that would weaken Stroessner's position in the last years of his rule.

Stroessner has been described as 'a personalist dictator, totally dominating the political regime', and another analyst has described him as heading a military regime in which, although the army is 'not far from power, it does not govern and Stroessner is not its spokesman' (Sondrol, 1991: 619; Rouquié, 1987: 184). Whatever the exact degree of personalist rule, it was based upon a powerful personal position with several different structural attributes, including an official party as well as the powerful public office of President and a strong leadership position over the military (Sondrol, 1991, and 1992; Nickson, 1988; Rouquié, 1987: 181–4).

Stroessner established an official party by taking over the long-standing Colorado Party at the very outset of his regime. The military's young Commander-in-Chief had engineered his nomination as the party's candidate in the 1954 presidential election (which would be the first of his many dubious election victories), and soon purged the party of all unreliable groups and personalities. He also expanded it into a truly mass party which took on a controlling as well as electoral role. The party developed an extensive and powerful presence in the grassroots of rural society, and party membership became obligatory for all state and municipal officials and for military officers. The officer corps went even further by requiring that all officer cadets have a Colorado family background.

In addition to making himself leader of an effective official party, Stroessner strengthened his leadership over the military in a variety of ways. He not only retained his military post as supreme commander, but also had the military swear an oath of personal loyalty to him. Later, he developed an ideology of Stronismo (emphasising nationalism, communitarianism, and anti-communism) which formed the basis of indoctrination sessions within the military and was reflected in a reorientation of the military's mission, with a new stress on anti-communist internal security and on communitarian civic action and rural development programmes. But Stroessner also strengthened his hold over the officer corps through such prosaic means as cronyism, clientelism, and the provision of lucrative opportunities for corruption, smuggling and black-market racketeering. As a final precaution he established a particularly reliable and personally loyal military unit, the elite Presidential Escort Regiment. It did in fact put up fierce resistance to the coup in 1989 that revealed the decline in Stroessner's hold over the military and finally ended his personalist rule.

However, an important factor in the demise of Stroessner's personalist rule seems to have been his lack of a strong leadership position over the official party. For the loosening of his hold over the military has been ascribed in part to divisions within his Colorado Party (Snyder, 1992: 391), which could not be contained by his indirect and informal type of party leadership.

Stroessner could not prevent the party's disintegration into a virulent factionalism that became very obvious at the 1987 Party Congress (Nickson, 1988). The 'militant' faction (which was committed to continuing Stroessner rule even if it meant having the now elderly ruler succeeded by his mediocre son) prevailed over the small group of pro-democratising 'ethicals' and the large 'traditionalist' faction, which was concerned about the historic Colorado Party's future prospects now that the end of the Stroessner era seemed to be looming. When Stroessner fell out with his senior army commander in 1989, he used General Rodriguez's sympathy with the traditionalist faction of Colorados as a pretext for demanding that he either retire or relinquish command of his troops and become defence minister (Sondrol, 1992: 112). Rodriguez responded by staging the successful coup that sent the elderly President into exile and led on to the democratisation of Paraguay.

As was noted in an earlier chapter, Pinochet's regime in Chile has been used as an example of how neopatrimonial regimes differ from the bureaucratic-authoritarian form of dictatorship (see Chapter 1). Pinochet's regime was described in typically personalist terms as one 'where power has been concentrated in the hands of a single individual at the expense of rule by the military as an institution', and it was argued that Pinochet had by 1976 created 'a government that was eminently personal in nature and not responsive to pressures from the officer corps' (Remmer, 1989: 149, 161). However, Pinochet's success in establishing some degree of personalist rule was based upon a personal position which seemed to include only the public office of President, an increasingly strong leadership position over the military, and an alliance with some civilian groups – notably the 'Chicago boys' monetarist economists (see Remmer, 1989; Garretón, 1986).

The degeneration into personalist rule began soon after the military seized power in 1973 through a violent coup against Chile's long-standing democracy (see Exhibit 3.2). The following year saw the army's commander, General Pinochet, become President of the country and president of the ruling military junta, which lost some of its significance as a governing body and control organ and no longer met on a weekly basis. The creation in 1974 of the notorious DINA (the highly repressive centralised military intelligence/security organ which reported directly to the President) also gave Pinochet a powerful tool for controlling the military as well as civilians.

Moreover, he acquired substantial control over military appointments and even retirements, so that politically unreliable officers could be transferred to remote areas or prematurely retired. His ability to use the carrot as well as the stick would be increased by the regime's increasingly large defence expenditure and number of generals – which would both be doubled in the years ahead. Furthermore, the military's colonisation of state and society allowed Pinochet to offer new varieties of carrot to the officer corps in the form of (active-service) appointments to a wide range of government, state and other civilian offices, including university rectors!

Although Pinochet's regime lacked an official party, the support his regime received from civilian conservatives became another means of strengthening his personal position. This civilian support provided 'sources of experienced and committed personnel, ideological support, and legitimation' that were not available to other right-wing South American military regimes of the time (Remmer, 1989: 161). In particular, Pinochet established a mutually reinforcing relationship with the 'Chicago boys', the civilian economists who propounded monetarist neoclassical economic theories developed at Chicago University. In return for providing Pinochet with an independent, personal source of policy expertise and expert personnel, they received his backing in pushing through monetarist and economically liberal policies that were not supported by mainstream opinion in the Chilean officer corps. In addition to its unusual economic policy Pinochet's regime became distinctive for its durability, as his personalist rule outlived all the other South American military regimes except Stroessner's long-standing 'democratic' military-party regime. And Pinochet's rule was ended in 1988–89 by a peaceful democratisation rather than the violent coup that overthrew personalist rule in Paraguay.

Saddam Hussein

The highly personalist rule of Saddam Hussein is an awkward case because, although he is a civilian party leader, he rose to power through a military dictatorship (see Brooker, 1997: 114–22; Karsh and Rautsi, 1991). The Iraqi Baathist regime originated in a 1968 military coup that led to the General Secretary of the Baath party, a well-known military man, becoming the country's president and Chairman of the Revolutionary Command Council junta. President/Chairman Bakr in turn quickly bestowed an increasing amount of power upon his young civilian protégé, Saddam Hussein. Several years earlier Bakr had installed Saddam as Assistant General-Secretary of the party, and soon after the 1968 coup he made Saddam the Deputy Chairman of the RCC, which was being transformed into a largely civilian junta as part of what became a true civilianisation of the regime.

During the 1970s the interrelated processes of (a) civilianisation and (b) Saddamisation dominated the regime. For while the civilian wing of the party gained increasing control over the military as part of a Leninist-style strengthening of the party's hold on state and society, Saddam secured his hold on the party through Stalin-style control of party administration and Himmler-like control of party and state security/intelligence organisations. By the mid-1970s President Bakr had relinquished his policy-making role to Saddam and was becoming only a ceremonial, figurehead leader. But it was not until 1979 that Saddam finally assumed the public and party offices of President, Chairman of the RCC, and General Secretary, complete with a stage-managed handing over of power from Bakr to his successor and then a violent purge of the party.

Having acquired these supreme public and party offices,

Saddam quickly moved to strengthen his personal position in other areas, such as by giving himself the supreme military rank of Field Marshal. His role as military and national leader was boosted by his invasion of Iran in 1980 and the resulting Iranian counter-invasion, which also created a conducive atmosphere for introducing a range of other measures that strengthened his already powerful personal position. The Baath party and ideology formally acknowledged his position as the individual leader of the party (rather than head of a collective leadership), several of his kinsfolk were deployed in high-security posts, and he was formally recognised as President for life – with the crime of insulting the President being punishable by death. He had become a truly monarchical President and his personal misappropriation of power was symbolised by the monarchical ceremonial trappings that accompanied his triumphant celebration in 1988 of a victorious end to the eight-year war with Iran.

The Monarchical Presidency

Most personalist rulers have held the public office of President and have exploited its potential as an individual rather than collective (prime minister) or administrative (party secretary) leadership post. In fact even among democracies the powerful presidency may pose a threat of 'degeneration'; it has been depicted as being less conducive than parliamentary government to stable democracy and as being preferred, during transitions to democracy, by 'old regime elites' seeking to preserve their power and privileges (Linz, 1990; Easter, 1997). Among dictatorships the presidency has been used by aspiring personalist rulers as a means of establishing what has been termed a 'presidential monarchy' (Apter, 1965) but which is often better described as a 'monarchical presidency'.

Monarchical presidencies involve the misappropriation of the public office of president, with the dictator becoming his country's president 'for life', sometimes quite explicitly (even legally) and otherwise involving only ritualistic reelections by the public or legislature. (There have even been a few cases of hereditary succession, such as 'Papa Doc' and 'Baby Doc' Duvalier in Haiti and the Somozas in Nicaragua.) These presidencies' powers of office normally include those of

1. head of state and government;
2. titular Commander-in-Chief of the armed forces;
3. appointor of ministers, military officers and civil servants; and
4. wielder of decree powers and/or some legislative powers.

The office of President is so 'compatible' with personalist rule that even communist regimes, despite their emphasis on collective leadership and party rule, have seen personalist leaders establish powerful state presidencies for themselves. Among the notable examples were Ho Chi Minh in North Vietnam, Kim Il Sung in North Korea, Ceausescu in Romania, Castro in Cuba and Gorbachev in the Soviet Union. It is true that the most famous case of post-Stalin communist personalism, that of Mao Zedong in China, did not involve a presidency, but party Chairman Mao was also untypical in not holding the powerful party post of General Secretary.

Two of the early Third World examples of presidential personalism were Nasser in Egypt and Nkrumah in Ghana. Colonel Nasser had come to power in Egypt after a 1952 coup but did not institutionalise his personalist rule until he created a powerful presidency for himself in 1956 (Perlmutter, 1974: 143–4). Party leader Nkrumah, who was already Ghana's prime minister when it gained its independence from Britain in 1957, went on in the 1960s to create a super-presidency for himself (Brooker, 1995: 108–12). He greatly expanded the administrative Office of the President until eventually it rivalled the government ministries in size as well as importance, and he expanded the President's Own Guard Regiment to rival the regular army (though this move also strengthened the corporate self-interest motive involved in the 1966 coup that deposed him).

Few other Third World monarchical presidents have developed their public office in such an innovative and extensive fashion, most preferring instead to use their leadership of party and/or military to strengthen their personal position. However, some of them have developed new forms of carrot and stick to support these orthodox measures. The most marked innovation in the use of the stick was the counter-plot purge developed by President Touré of Guinea (*ibid.*: 116, 124–6). This party General Secretary went beyond Stalin in the use of purge terror, actually developing the theory of 'the permanent plot' (that

Guinea was faced by a permanent state of conspiracy by its domestic and external enemies) to justify a succession of supposedly counter-plot purges in the 1960s-70s. The purges' victims were a series of different groups of alleged plotters: teachers, traders, the military, the military plus ministers and veteran party militants, and finally a major tribal group.

Other monarchical presidents have preferred to innovate in the use of the carrot rather than the stick, notably in the form of material rewards and incentives. President Suharto of Indonesia developed a new form or method of delivering material incentives, rewards and resources. He used *yayasans* (charitable foundations not subject to public accounting) to channel funds to various civilian targets: buying off political challenges, providing additional aid funds to rural districts, paying supplementary allowances to the top-ranking civil servants, and being a major source of funds for the regime party, Golkar (Vatikiotis, 1993: 51–2, 58, 112). Moreover, Suharto was a pioneer in the use of a civilian form of patronage to strengthen the personal loyalty of fellow officers. He appointed senior officers to civilian posts in which they could use 'their influence to secure licences, contracts, credit, and other amenities for [business] enterprises with which they [or their families] were privately associated'(Crouch, 1979: 577). President Asad of Syria went even further by allowing not only fellow officers but also his party officials and civil servants to exploit business opportunities as well as the standard forms of corruption (Brooker, 1997: 110; Perthes, 1995: 185–6).

In such cases the monarchical president embodies two different aspects of patrimonialism, namely (1) the personal rule of a monarch or chief, and (2) the blurring of the public and the private (see Chapter 2). Suharto's regime was viewed by Crouch from the perspective of the 'persistence' or 're-emergence' of traditional patrimonial features dating back to the precolonial Javanese kingdoms, such as the ruler's securing the loyalty of crucial elements of the political elite by satisfying their material aspirations (Crouch, 1979: 571–3). More explicitly, Perthes described Asad's regime as patrimonial and as seeing the state treated as private property (1995: 180, 186). In fact Medard's (1982) analysis of neopatrimonialism in African states argued that the lack of any distinction between the public and the private domains is central to traditional patrimonialism and its modern version, neopatrimonialism – pointing to such examples as corruption and patron–client relations (or 'clientelism').

African presidents provided many examples of this aspect of neopatrimonialism as well as the monarchical aspect, with perhaps the most striking case being the more than 30-year reign of President Mobutu of Zaire. In addition to misappropriating public funds to feed his own private fortune (of eventually many billions of dollars), Mobutu allowed his political supporters and their clients to indulge in such massive misappropriation of funds and institutionalised corruption that his regime has been labelled a 'kleptocracy' (Leslie, 1993: 35–6). However, there were marked variations in the degree of neopatrimonialism to be found in Africa (Van de Walle, 1994). In particular, there was variation in the degree to which presidents resorted to allowing their regime 'barons' (as Van de Walle termed them) to exploit the opportunities for enrichment involved in heading a state agency that is a major source of revenue (*ibid.*: 134). These 'barons' were recruited from family, friends, political allies, and even former political enemies, and they helped the ruler to manage a patron–client pyramid that extended down to the village level.

However, this analogy with medieval barons also raises the issue of whether these were typically 'feudal' barons, in the sense of having misappropriated public powers as well as revenue (see Exhibit 6.1). A modern version of feudalism and its misappropriating tendencies would involve not only corruption but also a wider misuse of public powers. They would be used by powerful officials in a manner indifferent or even contrary to the personalist ruler's desire, and as if these powers were the personal 'property' of the official. Therefore the degeneration into personalist rule would have spread from the top of the regime downwards and outwards, with personalist rulers to be found in the central administration and in the provinces as well as in the presidential palace.

An early African example of a monarchical presidency suffering from quasi-feudal misappropriation arose in Nkrumah's one-party state of the early 1960s (Brooker, 1995: 104–7). His key territorial agents were the Regional Commissioners, who combined state and party powers in their role as informal regional governors, and the District Commissioners, who were party/state officials that tightly controlled the party's local branches

Exhibit 6.1 Feudalism, Benefices and Prebends – Old and New

Feudalism is the most famous variety of what Weber termed 'decentralised patrimonialism', in which a patrimonial ruler's officials personally appropriate the 'fief' or 'benefice', often a landed property, that has been attached to their administrative office as a means of support or reward for the office-holder (Weber, 1964: 351–3, 373–7). An administrative staff systematically supported by such benefices was said by Weber to be based on 'prebends'. This notion of prebendal administration has been applied to such modern Third World countries as Nigeria, just as the notion of 'patrimonial benefice' has been applied to Mobutu of Zaire's distribution of expropriated businesses to his officials – whose salary might constitute as little as 2 per cent of their earnings (Joseph, 1987: 55–6; Young, 1982a: 249, 302).

The application of such archaic terms as 'prebend' and 'benefice' to modern 'neopatrimonial' countries can be quite illuminating (see Chapter 2). For example, Weber referred to corruption in a patrimonial system as simply a disorganised, unregulated system of (benefice) fee-paying by the public (1964: 357). But applying the notion of feudalism to a modern country implies something more politically significant than just corruption. For feudalism typically involves a special kind of landed benefice, known as the 'fief', which incorporates the exercise of the ruler's judicial and other public powers over his subjects.

More importantly, although there is a feudal oath-bound tie of personal loyalty between the patrimonial ruler and the 'vassals' upon whom he bestows fiefs, it is usually not sufficient to prevent these officials from misappropriating the public powers bestowed upon them. Weber pointed to the tendency for patrimonial rulers to lose control over their feudal vassals; the ruler's control over a vassal never in practice attains the feudal ideal or is more than temporarily effective (1964: 376) In other words, there is a tendency for the feudal official to usurp power through misappropriating the public powers that have been bestowed/devolved upon him.

and dominated local government. However, although the RCs were supposedly personally responsible to Nkrumah, he was plagued by a breakdown in the chain of command between himself and the regions. The RCs tended to act independently of and sometimes in opposition to his instructions, and most of the many policy statements and decisions made at regional and local levels actually contradicted Nkrumah's policy pronouncements. He responded only with ineffectual warnings against any repetition of this disloyalty, which had seriously undermined his monarchical presidency's control over the regions. On the other hand, the principal function of his regional and local officials 'was to keep the peace in the countryside', and as long as they kept the countryside quiet, they at least allowed Nkrumah to concentrate upon his predominantly urban and industrial concerns (Jones, 1976: 91).

In contrast, to lose control of the regions of such a massive country as the Soviet Union meant losing control of not only the countryside but also most of industry and of the urban population. And on his way to becoming a highly personalist ruler Stalin made sure that he eliminated the danger of a quasi-feudal misappropriation of power by regional officials. As early as the 1934 Party Congress, Stalin had publicly complained about party officials in the regions not fulfilling the decisions of the party's central organs (the country's *de facto* central government). At the February 1937 meeting of the Central Committee, Stalin complained again about the regions' unresponsiveness and also accused the party's powerful regional secretaries of forming mutually protective 'family groups' (of personally loyal party and state officials) whose existence would increase the secretaries' independence from the central party organs (Getty, 1985: 145). Therefore it is not surprising that these regional officials became a prime target of the Great Terror or Great Purge that Stalin launched in mid-1937 – by the end of the year nearly all of them had been removed and either executed or imprisoned (*ibid.:* 173, 257 n. 5).

However, such a violent elimination of quasi-feudal misappropriation is based on the ruler's continued control over the police and military. In Nasser's Egypt the monarchical president was faced with a quasi-feudal loss of power over the military itself. After the 1952 military coup, Colonel (later President) Nasser had ensured that the military bestowed the post of

Commander-in-Chief on his close friend, Brigadier (later Field Marshal) Amer. Yet, by the early 1960s Amer had substantially weakened 'presidential authority over the military, which he had run as his personal fief' (Dekmejian, 1971: 255). And the increasingly independent position enjoyed by the military during the mid-1960s posed a real threat to Nasser's own, personal position within the regime. He was unlikely to be removed from power but 'a gentler process of "kicking him upstairs" into some purely honorific position did appear to be a real possibility' (Baker, 1978: 95). Nasser eventually regained control over the military, thanks to its humiliating defeat in the 1967 war with Israel, but for several years there had been a real prospect that he would be transformed into an only ceremonial, reigning rather than ruling, monarchical president.

7

Policies and Performance

The policies and performance of dictatorships can be viewed as simply a question of how these regimes *use* the public offices and powers that they have seized or misappropriated. Such an approach seems particularly appropriate when focusing on their key policy programmes, which may appear only once in a regime's lifetime. (More wide-ranging descriptions and assessments of the policies of specific types of dictatorship, such as communist or Nazi policies, can be found in works listed in Further Reading.) For example, Hitler's genocidal programme of physically eliminating Europe's Jews can hardly be viewed as just one of the 'outputs' of the Nazi government. Indeed the use of power to perpetrate a 'crime against humanity' is most appropriately analysed by applying the forensic motive/means/opportunity framework. In this case there was ideological motive, SS means and wartime opportunity – the conquest of most of Europe plus the availability of wartime conditions of secrecy and control.

However, this framework cannot readily be applied in any systematic fashion to the policies of dictatorships; even their key policy programmes are much too diverse in nature and background – and only some of the programmes could be considered 'criminal'. Instead, this chapter will focus on identifying the distinctive and key policy programmes, such as the establishing or dismantling of a communist economy. Then it will go on to examine personalist and non-personalist policymaking and styles of government, before concluding with an assessment of governmental 'performance' and policy implementation.

Distinctive Policies

Identifying the distinctive (key) policy programmes of dictatorships involves sifting out those key programmes that have been instituted by one or more dictatorships but not by a democracy. (It also means excluding distinctively high commitment of resources, such as the rearmament programme instituted in Nazi Germany and the health-care programme established in Communist Cuba.) There can be problems, though, in distinguishing between the dictatorships' and the democracies' versions of seemingly quite similar policy programmes or approaches.

For example, the theory and institutions of corporatism are historically identified with the Italian Fascist regime's doctrine and institutions of the Corporate (or Corporative) State. In theory this corporatism was a state-supervised system of representation and self-government by economic interest groups. Instead of labour unions, farmers' unions, professional associations and employer/industry associations, there would be legally recognised 'syndicates' or 'corporations' – each representing and to some extent controlling a major industry or sector of the economy – which would collectively join with the state to organise the economy as a whole (see Exhibit 7.1).

But the actual practice of corporatism seems to have been much more prevalent in some European democracies in the 1950s–70s than in Fascist Italy and other corporatist dictatorships. Schmitter resolved this paradox by drawing a detailed and famous distinction between the 'state' corporatism imposed by some dictatorships and the 'societal' corporatism that had developed in some democracies (1974: 113, 103–4). State corporatism was often more of a control/repression mechanism and ideological symbol than a 'working' economic or social programme, but it retains its significance as arguably the sole distinctively 'non-democratic' policy programme to have been instituted by military as well as party dictatorships.

Military Regimes

As Finer pointed out in the 1980s, military regimes do not have any common or distinctive approach to economic (and social) policy. Of the then existing military regimes he classified nine as being market-capitalist in approach, 10 as

Exhibit 7.1 The Fascist Corporate State and Other Forms of State Corporatism

As a first step towards attaining its ideal of a Corporate or Corporative State the Fascist regime initially established an extensive system of state-supervised syndicates that had a legal monopoly to represent (separately) employers and employees in each sector/industry of the economy (Brooker, 1991: 150–1, 193–7). In the case of the employee syndicates, for example, there was a Confederation of Syndicates of Industrial Workers which incorporated the national syndicate of textile workers which in turn was a federation of provincial textile unions. But such employee syndicates were prevented from operating as true labour unions by the legal prohibition on strikes and by unenthusiastic government-appointed leaders.

The supposedly definitive structure of the Corporate State was not established until the mid-1930s and was more of an ideological symbol than a set of working institutions. The government created 22 sector/industry national corporations, each comprising representatives of the relevant employer and employee syndicates and of the Fascist Party and state. The corporations were given token powers over production, pricing, wages and labour disputes, but had scant effect on the Fascist government's economic policy or even on the continuing activities of the employer and employee syndicates.

Several other dictatorships have implemented a degree of state-controlled corporatism (as in Franco's Spain and military-ruled Brazil) which has been similarly biased against workers' industrial and political power (Schmitter, 1974: 124). The use of a state-controlled corporatist system to control or contain labour and exclude it from power has been described by Stepan as 'exclusionary' corporatism (1978: ch. 2). However, he identified another form of state-controlled corporatism, 'inclusionary' corporatism, which is aimed at integrating or incorporating the workers and peasantry into society.

For example, the Peruvian military regime's inclusionary corporatism of the early 1970s sought to establish a new structure of 'decentralized, participatory, self-managing groups' in agriculture, industry and urban squatter settlements (*ibid.*: 120). The regime apparently hoped that the success of these new groups, in conjunction with other social policies, would lead to the withering away of the country's labour unions. However, both inclusionary and exclusionary corporatist methods differ from the state-imposed economic liberalism of the Pinochet regime in Chile, which used coercion and a freed-up labour market to control workers and exclude them from power (Schamis, 1991: 206).

capitalist-statist, 12 as capitalist-socialist and four as socialist (Finer, 1988: 296–7). In general, the military regimes have been less extreme than the party dictatorships in their economic and social policies. Not only are many of them 'centrist' in approach, but also the rightist and leftist extremes are milder than their fascist and communist counterparts. The rightist Franco regime in Spain did not develop into a fully fledged fascist regime and a similar pattern is evident among the leftist military regimes. The Burmese socialist regime copied only parts of the ortho-dox communist economy, while the avowedly Marxist–Leninist African military regimes failed to institute even a centrally planned economy, let alone the collectivisation of agriculture.

In comparison, the Peruvian military regime's populist programme of the early 1970s seems quite radically socialist. The self-proclaimed revolution of the Revolutionary Govern-ment of the Armed Forces went beyond the nationalist/social-welfare approach of nationalising foreign companies and improving the provision of health care and education. The masses' integration into the national society – and desisting from class conflict – was also to be promoted by a land reform that transferred ownership of the large estates to the labourers who worked them; while in industry there was to be some worker participation in management and a gradual transfer of 50 per cent share-ownership of industrial enterprises to their workers (Stepan, 1978: 120, 274). Combined with some unusual organ-isational, mobilising features (see Exhibit 7.1), this social programme was one of the few distinctive policy programmes developed by a military regime.

Another distinctive policy programme, economic as well as social, was developed by what O'Donnell termed the 'bureau-cratic-authoritarian' regimes (extensively described in Chapter 1). But the pure form of bureaucratic-authoritarianism was almost as rare as the left-wing Peruvian regime's programme. More common was the monetarist, economically liberalising (or 'neo-conservative') programme instituted by Pinochet's regime and to a lesser extent by its contemporaries in Argentina and Uruguay (Schamis, 1991). However, this programme soon lost its distinctiveness. For although a programme of monetarism, econ-omic deregulation and privatisation of state-owned assets was adopted in Chile 'earlier and more intensively than in, say, Margaret Thatcher's Britain', this programme lost its non-democratic distinctiveness when Britain and other democracies adopted similar policies (*ibid.*: 251).

Fascist Regimes

The party dictatorships have been more diverse, innovative and extreme than their military counterparts. To begin with the most notorious case, the Nazi policy of anti-Semitic genocide is too distinctive to be viewed as even a typically 'fascist' policy – the Italian Fascist regime did not even adopt anti-Semitic doctrines until the later 1930s. However, both regimes were committed to an imperialist foreign policy. The Fascists openly proclaimed their intent of establishing a new Roman empire around the Mediterranean, while the Nazis were secretly committed to the goal of conquering Lebensraum (living space) in Eastern Europe and the Soviet Union. In terms of economic policy, this meant an economy oriented towards military needs and in turn encouraged a policy of autarky – of economic self-sufficiency.

But it was in social policy that both regimes pursued a distinctive and ambitious goal that was linked to their imperialist aims. Both sought to indoctrinate their societies in an ideology that would strengthen the social solidarity and political loyalty of what would be the 'home front' in another total war like the First World War (Brooker, 1991). To carry out this social policy the regimes constructed an array of indoctrinating organisations that went well beyond anything developed by nation-building regimes seeking the more limited goal of instilling a degree of national consciousness in their societies. In the Fascist case, the militarist/imperialist aspect of this social policy was displayed in such features as Mussolini's description of Fascism as 'education for combat' and the 'reform of custom' (such as replacing the handshake with the Roman salute) that sought to transform Italians into an 'imperial people' (Brooker, 1991: 62–3, 158). In the Nazi case the militarist/imperialist dimension was less prominent, in conformity with the propaganda portrayal of Hitler as a man of peace and of Germany as seeking only legitimate nationalist goals (*ibid.*: 59).

Communist Regimes

By far the most distinctive policy programme of the communist party dictatorships was the introduction and operation of a centrally planned economy based on state-owned industry and collectively owned agriculture – the orthodox communist economy (see Exhibit 7.2). As most communist regimes adopted this type of economy, it became the most common of the distinctively 'non-democratic' policy programmes. However, there were some marked variations on the theme.

The leftist variation involved a downplaying of the material incentives that are included in the orthodox communist economy. (These are justified ideologically by referring to the Marxist doctrine that during the socialist transition to full communism, individuals are to be rewarded according to the quantity and quality of work which each contributes to society.) The incentives take the form of not only production bonuses and other output-related income, but also wage differentials and sizeable differences in income between manual workers and senior managers – sometimes as high as a ratio of 1:5 (Kornai, 1992; 324). Several communist regimes have sought to be more egalitarian and to shift the emphasis from material to 'moral' incentives. In Cuba in the 1960s this took the form of ('socialist emulation') competition between work groups and the presentation of symbols of collective achievement to high-performing work groups, but in North Korea the mobilisation of effort from the workforce went beyond such methods to eventually include military-style 'speed battles', in which an economic task was transformed into a battle to be won within a specified number of days (Brooker, 1997: 88, 73–4).

However, in China leftist experiments with the communist economy went beyond deviation and produced an actual mutation – the Great Leap Forward of 1958–60. The peasantry were herded into massive 'people's communes', whose highly communal life-style and economic self-sufficiency (including small-scale industrial production) led to official pronouncements that a fully communist society could be achieved within these rural communes instead of in the urbanised/industrialised setting envisaged by orthodox Marxism (Brooker, 1995: 92–3). Although such rural-utopian visions were abandoned after the Great Leap Forward produced massive famine, less than a decade later China

Exhibit 7.2   The Orthodox (Stalinist) Communist Economic Model

The basic model of an orthodox communist economy was established by the Soviet Union's first Five-Year Plan instituted in 1928–32 under Stalin's leadership. (However, the model sketched here highlights the essential and distinctive features rather than providing an exact description of this original case or any of the various copies that emerged in other communist countries.) The institution of an orthodox communist economy requires a massive restructuring of economy and society. The state takes over the ownership and operation of all industry, commerce, finance and international trade; and this wholly state-owned urban economy is operated as a command-planned economy, with the country's official Five-Year Plan setting targets for annual and five-yearly production that emphasise the rapid growth of heavy industry. Plan-implementing directives are sent by the various economic ministries (each administering a particular economic sector or industry) to their state-owned enterprises, which are operated as individually managed factories or firms. Prices of goods and services are set by state officials involved in the administration of the planned economy, and state (international) trading arms conduct all exporting and importing.

However, the state does not take over ownership and operation of all agriculture. Only a small proportion of agricultural land is transformed into state-owned farms worked by wage-earners; the rest is 'collectivised', replacing individual or household ownership with collective ownership of a very large farm by a large number of individuals/households. Each receives a share of the farm's returns and/or produce, but the size of that share is linked to the contribution, such as the number of days worked in the fields, that the person/household has made to the collective effort of operating the farm (which is directed by the farm's elected management committee).

The peasantry are also forced to relinquish control over marketing, as the collective farms have to sell their produce to the state at prices set centrally by the economic administrators. Furthermore, the collective farms are set annual 'production quotas', similar to those of state-owned industry, specifying the types and quantities of produce to be sold to the state. However, a small 'private plot' of land (less than an acre) is allocated to each household belonging to a collective farm, and produce from this plot can be sold privately by the household to urban consumers in the farmers' markets of local towns.

experienced the equally radical Great Proletarian Cultural Revolution. This leftist mutation did not involve such drastic social restructuring – it was a 'cultural', consciousness-changing revolution – but it had an egalitarian, populist and anti-bureaucratic theme which attacked material inequality as well as bureaucratic/technocratic attitudes and authority (*ibid.*).

A mutation which emerged in Kim Il Sung's North Korea in the 1960s, the theory and practice of Juche, is more difficult to classify as leftist because (despite official denials) it had nationalist connotations. Juche is usually translated into English as national 'self-reliance', and this is certainly how it affected economic policy, but Juche had a wider concern with national 'self-identity' which produced a distinctly nationalist influence upon cultural matters and historical interpretation (Brooker, 1997: 72–3). Another mutation which is difficult to classify as leftist is the ruralist, virtually anti-modern communism of the 1975–79 Khmer Rouge regime in Cambodia (Kampuchea). Not only was the urban population made to evacuate the cities and seek a new life among the collectivised peasantry, but also the professional as well as capitalist middle classes seemed to be targeted for extermination, with the result that out of a population of less than eight million, some quarter of a million were executed and a half a million others killed by starvation and similar 'natural causes' (Holmes, 1986: 67–8).

From the perspective of orthodox communism, the regimes which instead sought to liberalise their economies have produced 'rightist' mutations. The liberalised version of communism which was developed in Tito's Yugoslavia in the 1950s–60s (often referred to as Titoism) included an innovative restructuring of the state-owned industrial sector of the economy. The new industrial strategy involved not only using market forces instead of planning commands, but also allowing the workers' elected councils an increasing say in the management of their factories – so that by the 1970s these self-managed enterprises 'enjoyed most of the real powers ownership brings with it' (Swain and Swain, 1993: 138). The Hungarian regime's 'market socialist' New Economic Mechanism of 1968 followed the Yugoslav approach of replacing the Plan's commands with market prices and profits – though it stopped short of adopting Yugoslavian-style workers' self-management. As will be seen later, China and Vietnam would follow a similar path in the 1980s and implement extensive liberalisations of their economies.

Socialist Dictatorships

Party dictatorships have also developed various forms of non-communist socialism. Often they have opted for a state-dominated 'mixed' economy (with its mixture of state controls and market forces, state ownership and private ownership) which seems quite similar to the mixed economies developed by some Western democracies – differing only in degree and/or sophistication. However, the MNR revolution in Bolivia and the Sandinista revolution in Nicaragua led to distinctive agrarian reforms that redistributed land to peasant producers (Malloy, 1971; Gilbert, 1988: ch. 4). African socialism, too, produced a few distinctive policies. Touré's regime in Guinea launched a Socialist Cultural Revolution that had a more narrowly cultural focus than its Chinese model and campaigned against colonial and Western cultural influences, including mini-skirts and hippies (Brooker, 1995: 116). In Tanzania the distinctive socialist programme developed a strong emphasis on national self-reliance, an egalitarian 'leadership code' (to prevent public and state officials enjoying a too affluent lifestyle), and a rural programme of 'socialism in the villages' that forced peasant farmers to abandon their scattered homesteads and form village settlements – in which collective agriculture was an optional extra (Young, 1982a: 104–22).

Personalist Government and Policy-Making

Many of the distinctive policy programmes introduced by dictatorships have originated under the auspices of a personalist ruler. For example, the core of Tanzania's socialist programme, the 1967 Arusha Declaration, was the practical application of Nyerere's 'moral vision' of African socialism – and was implemented under his mild personalist rule (*ibid.*: 104). Pinochet's support for the 'Chicago boys' monetarist economic policies is a military example of this personalist influence (see Chapter 6) and so, too, is the support that General Velasco gave to the socialist programme implemented by the Peruvian military regime. As President and 'Head of the Revolution', Velasco provided vital support to the regime's socialists until his 'increasingly personalist leadership' and lack of concern for 'the collective interests of the military' led to his removal in 1975 – and to the Revolution entering a new, consolidating phase (Cotler, 1986: 156–8). In fact from the perspective of strategic, programmatic policy-making, the distinction between personalist and non-personalist government may be more significant than the distinction between military and party government.

The autonomous and possibly absolutist power enjoyed by a personalist ruler would seem to allow him to indulge his ideological prejudices and fantasies much more readily than can a non-personalist government. The obvious example is Hitler's genocidal policy towards the Jews and his Lebensraum policy of establishing a racial empire in the east by right of conquest. But many examples of personalist government have not been very innovative or extreme in their policies, except perhaps in those aimed at keeping the regime going – sometimes quite literally as a 'paying proposition' for the ruler and his cronies. This distinction was conceptualised by Linz in terms of the difference between the totalitarian and the sultanist ruler, and by Jackson and Rosberg in terms of the difference between the ideological 'prophet' and the other types of personal ruler, especially the tyrannical type (see Chapter 2). The key factor is not so much the presence or absence of ideology (as even Mobutu's lucrative kleptocratic regime in Zaire espoused an ideology), but whether the ideology motivates policy.

However, even among the ideologically motivated cases of personalist government there seems to be little relationship between the degree of personalist rule – its autonomy and absolutism – and the innovative or extreme nature of the policies. Although the Holocaust genocide and Lebensraum imperialism were instigated by Hitler only after he became a highly personalist ruler, Stalin had not yet established an even weak personalist rule over the Soviet Union's communist regime when it launched the first Five-Year Plan in 1928.

The two most extreme mutations of communism, the Great Leap Forward and the Cultural Revolution, were both launched by Mao Zedong before he had become a highly personalist ruler. A Western biographer who depicts Mao as a modern counterpart of China's long line of Emperors (and as having sought to learn from their example) describes him as having become increasingly Imperial in style of rule by the late 1950s (Salisbury, 1993: xiii, 8–9, 52–3, 170). But Mao did not become a highly personalist ruler until after he launched the Cultural Revolution in 1966, which led to his enjoying the informal status of an absolutist monarch until his death 10 years later.

There are several other examples of personalist rulers insti-gating relatively extreme policies some years, even decades, before their personal power has peaked. And it seems likely that in some cases, such as with Pinochet in Chile, they initiated these policies partly as a means of strengthening their personal posi-tion. (In other cases, they may also have been acting as the standard-bearer of a faction or body of opinion within the party or military.) Another implication of personalist rulers' initiating key policies early in a lengthy reign is that their country may well be condemned to many years of policy stagnation, with an aging but powerful personalist ruler maintaining the policies he introduced a decade or more ago.

Style of Government

Personalist rule does not always involve what is popularly en-visaged as a 'monarchical' *style* of government. Even such a highly personalist ruler as Hitler showed some tendencies that hardly seem compatible with a monarchical style. He had a 'hands off' approach to personalist rule that devolved exten-sive policy-making powers onto the ruler's personally known and trusted subordinates (Hiden and Farquharson, 1989: 62–76). He devolved most party and state decision-making on to his administrative secretaries, such as party administrators Hess and Bormann, on to his regional party officials (Gauleiter), and on to his personal lieutenants, such as security chief Himmler and propaganda chief Goebbels. While Hitler dominated decision-making in foreign policy, he intervened only fitfully (but authoritatively) in matters of domestic policy and admin-istrative routine.

Hitler's system of devolving power had the advantage of pro-moting the indispensability of the leader-ruler 'as a source of appeal and as the arbiter of exponents of conflicting interests and power groups' (Broszat, 1981: xiii). But he gave his system an added complexity by virtually encouraging rivalries among his subordinates by giving them similar authority and vague powers 'and letting them fight it out'; he believed that 'the strong would survive and the stronger should have the authority'

(Peterson, 1969: 12). The same approach seems to be evident in his creation of Supreme Reich Authorities and 'supreme' party/state organisations that competed with increasingly autonomous ministries in an administrative 'polyocracy' which seems to have descended into squabbling anarchy (Broszat, 1981: 286; Peterson, 1969: 32–3).

Yet although Hitler's system was long ago analysed as being 'neo-feudal', complete with vassals and chieftains (Koehl, 1960), there was no quasi-feudal misappropriation of power by his personal or bureaucratic subordinates (see Chapter 6). He may have been loathe to dismiss personally loyal appointees (even those who had proved incompetent or obnoxious), but he certainly retained the power to do so and he had no difficulty in having his decisions implemented whenever he did intervene in matters of domestic policy (Peterson, 1969: 11–12; Hiden and Farquharson, 1989: 76, 62). If Hitler's various bureaucratic and territorial agents acquired a degree of personalist rule over their own spheres of control, it was a weak 'free agent' autonomy rather than a quasi-feudal misappropriation of power.

Stalin's style of government was quite the opposite of Hitler's. Stalin opted for a workaholic administrative (over-)centralisation that promoted the administrative as well as political indispensability of the leader-ruler. He made a mass of routine and often trivial decisions over a huge range of matters; he actually 'enjoyed settling such trivial issues' and 'got used to the idea that people couldn't manage without him, that he must do everything' (Volkogonov, 1991: 147; see also pp. 220, 232, 240–1). In Hitler's Germany the regional party officials, the Gauleiter, could defy central authority without conscious disloyalty to Hitler because they were defying only his subordinate party and state officials, not the personal will of their leader (Peterson, 1969: 18, 341, 351, 434). But in Stalin's Soviet Union the ruler's 'hands on' style of personalist government meant that regional officials' lack of response to directives from the party Secretariat would be viewed as a direct defiance of the leader-ruler.

The typical personalist style of government lies somewhere between the Hitler and Stalin extremes, as can be seen in the case of two of the most famous Middle Eastern personalist rulers, Nasser and Asad, who were both military men rather than party leaders. President Nasser of Egypt employed a more coherent version of Hitler's system of devolving power. He entrusted key administrative responsibilities to individuals in whom he had confidence and then allowed them substantial autonomy in carrying out these responsibilities. Baker described this system as 'bureaucratic feudalism' and argued that division of the civil service into squabbling 'functional fiefdoms' enabled Nasser to assert some control over this bureaucracy as well as promoting his indispensability as an arbiter and integrator (Baker 1978: 55, 70, 75–6, 81, 86–7). But, like Hitler's system, it did not in fact involve any quasi-feudal misappropriation of power, and Baker himself acknowledged that Nasser retained control over appointments and that his appointees' power depended upon their personal relationship with the President. It was in relation to command of the military rather than control over sections of the civil service that Nasser experienced a quasi-feudal expropriation of his power (see Chapter 6).

President Asad of Syria provides a good example of a more 'middle ground' personalist style of government, but even he is closer to the Hitler than the Stalin extreme (Perthes, 1995: ch. 5). In the nearly 30 years since the Syrian Baathist regime's Defence Minister, General Asad, staged his intra-regime countercoup he has established a system that is perhaps best described as 'prioritised' policy-making. As befits a personalist military regime, the military as an organisation is not involved in policy-making about civilian society, and even such national-security issues as the military budget are decided by President Asad. Nor does Asad allow the official party more than a consultative role in policy-making. The Baath party's equivalent of a Politburo, its Regional Command, holds weekly meetings in which it discusses the government's proceedings and issues but it is not a decision-making body, and Asad (the party's General Secretary) attends meetings only when he wishes to consult with the Regional Command about important policy issues before making the final decision. And the President takes personal and sole charge of policy-making in the areas of foreign policy, defence and internal security.

On the other hand, Asad devolves a large amount of what he considers the less important areas of domestic policy-making (see Perthes, 1995: ch. 5). His directives or guidelines are frequently mentioned by government, party and media, but these are not specific, clear-cut instructions and allow his government, the Council of Ministers, and state/party bureaucracy room to manoeuvre in administering Syrian society. Although he heads an avowedly socialist regime that retains extensive state control over the country's mixed economy, Asad views even economic policy as quite secondary, as only serving his 'high policy' national-security and internal-security goals. He takes part in economic policy-making only when

1. there is a significant change in policy (for him to approve);
2. there is a major conflict of interest (for him to arbiter), or other 'political' implications; or
3. there is a need for a very rapid decision to deal with a crisis.

Economic Policy-Making

In Asad's Syria, therefore, economic policy-making is usually left in the hands of his prime minister, minister of the economy and guidance committee, which includes representatives from the party, the labour unions, and the business sector (*ibid.*). The ministers and their officials do not seem to have prepared any agendas for sweeping economic change, whether because technocrats and the IMF have little influence or because of the anticipated negative reaction of Asad to politically disruptive economic changes. Instead, in the 1980s–90s there has been a gradual, pragmatic and limited liberalisation of the economy (Brooker, 1997: ch. 6).

In comparison, the personalist ruler of the Baathist regime in neighbouring Iraq, Saddam Hussein, appears to have instituted a much more dramatic economic liberalisation in the late 1980s (Brooker, 1997: 126–9). But he, too, viewed economic policy as secondary to national-security and internal-security concerns. Liberalisation of the mixed economy (as in the privatisation of state-owned businesses and the reductions in state subsidies) helped to free up resources for his massive programme of military expenditure, which had been stimulated by the war with Iran and been hampered by a dramatic fall in Iraq's oil revenues. Furthermore, although his economic liberalisation was an affront to long-standing socialist ideology and vested interests, any potential threat to internal security had been reduced by his important subordinates' preferential access to privatised state assets and by his (presumably) increased support from a less state-controlled business sector. When the liberalisation led to politically awkward levels of inflation, he sacked ministers and reinstituted some of the former state controls and subsidies – exactly the sort of embarrassing policy reversal or cycle that Asad had avoided through his more gradual approach.

The economic policies of Asad and Saddam Hussein also offer two Middle Eastern 'test cases' of Haggard and Kaufman's theory that having a personalist government increases a dictatorship's capacity to carry out a programme of liberalising economic reform (1995: 12, 270–6). They argue that a personalist or 'single' ruler is less likely than a collective/collegial government to be afflicted by factional divisions which (a) in military regimes lead to policy stalemate, and (b) in party regimes lead to ambiguous policy decisions that hamper policy implementation by providing administrators with the opportunity to appeal or challenge commands that they do not wish to implement.

However, their theory recognises that the presence of personalist government provides only a *capacity*, not motivation, for economic reform (*ibid.*: 271–4). Effective and institutionalised policy reform also requires that the ruler be committed to reform and be prevented from backsliding. And the prevention of backsliding requires in turn that the ruler's power be 'checked', be limited, by a strong and independent private sector and by his delegation of policy-making authority to technocrats who are to some extent 'insulated' from his short-term demands. Therefore it is hardly surprising that Saddam Hussein's (reform-reversing) government is 'erratic and economically self-destructive'; Saddam would never allow technocrats to check his power, and Baathist Iraq is one of the Middle Eastern regimes that 'severely circumscribed' their private sectors (Haggard and Kaufman, 1995: 269, 273). But in the more interesting case of Asad's similarly 'unchecked' personalist government, his preference for gradualist and *ad hoc* liberalisation suggests that an unchecked ruler's priorities and assessment of the political situation may lead to not erratic but gradual and limited policy reform.

The personalist ruler can actually be a 'major impediment' even to gradual and limited reform, as in the case of Kim Il Sung's 'surprisingly stable, yet highly inefficient and myopic' rule over North Korea (*ibid.*: 271). He did very little to liberalise North Korea's troubled economy in the 1980s, and not long before his death he foreshadowed a swing to the left (converting the collective farms into state farms) rather than any liberalisation of the now collapsing economy (Brooker, 1997: ch. 4). Similarly, Fidel Castro responded to Cuba's 1980s economic difficulties by initiating a leftist/moralist Rectification campaign, and he was clearly unenthusiastic about the few liberalising measures that were finally introduced in the 1990s (*ibid.*: ch. 5).

Non-Personalist Government and Policy-Making

Although most examples of non-personalist dictatorial government are found in military regimes, the best examples are provided by long-standing party regimes. Many of the military non-personalist governments have within a few years either handed power back to civilians or been transformed into at least weakly personalist rule. And during their time in power these governments have usually been content with 'muddling through' and *ad hoc* policy-making rather than being guided by ideological goals or a programme of 'reforms'. The long-standing party regimes therefore provide a better range of examples of non-personalist government – offering useful comparisons with their personalist counterparts.

Economic Liberalisation

Communist China and Vietnam in the 1980s offer particularly useful comparisons, having been engaged in economic liberalisation during the same period as Baathist Syria and Iraq. Although neither China nor Vietnam enjoyed the supposed capacity-enhancing benefits of personalist government, both countries were acknowledged by Haggard and Kaufman to have carried out successful economic reform programmes in the 1980s (1995: 269). As these theorists' focus was on middle-income non-communist countries, they did not investigate how the Chinese and Vietnamese policy reforms were affected by, and overcame, the handicaps of non-personalist, collective/collegial government – which in party regimes take the form of 'ambiguous' policy-making and resulting problems with implementation. Instead they looked to the Mexican party regime for a straightforward case of weakly personalist government instituting a successful economic reform, thanks in large part to the 'enormous personal power' and 'concentration of power' enjoyed by Mexican presidents during their single term of office (*ibid.*: 272–3, 286–7). But this makes the comparable successes of the non-personalist Chinese and Vietnamese governments all the more intriguing.

Any comparison between the Chinese/Vietnamese economic liberalisations and those in Syria, Iraq and Mexico must take into account the high priority that communist regimes give to economic policy. As economic success and structure is central to their ideological claims to legitimacy (see Chapter 5), Communist China and Vietnam could be expected to be more concerned about economic policy than these three non-communist regimes. On the other hand, the Chinese and Vietnamese governments were tackling a more difficult reform than were their counterparts in Syria, Iraq and Mexico; the two communist regimes were seeking to liberalise a state-owned/ planned rather than just state-controlled/mixed economy. (Tito's personalist liberalisation of Communist Yugoslavia decades earlier had been more innovative, though, especially in his unique system of having factories managed by their workers.) The Chinese and Vietnamese programmes would involve:

- replacing collectivised agriculture with a household-based system;
- having state-owned industry increasingly operate in the market rather than planned sector of the economy;
- encouraging the development of privately owned businesses; and
- stimulating much more international trade and foreign investment.

It is therefore not surprising that the Chinese and Vietnamese reform programmes experienced (and overcame) decision-making and policy-implementing problems that Haggard and Kaufman would consider typical of collective/collegial dictatorships. However, the Chinese and Vietnamese style of non-personalist government also devolved policy-experimenting power upon lower-level administrators and this 'experimental and bottom-up' approach seems to have offered a significant advantage to their reform programmes.

China Communist China in the midst of the 1978–88 decade of economic reform offers a rare example of the combination of individual and collective regime leadership. Deng Xiaoping was publicly recognised as the regime's senior or paramount leader despite his lack of such individual leadership posts as party Chairman or General Secretary. He exercised a veto over Politburo decisions (even after retiring from it in 1987), had the right to intervene in any policy area, and was the final arbiter of disputes, including allocating key offices and responsibilities among the various party factions/followings of less senior party leaders (Brooker, 1997: 25–6). However, Deng was not even a weakly personalist ruler enjoying an at least 'free agent' autonomy. He had to govern in conjunction with a collective leadership comprising not only his most powerful protégés, who held the posts of General Secretary and Premier, but also his fellow 'elder statesmen' of the party who, like him, owed their power to venerable prestige and personal contacts rather than holding powerful offices.

The leaders' sharing of power was embodied in the policy-making processes of the regime. Within the individual/collective leadership there was a strong tendency towards policy specialisation, with particular leaders assigned to supervise a particular, specialised policy area. They would bring information and recommendations (from the relevant party and state organs) to the standing committee of the Politburo, which would approve a policy option that would in turn be ratified by the monthly meeting of the full Politburo (Hamrin, 1992: 100, 102, 114). The regime leadership also tended to devolve a large amount of policy-making to lower levels of administration (Zhou, 1995: 157). Once the party Politburo had formally issued directions or guidelines for a particular policy area, it delegated the specific policy-making to the legal government (the State Council), which in turn delegated decision-making to the ministries/commissions and the provinces. Although the tendency to delegate led to some policy-implementing problems, it also meant that the regime's economic liberalisation had an 'experimental and bottom-up nature', in the sense that nearly every liberalising measure 'was first given a localised dry run, with local authorities and enterprises taking the initiative in the experiment' and then the central authorities seeking to implement the successful measure on a nationwide basis (*ibid.*: 154–5).

However, Deng and the other economic liberalisers were constrained by conservative (orthodox communist economic) opinion within the collective leadership and by vested interests within the administration. Therefore the liberalising process displayed a cyclical tendency, with the liberalisers running into a conservative counterattack which would force them to compromise or to weather a conservative propaganda campaign before regaining the initiative (Brooker, 1997: 39). The process also tended to be gradual and piecemeal, as the liberalisers avoided taking on too many vested interests all at once – and avoided taking on the strong heavy-industry lobby within the party and state bureaucracies (*ibid.*: 34–5). In fact the economic liberalisers used an 'outflanking' strategy in

1. opening up a new market sector alongside rather than in opposition to the traditional planned sector of the economy (and encouraging industrial enterprises to develop a vested interest in the opportunities offered by the market sector); and
2. 'playing to the provinces' by decentralising revenue gathering and public spending to the provinces, so that provincial leaders would have a vested interest in economic liberalisation as a means of boosting the revenues of their provinces (*ibid.*: 38–9).

Vietnam   The Vietnamese regime took the communist principle of collective leadership to the furthest extreme seen in any communist regime. Following the death of Ho Chi Minh in 1969, the remaining Politburo members served together as a collegiate and outwardly unified collective leadership until the 1980s and then began a two-stage, 1982/1986 handover of power to a younger generation of leaders. Moreover, the long-standing emphasis on maintaining consensus within the party meant that any controversial policy would be promulgated in vague or ambiguous language and/or would be allowed to be delayed, modified or even ignored by administrators responsible for implementing the policy (Brooker, 1997: 56).

On the other hand, the imprecise policy guidelines and loose policy implementation also allowed ample opportunity for an 'experimental and bottom-up' approach to applying policy, with the initiative shifting from the central administrators to the provinces and even to the farm or factory level. In fact economic liberalisation 'produced a number of cases of reliance on local experiments to find "models" for broader application', as when Long An province's experiment with a market-based pricing system was implicitly approved by the party leadership as 'a generally valid model' (Porter, 1993: 121, 124).

The Vietnamese regime's programme of economic liberalisation was initially inhibited by the absence of a powerful group or faction of committed economic liberalisers within the leadership. There was a tendency for liberalisers and conservatives 'to benefit from shifting currents of opinion within the Party mainstream' (Brooker, 1997: 56). Therefore, although economic liberalisation began in 1979, it experienced a major cyclical reversal in the early 1980s which lasted longer than any of the cyclical reversals experienced by the Chinese liberalisers. The programme did not regather its momentum until 1984–85 and at first met with disaster, being associated with an unprecedented (for any communist regime) bout of hyper-inflation. But the party was not deterred and made a collective commitment to economic renovation (*doi moi*) at the 1986 Party Congress. With the party and the regime having staked their reputations on carrying through a sweeping economic liberalisation, the regime made up for lost time in the later 1980s and began to catch up with China's programme.

Performance and Policy Implemention

An 'unbiased' assessment of how well the non-democratic regimes have performed as governments has several issues to contend with. Is it best to assess performance by (a) specifying a few key areas of government performance, such as promoting economic growth, or (b) using the check-list approach of examining a wide range of government 'outputs', or (c) evaluating performance in terms of a regime's own (self-proclaimed or self-evident) preferred goal or set of goals? The diversity of non-democratic regimes makes it impractical to use the checklist approach in the limited space available. On the other hand, specifying just one or a few areas of policy-making/implementation as somehow more important or crucial than others may lead to accusations of arbitrariness or bias and of not understanding that government involves setting priorities – that giving priority to any particular goal or area will produce 'performance costs' in other areas.

For example, many highly repressive military regimes would have claimed that their abysmal human-rights record was an inevitable part of their emphasis upon laying the foundations for stable (and true, real, incorrupt or effective) democracy. Another example is that proponents of the orthodox communist economy could claim that it was aimed at securing high levels of economic growth and should not be pilloried for the inevitable side-effects of this prioritising. In fact the side-effects of this system of 'forced growth' and 'over-investment' have included a relative lack of concern not only for consumer goods but also for quality control, the service sector, shortages of goods and materials, and protection of the environment (Kornai, 1992: 197–8; Nove, 1977: 155–9).

Therefore the least contentious approach to assessing performance, at least as an initial approach or starting point, is to evaluate regimes in terms of their own priorities and goals. How well did they perform according to their own standards, in achieving their key goal or set of goals?

The Performance of Military Regimes

Although most military regimes have claimed to be intent on establishing a stable and 'true' democracy, they have proved to be dismal performers in this area. While they may be able to remove (at least temporarily) some types of civilian threat to democracy, they are much less successful in removing the military threat. As Nordlinger pointed out, the historical evidence suggests that 'the most frequent sequel to military coups and government is more of the same' (1977: 207). Those military regimes that came to an end in the 1980s–90s seem to have been more successful in laying the foundations for stable democracy but it is still too early to be sure and to assess whether the military did contribute, even if only inadvertently, to establishing stable democracy (see Chapters 3, 8 and 10).

Military regimes' performance in their usually high-priority area of economic development has certainly been no better than that of civilian regimes. As was seen earlier, the military regimes have not had any truly distinctive economic policies, in the sense of differing from any of the policies ever implemented by civilian governments. But the military may have been better than civilian governments at *implementing* policy, and in the early 1960s a few Western political scientists expressed some confidence about the military's ability as administrative 'modernisers' of 'underdeveloped' countries (Shils, 1962; Pye, 1962). In the mid-1970s, though, cross-national statistical studies failed to find any significant relationship between military rule and economic performance (McKinlay and Cohan, 1975, 1976; Jackman, 1976; see also Kennedy and Louscher, 1991).

Moreover, military regimes proved no more successful than other regimes in coping with the economic crisis that hit the Third World in the early 1980s. Even the supposedly technocratic and successful South American military regimes – those of Brazil, Argentina, Chile and Uruguay – seemed unable to cope with the new situation, experiencing a combination of recession, currency devaluation, renewed inflation and a foreign-debt crisis. According to Epstein's (1984) assessment of these four regimes' performance, 'none has been able to do well under the particular conditions of the early 1980s'; their previous economic success 'seems to have been for nothing' and 'the perception of failure has been all the more intense' (*ibid.*: 52, 43, 40).

The Performance of Fascist Regimes

The party dictatorships show quite a varied range of goals, depending upon whether a regime is fascist, communist or an African one-party state. In the case of the two fascist regimes, assessing their performance in terms of their own goals could be taken to mean their performance as imperialist conquerors – of Lebensraum or of a new Roman Empire. But as the emphasis here is on domestic rather than foreign policy, their performance will instead be assessed in terms of their distinctive goal of preparing Italian or German society for the rigours of total war.

The fascist regimes' policy of strengthening social solidarity through indoctrination in fascist ideology appears to have largely failed to instil the ideology and to strengthen wartime solidarity. It seems to have been an abject failure in the Italian case and to have been at most only partially successful in the German case (Brooker, 1991: 303–8). During the Second World War

Mussolini acknowledged privately that the regime had failed to militarise Italian society, and his pessimistic view of Italian morale deterred him from mobilising Italy for 'total war' – a much smaller proportion of the economy was converted to war production than in the First World War (*ibid.*: 308).

In Nazi Germany the home front proved very resilient during the war and, unlike in 1918, did not collapse into revolution. But this was probably due much less to any shared belief in Nazism than to the repressive capacities of the Gestapo/SS and to 'the regime's reluctance, in the light of the experience of 1917–18, to depress living standards too far' – deficiencies in the food supply and welfare services 'never came remotely near plumbing the depths' of the First World War (*ibid.*: 313–14). In fact the Nazis showed some of the Fascists' timidity about giving the public cause for grievance. 'Hitler and the Nazi leadership were anxious, now as before the war, not to invoke a serious loss of popularity through imposing stringent restrictions on consumption' (*ibid.*: 300–1). Germany was not officially put on a 'total war' footing until 1943, and even then the mobilisation of women into the workforce was less extensive than in Britain; the belated conscription of female labour was by no means thorough, and 'the armaments industries still had difficulties in finding women employees' (*ibid.*: 296, 308).

However, the Nazi dictatorship's organisational deficiencies were the main source of its surprisingly weak performance in mobilising resources for total war. Overy has emphasised that the Nazi regime was a markedly less efficient mobiliser than its communist counterpart in the Soviet Union. Germany produced much less war material from a much larger industrial base (after the German conquests of 1940–41) than the Soviet Union's, and this difference in mobilisational efficiency was only partly due to the communist regime's ability to elicit a greater effort and sacrifice from its people (Overy, 1995: 181–4, 188–90). He suggests that the failure was basically organisational and in large part due to the regime allowing the military to dominate arms procurement and production (*ibid.*: 203–4). For the German military sought a variety of high quality and advanced weapons rather than concentrating on the mass production of proven designs. A trebling of weapons production was brought about only after Hitler intervened in 1941–42 to shift the emphasis to mass production and to shift control over armaments production to the industrialists and his new Minister of Armaments, Speer. But this increase took years to bring about and was constantly hampered by

> a web of ministries, plenipotentiaries and Party commissars, each with their own apparatus, interests and rubber stamps, producing more than the usual weight of bureaucratic inertia (Overy, 1995: 201).

Hitler's overly complex system of devolving power therefore proved to have administrative disadvantages when compared to even the opposite extreme – Stalin's overly centralised style of government. In the titanic clash of styles in 1941–45, Stalin's proved more adaptable and efficient as he was able to decentralise his system more easily than Hitler was able to impose hierarchical control over Nazi Germany's administrative polyocracy. Hitler was left with only one great organisational and policy 'success' – his genocidal anti-Semitic 'Final Solution'. But the Holocaust is a historic warning that even an inefficient non-democratic regime can still be horrifyingly efficient and effective in achieving a particular goal.

The Performance of Communist Regimes

Assessing the performance of communist regimes in terms of their own goals means assessing not their war record but their success in promoting peacetime economic growth. Economic performance is central to a communist regime's claim to legitimacy (see Chapter 5), its propaganda and its policy-making priorities. In fact the emphasis on growth (especially of heavy industry) has led to the orthodox communist economy being characterised as a 'forced growth' system (Kornai, 1992: 197).

This system has usually produced impressive results in the early years or decades of communist rule, notably in the Soviet Union's first Five-Year Plan and in North Korea in the later 1950s. But usually there is also a decline in the rate of growth as the economy becomes more advanced and shifts to what the Soviet Union referred to as 'intensive growth' – based on increases in efficiency and productivity rather than mobilising increasing amounts of labour and capital to meet the planners' priorities and targets (Nove, 1977: 162). A crucial example of this tendency was the manner in which the Soviet Union outperformed the United States in the 1950–73 period, by 5 per cent average annual growth compared to 3.7 per cent, but then fell behind in 1973–88 as its growth rate sank to an annual average of only 2.1 per cent compared to the US rate of 2.5 per cent (Kornai, 1992: 201, table 9.2).

By the 1980s the Soviet Union and the East European states were experiencing only mediocre economic growth, with their average annual growth rates having fallen to only 2 per cent or below (*ibid.*: 200, table 9.12). The decline in growth performance was so significant that it undermined the communist regimes' claims to ideological (and performance) legitimacy. During the first half of the 1980s a wide range of Western analysts were presenting an 'apocalyptic view' of the 'crisis' facing the Soviet Union and Eastern Europe, with these countries' economic deterioration being depicted as underlying 'the "crisis" in their legitimacy' (White, 1986: 465).

The main reason for the decline in growth rates seems to have been the orthodox communist economy's inability to adjust to the requirements of 'intensive growth'. The continual technological improvement, efficient management, and concern for quality that were required for this type of economic growth were not encouraged by the state-planning system of quantitative targets and production-based incentives – which actually hampered factory/farm-level initiatives and led to low productivity and inefficient allocation of resources (Nove, 1977: 162–4, 379).

The communist regimes were well aware of these problems, and several different types of solution were attempted in the 1960s–70s. While the Soviet Union sought to devolve more decisions down to the factory level, the leftist North Korean economy was reinvigorated by simply importing Western technology and plant – until the regime exhausted its sources of foreign ('hard') currency. The Hungarian shift to a form of market socialism was the most radical solution but, like the earlier and more innovative Yugoslavian economic liberalisation, it was unable to deliver more than mediocre growth in the 1970s–80s. The Hungarian system eventually ran into difficulties with its trade deficit and foreign debt, while the Yugoslavian system was also plagued by inflation, unemployment and firms/enterprises loading themselves up with bank debts (Stokes, 1993: 79–80; Swain and Swain, 1993: 137, 167–70). Only the liberalised form of communist economy developed by China in the 1980s seemed to offer a long-term solution, as it increased China's already high 1965–80 growth rate to the impressive level of more than 10 per cent (Kornai, 1992: 201, table 9.13). But the Chinese model also appeared to be just another variant of the mixed state/private, planned/market economy seen throughout the Third World – not a distinctively communist type of economy.

The Performance of African One-Party States

Finally, there is the remaining type of party dictatorship – the African one-party state. Identifying and assessing the goals of these party regimes is complicated by the fact that while many espoused some form of African socialism, several others, such as Kenya and the Ivory Coast, were more capitalist than socialist. Young's 1982 check-list assessment of the link between African military and party regimes' ideology and their performance did contain two criteria (out of six) which were said to have been espoused by all African regimes, namely, economic growth and (nationalist) autonomy/self-reliance (1982a: 15–19). However, he did not include the goal of nation-building, which seems to have been publicly espoused by all the one-party states and was actually one of their justifications for one-partyism (see Exhibit 5.2). Assessing their performance as nation-builders is much more difficult than scanning a set of statistics on economic growth, but in another work Young (1982b: 176) implied that the one-party states had been no more successful as nation-builders than had the Nigerian military regime.

As for the other two goals proclaimed by the regimes themselves, Young was dubious about most African regimes' success in the area of autonomy/self-reliance, and he gave the one-party states a mixed report as promoters of economic growth. Among the one-party states that he mentioned in assessing autonomy and self-reliance, the Ivory Coast had actually opted for close ties with France, and even such vocally self-reliant or autonomous countries as Tanzania and Guinea were dependent upon, respectively, foreign aid and mineral exports organised by foreign companies (1982a: 312–3).

Of the one-party states that he mentioned in assessing economic-growth performance, only the relatively capitalist Ivory Coast, Kenya and Malawi were given high marks. Socialist Tanzania was viewed as, at best, a moderate success, while socialist Ghana, Guinea and Mali were labelled 'mediocre' – a failure largely due to 'ill-chosen state-run industrial projects' and to 'social-ist-inspired rural policies' that had proved economically counterproductive (1982a: 300–1). This mixed report on economic performance accords with a statistical survey, based upon the relatively prosperous years of 1958–66, which showed no significant difference in the rates of growth achieved by African one-party systems and those achieved by multiparty and no-party systems (McKown and Kauffman, 1973: 60–1).

During the 1980s Africa entered a severe economic crisis in which assessments of relative economic success seemed irrel-evant. At the beginning of the decade Young could still depict Africa's economic problems in terms of stagnation (1982a: 6), but in the 1980s most African economies were actually shrinking – during 1980–87 the overwhelming majority of sub-Saharan African states experienced a *negative* average annual 'growth' rate (Tordoff, 1993: 258–60, table 10.1). Therefore 'far from being "developmental dictatorships", African regimes [had] faced a twenty-year downturn' and by the 1980s were having to im-plement 'drastic austerity measures to curb imports and cut government spending' (Bratton and Van de Walle, 1992: 429).

The economic failings of so many African regimes confirmed that dictatorship offered no simple solution to the problems of economic development. In recent decades the many countries of Africa had seen more military and party dictatorships than any other region of the world, and by the 1980s few examples of democracy remained. Yet the shift from democracy to dictator-ship, which had begun as early as the 1960s, had not prevented a calamitous failure in performance by many African govern-ments. Most analysts agreed that the failure was only partly due to external economic forces and other factors beyond a government's control. The standard of African government had in many cases fallen well below what might have been expected in the circumstances; there had been widespread incompetence and some cases of 'criminal negligence' or worse. An analyst of the politics of Africa's economic stagnation claimed that most regimes had actually discouraged the mobilisation and productive investment of resources (Sandbrook, 1985: 35). Moreover, the African experience suggested that the performance failings of dictatorship might be due to not only the 'wrong' policies, but also a 'weak' *implementation* of policy.

Problems in Policy Implementation – the Weak State

These difficulties in implementing policy were quite different from any implementation problems that might arise from the style of government or the lack of personalist government. Personalist dictatorship (in diverse forms) was common in Africa but, as Jackson and Rosberg pointed out, it was characterised 'by the seeming paradox of relative freedom or autonomy for the ruler and his clique to make policies but great constraint and incapacity to implement or enforce them' (1982a: 30). They explained that this was primarily because African governments lacked sufficient resources, and possibly lacked sufficiently 'able, well-trained, or diligent' officials to deploy their limited resources efficiently (*ibid.*: 31). African governments certainly had fewer resources than those of governments in wealthier regions, but this was only one reason why African rulers were unable to have policies properly implemented by their state machinery – by the state's ministries, local administrators, police and army. For although their governments were able to secure substantial increases in the funding and size of their state machinery, this had not produced the expected increases in the state's capacity. By the 1980s the 'weak' African state was becoming a classic example of the failings of dictatorship.

Until then the great debate over the nature and role of the state in Africa had been between those who viewed the state as the prime mover of economic and social development, and those who viewed it as an actual obstacle to development (Doornbos, 1990). The latter view had arisen in the 1970s when the increasingly large state bureaucracy had been termed the 'over-developed' state and had been accused of syphoning off public revenue to further its officials' corporate and individual self-interest; some Marxists argued that in fact a (state) 'bureaucratic bourgeoisie' was playing the 'dominant and exploitative role' played by the financial/industrial bourgeoisie in wealthier capitalist economies (Doornbos, 1990: 184–5). Non-Marxists tended to describe such states as neopatrimonial and to acknowledge that the state had in some cases been transformed into a parasite or even a predator upon society (Young, 1982a: 5, 19).

Jackson and Rosberg were among the first to emphasise the actual *weakness* of many African states. They contended (1982b) that many persisted only because of their 'juridical' role or existence – because of their place in the international state system and of the recognition and support they received from other states. By the later 1980s the weakness of 'the African state' was widely acknowledged, and even some proponents of its older image as a powerful institution now admitted that 'the rule of state leaders has extended beyond the capital city or the main port only in the most tenuous and intermittent way' (Migdal, 1988: 7). It was argued that in some African countries, such as Ghana and Guinea, the ordinary people were actually 'disengaging' from the 'enfeebled' state in various ways (Azarya and Chazan, 1987). A wide-ranging assessment concluded that among its several failings the African state had:

1. been unable to achieve (ideological) legitimacy;
2. failed to 'penetrate' society, in the sense of having failed to establish control over political actors and social units at local (elders/village) level, or even intermediary (chief/ethnic) level; and
3. been only partially successful in extracting resources, by taxes and other means, from its largely peasant economy (Forrest, 1988).

However, by now the Third World as whole, not just Africa but also Latin America, Asia and the Middle East, was being depicted as lacking strong states. Migdal (1988) argued that most Third World states had achieved only a weak or middle-level capability to control society and implement their social policies, and that their lack of social control was related to the structure or 'strength' of their society. A 'web-like' social structure comprising ethnic groups, linguistic groups, tribes, clans or other social segments was not only very resilient but also provided a strong basis for its leaders – the 'chiefs, landlords, [political] bosses, rich peasants, clan leaders', or other local 'strongmen' – to resist attempts by the state to establish social control (Migdal, 1988: 37, 33). The state's leaders and administrators therefore reached accommodations with the local strongmen. 'In exchange for resources and minimal interference' from the state, the 'strongmen have ensured a modicum of social stability in the cities and countryside' (*ibid.*: 265). If the rulers and administrators of such countries as Mexico and Egypt were apparently still relying on local strongmen, it is hardly surprising that African states had failed to penetrate their much more web-like societies, with their strong ethnic, tribal, clan and village loyalties.

Assessing the Performance of Dictatorships

By the 1980s dictatorships seem to have been experiencing a 'performance crisis', which helps explain why so many would soon succumb to democratisation (see Exhibit 7.3). For in addition to most Third World dictatorships being plagued by incapable state machinery:

- South American military regimes were facing economic crisis;
- Communist regimes were experiencing declining rates of economic growth; and
- African regimes were facing economic crisis following long-term economic failure.

However, the credibility of the non-democratic regimes as 'performers' was maintained by their success in creating a group of capitalist 'newly industrialising countries' (NICs) in Latin America, notably Brazil and Mexico, and in East Asia, namely South Korea, Taiwan, Singapore and Hong Kong. The Asian cases seemed particularly impressive because they had carried out an export-led (rather than import-substituting) industrialisation and had avoided the debt crises and other economic problems that afflicted Brazil and Mexico in the 1980s. In his famous work on these six NICs Haggard (1990) pointed out that not only the Latin American but also the East Asian cases of industrialisation (except Hong Kong) had been guided and assisted by the state – and in each case the state had been implementing the policies of a government that was at most only partly democratic. The term 'authoritarian' was used to describe the wide variety of regimes to be found among the NICs: party dictatorship in Mexico, military dictatorship in Brazil and South Korea, semidemocracy in Singapore, and British colonial rule in Hong Kong.

Despite the economic success of these authoritarian NICs, Haggard maintained that there were 'no theoretical reasons to think that authoritarian regimes are *uniquely* capable of solving the collective-action problems associated with development' (1990: 256). Nor did he see any plausible direct link between authoritarian politics and the Latin American import-substituting approach to industrialisation: 'ISI [import-substituting industrialisation] occurred under a variety of different political

Exhibit 7.3   Performance and Democratisation

Long before the 1980s, dictatorships' performance failures had contributed to their demise, whether an African one-party state falling to military coup or a military regime returning power to the people through democratisation. When many party dictatorships, too, were democratised in the 1980s–90s, it appeared that the performance-failure factor could also be applied to their transferral of power to the people. The link between communist regimes' declining rates of economic growth and their democratisation seems quite straightforward, especially as the economically rejuvenated Chinese and Vietnamese regimes escaped the democratisation that overtook Eastern Europe. However, the economically crisis-ridden Cuban and North Korean communist regimes also escaped democratisation, while the African one-party states – despite their disastrous economic performance – at least survived a few years longer than the East European communist regimes.

Therefore it is not surprising that Haggard and Kaufman had some difficulties in applying the economic-performance factor to party as well as military dictatorships. In the case of military regimes, economic failure leads to the defection of the regime's allies in the private sector and to widespread opposition among the public; which in turn aggravates conflict within the military about whether it is worth staying in power; and typically leads the military to attempt to negotiate a withdrawal from power as a solution to its various internal and external difficulties (1995: 12; see also Epstein, 1984; O'Donnell and Schmitter, 1986). But their Taiwanese case-study of a party dictatorship engaging in a (very lengthy) process of democratisation was based not upon economic failure, but upon long-term economic success! They argued that such success increases the willingness of party leaders to risk democratisation because they are more confident that they can retain power under these more competitive rules of the game (*ibid.*: 291–2).

It is only in a brief analysis of the East European communist regimes' rapid democratisation that 'poor economic performance' was presented as playing a similar, central role in transitions from party dictatorship to democracy as it does in transitions from military dictatorship (*ibid.*: 372). However, they also acknowledged that party dictatorships are more politically durable than military dictatorships, and a series of five or more political and social, not performance, factors were mentioned or implied to explain (a) why even durable communist regimes succumbed to democratisation, and (b) the cross-national variations in the East European regimes' transitions to democracy. Clearly the transition from dictatorship to democracy is not easily explained by performance alone – as will be confirmed in Chapter 8.

arrangements' (*ibid*.: 255). But he acknowledged that there was a more plausible link between authoritarian politics and the East Asian *export-led* approach to industrialisation, which had focused attention (1) on the role of labour in maintaining the country's international competitiveness, and therefore (2) on the economic advantages of controlling or at least politically excluding the working class.

His own research, though, provided little evidence of such a link; his historical/comparative studies of the four East Asian cases had pointed to a clear link between labour control and export-led growth only in the case of Singapore (*ibid*.: 111–2). Moreover, he had also noted that the labour-market conditions in these East Asian countries might have prevented even strong labour unions from pushing up wages, which

> suggests that repressive and exclusionary policies were by no means necessary for export-led growth. But it is plausible that political coalitions that included labor would have in-fluenced the overall direction of policy and reduced the flexibility of both the private sector and the state. (Haggard, 1990: 233–4)

It seems, therefore, that the only plausible link between au-thoritarianism and East Asian export-led growth is that the presence of non-democratic regimes prevented labour from interfering with technocratic policy-making and business flexi-bility. This is the rather flimsy basis for any claims that authoritarianism is a precondition for such 'economic miracles' as have been seen in East Asia. In contrast, there is conclusive evidence that authoritarianism is by no means a guarantee of economic progress – as many African countries can testify! Haggard himself warned against a 'selection bias' which dwells upon authoritarianism's 'East Asian success cases' and overlooks such 'patrimonial states as Zaire' (1990: 263–4).

Haggard also noted how the diversity to be found within the category 'authoritarian regime' helped to explain why statistical studies of the relationship between regime type (democracy/authoritarianism) and economic performance had produced only weak and contradictory results (*ibid*.). There had already been at least 13 cross-national statistical studies into the rela-tionship between democracy and economic performance, but the only consensus seemed to be that there was the possibility of a minor negative effect – that lack of democracy might be slightly advantageous to economic performance (Helliwell, 1994: 235–6). A later and seemingly definitive statistical examination of this issue failed to find 'any significant linkage between the level of democracy and subsequent economic growth', and raised the issue of whether the economically key differences between regimes might be found *within* each of the two categories, 'democratic' and 'non-democratic' (*ibid.*: 241).

The same issue had arisen in a cross-national study of Third World countries embarking on (socially painful) economic stabilisation or restructuring programmes (Nelson, 1990). The study discovered that 'regime type' was of little use in explaining why some governments in the sample responded to their country's economic problems with less delay and broader remedial programmes. For these decisive governments were found in a *variety* of types of regime – 'established democracies, transitional democracies and authoritarian systems' – and their decisiveness was best explained by their 'political institutions and circumstances', such as broad political support for the government (Nelson, 1990: 328). Successful implementation of stabilisation/restructuring programmes showed a similar pattern, with 'regime type' again proving irrelevant and the key political factor being support for the government, especially its leader, and the disabling of opposition (*ibid.*: 340–1). For example, in the African country of Zambia the authoritarian government of unpopular President Kaunda abandoned an economic programme whose implementation had been plagued by not only administrative incompetence, but also strong resistance from state officials who could not be sacked because they constituted a major part of his remaining political support (*ibid.*: 321, 340).

Clearly, therefore, there is a need to go beyond the democracy/authoritarian performance issue and look for institutional (and other) factors which distinguish 'strong' from 'weak' authoritarian regimes (Haggard, 1990: 264). But even when the strong authoritarian regimes have been identified, there are likely to be some performance anomalies. The 'conventional wisdom' that strong non-democratic regimes are likely to be better economic performers than democracies is usually based upon an image of removing the democratic limits and pressures upon the government or state machinery of an (often existing) democracy:

Weak legislatures that limit the representative role of parties, the corporatist organization of interest groups, and recourse to coercion in the face of resistance should all expand governments' freedom to maneuver on economic policy. (*ibid.*: 262)

But this could also be describing the early stages of Mussolini's fascist regime, which used its freedom of manoeuvre to impose a state-controlled and autarchic, military-oriented economy on Italy! Haggard pointed out that any argument which focuses attention on a regime's capacity to make and implement policy must be accompanied by an argument that shows why political leaders have an incentive to promote economic well-being – that explains why a strong authoritarian state will necessarily be 'optimal or efficient' rather than 'predatory' in its policy-making (*ibid.*: 263).

Moreover, the alternatives to economically efficient authoritarianism include more than just a materially self-interested predatory regime. As was described earlier in the chapter, there is also the nightmare alternative of an ideologically motivated regime inflicting economically and socially damaging, even horrific policies upon its people.

8

Democratisation

The Demise of Dictatorships and Birth of Democracies

Dictatorships come to an end in various ways. They can be ended by such 'accidental' events as the death of a personalist dictator, or a foreign invasion that conquers the regime's country. More purposefully, a regime leader may end a party's rule by misappropriating power (see Chapter 6), or the party's expropriation may instead arise from a military coup or a spontaneous revolution by the people. But there have also been many cases, especially among military regimes, of relatively voluntary handing over of power to the people – a relinquishing of public offices and powers.

Relinquishing involves a voluntary transferral of power rather than a biological loss of power through death in office, or a political loss of power through being expropriated by seizure or misappropriation. However, various forms of force or pressure, such as armed insurrection or demonstrations of popular discontent, may contribute to the decision to relinquish power, if only by altering the regime's assessment of whether holding power is worth the effort or odium. Therefore relinquishing power involves degrees of 'voluntariness' and in extreme cases may mean little more than making the best of a virtually hopeless situation, with the regime's opponents likely to seize power in the near future. Such a situation comes very close to being a case of orderly expropriation rather than relinquishment – of being a surrender rather than a transferral. But in cases of orderly expropriation, in which the seizure of power ends in surrender negotiations and agreements, the regime has already lost the use of its public powers – it has lost control of the streets and of society – and its public offices are all it has left to surrender.

Whether ended by death, expropriation or relinquishment, a dictatorship has often been replaced by simply a different type of non-democratic regime. The death of a personalist ruler has often resulted in a return to the preceding party or military type of dictatorship. And the ending of a party or personalist dictatorship by military coup has often resulted in the establishment of a military regime.

However, in recent decades democratisation has become the most common result of a dictatorship's demise. Democracy, even if only short-lived, has always been a common ending of military dictatorships, but it became the common ending of party and personalist dictatorships, too, when most of the existing examples of these regimes were democratised in the 1980s and early 1990s as part of what has been termed history's 'third wave' of democratisation.

The Third Wave of Democratisation

In the early 1990s Huntington used this term to describe the wave of democratisation that was still sweeping through the world and which he viewed as having begun in 1974 with the pro-democracy military coup that overthrew Portugal's long-standing dictatorship (Huntington, 1991: 3). He referred to it as the *third* wave to distinguish it from the two earlier periods of relatively frequent transitions to democracy: the first, 'long' wave of democratisation in 1828–1926, and the second, 'short' wave in 1943–62 (*ibid*.: 16). He pointed out that in 1990 the actual proportion of democratic states in the world (45 per cent) was still no higher than its previous peak in 1922 (*ibid*.: 26). But the democratisation of numerous states in Africa during the early 1990s would give the democratic states a large majority – compared to being very much in the minority (25 per cent) before the onset of the third wave of democratisation.

Huntington also made an impressive attempt at explaining why this wave of democratisation occurred. He suggested that five 'independent variables' played significant roles in bringing it about:

1. authoritarian regimes' increasing legitimacy problems, including problems with (economic) performance legitimacy;
2. the social effects of the 1960s rapid economic growth, such as the expansion of the middle classes;
3. changes in the political attitudes of the Catholic Church, which nationally and internationally became opposed to authoritarian regimes;
4. changes in external actors' policies, such as the Soviet Union abandoning its policy of intervening militarily to maintain communist rule in Eastern Europe; and
5. the 'snowball' or 'demonstration' effects (see Exhibit 8.1), enhanced by increasingly effective international mass media, as earlier transitions in the wave of democratisation stimulated people in other countries to attempt similar regime changes (Huntington, 1991: 44–5).

However, explanations or explanatory theories of democratisation have their limitations when used to analyse the ending of dictatorship – the expropriation or relinquishing of power – that has led to the birth of democracy. They seldom provide a systematic analytical framework that (a) focuses on a few crucial elements in the ending of a regime, such as the strength of opposition to the regime, and (b) defines these elements in sufficiently broad terms to incorporate a wide range of more specific, explanatory factors – such as the changes in the political attitudes of the Catholic Church and the 'snowball' or 'demonstration' effects of democratisation.

Another limitation of theories of democratisation is that they usually do not explain important regional or regime-type variations in the way that dictatorships are democratised and in their vulnerability to a wave of democratisation. Usually theories of democratisation have to be supplemented by explanations of democratisation in a particular region or in relation to a particular type of dictatorship. (The regional explanations may take the form of theories explaining why democratisation occurred in a particular region, such as in Latin America or Africa, or they may take the less explicit form of a general or global theory including explanations for regional variations.) The need for regional explanations can be seen in the regionally 'biased' manner in which the 1970s–90s wave of democratisation swept through the world. The lack of democratisation in the Middle

Exhibit 8.1   The Domino, Snowball or Demonstration Effect

An important factor in transitions from dictatorship to democracy is popularly known as the 'domino' or 'snowball' effect. The 'domino' metaphor had originally been used in Cold War rhetoric to high-light the danger that communist revolution would spread rapidly from one Asian country to another. By the 1980s, though, it was 'democratic dominoes' that were increasingly evident as many military regimes in Latin America and Asia succumbed to democ-ratisation. Starr's (1991) statistical analysis of 1974–87 democ-ratisation – a period in which transitions were predominantly from military rule – concluded that such a 'domino' effect did exist, though domestic factors made a country 'ready' for democratisa-tion or produced 'barriers' against this external democratising effect.

Moreover, his analysis indicated that the domino or snowball effect was evident regionally as well as globally, as it concluded that a powerful regional effect was evident in Latin American democratisation in 1984–86. The standard technical term for such a global and/or regional phenomenon is 'diffusion effect', but it is also referred to as an 'emulation', 'modelling' and (most fre-quently) 'demonstration' effect (*ibid.*: 357, 360, 369, 377). A *demonstration effect* seems the best description of how the diffu-sion of democratisation globally and regionally can have a cumulative influence. For continual demonstrations of successful democratisation in other countries seem to both reduce the mili-tary's political self-confidence and raise the self-confidence of its civilian opponents (see Table 8.1).

East is an awkward anomaly that requires – and has produced – more in the way of explanation than simply pointing the finger at Islam (Salamé, 1994).

Furthermore, the third wave of democratisation swept through the other regions of the world in an almost sequential man-ner: southern Europe in the mid-1970s, Latin America and Asia in the later 1970s and the 1980s, Eastern Europe in 1989, and Africa in the early 1990s. In the African case the regional wave of democratisation not only removed the surviving African one-party states, but also virtually annihilated what had for decades been the world's largest body of military regimes. In 1989 more than 30 of the 48 countries of (sub-Saharan) Africa were ruled by some form of military regime, but six years later there were only three clear-cut examples of such regime (Wiseman, 1996: 1–2). Many experts on Africa have offered regional explanations for this dramatic democratisation (*ibid.*: 35–6; Bratton and Van de Walle, 1992) but what particularly needs regional explanation is why the African region lagged behind Latin America and Asia before so quickly making up for lost time.

Regional explanations are also required to deal with anomalies in the way that a particular variety of regime has succumbed to democratisation. The communist regimes show a distinct regional variation in their democratisation, for the three major Asian and sole Latin American examples of communism survived the global democratisation that brought down the other communist regimes (and also the other varieties of dictatorship in their own regions). Moreover, there is a sequential anomaly in the democratisation of the other communist regimes. For while the East European cases unexpectedly collapsed in 1989, both traditionally liberal Yugoslavia and the (for several years previously) liberalising Soviet Union lagged behind and were still not centrally democratised as late as 1991. This anomaly is partly explained by regional explanations of why the six East European communist regimes were so vulnerable to democratisation in 1989.

Regional explanations of the dramatic collapse of the East European regimes in late 1989 have tended to emphasise three factors (Berglund and Dellenbrant, 1991):

- There was a legitimacy 'crisis' arising not only from the regimes' lack of democracy and long history of being virtual client regimes of the Soviet Union (the seemingly puppet rulers of its East European satellite states), but also from the regimes' inability to meet economic aspirations encouraged by communist ideology and by comparisons with Western Europe (Holmes, 1986: 100, 102–3; Przeworski, 1991: 2).
- Secondly, there was the change in attitudes in a now liberalising and partially democratising Soviet Union, especially what appeared to be the abandoning of the long-standing Soviet doctrine of intervening militarily to preserve communist rule in Eastern Europe as in Hungary in 1956 and Czechoslovakia in 1968 (Karl and Schmitter, 1991: 158; Stokes, 1993: 21, 99; Przeworski, 1991: 5).
- Thirdly, a regional snowball or domino effect initiated by the Polish communist regime's willingness

(a) in early 1989 to formally negotiate with the pro-democracy opposition,

(b) in April to agree to a series of political concessions that included an almost immediate limited democratisation and promises of full democratisation in a few years time,

(c) in June to implement this agreement by allowing free elections to the agreed quota of seats in parliament, and

(d) in August to allow the installation of a predominantly non-communist government (Welsh, 1994: 386; Przeworski, 1991: 3–4, 55).

In addition to regional explanations there is also a need for supplementary theories or explanations that can account for why the military type of dictatorship – the apparently most powerful type – is actually the most vulnerable to democratisation. A striking anomaly of the 1970s–80s democratisation is that until 1989 many military regimes but virtually no party regimes had succumbed to democratisation. Moreover, the 1989 collapse of communism began with the military-led relinquishing of power in Poland (Przeworski, 1991: 4, 6, 78), where communism had been taken over by the military in 1981 (complete with all the trappings of coup, martial law, military junta and eventual 'civilianisation') and was still headed by a military man in civilian garb, General Jaruzelski.

As the military regime is so vulnerable to democratisation, the most likely place to find an analytical framework for examining the democratising demise of dictatorships is in the analyses of the demise of military regimes. After developing such a framework, the next step is to find a typology of transitions (from military dictatorship to democracy) that can provide the basis for a 'global' set of regional explanations of democratisation. Then attention will return to the other types of dictatorship, the personalist and party, which have been more reluctant than the military to relinquish the power they have seized or misappropriated.

The Military's Relinquishing of Power

The military has shown a much greater tendency than parties or personal rulers to *relinquish* power. In part this is because it is so difficult for any other organisation or group within society to seize power from the military. But the tendency towards relinquishment is more because the military has often seized power without intending to retain it for the longer term. As Nordlinger pointed out, the military's common lack of commitment to retaining power on a long-term basis 'helps to account for the low average life span of military regimes', which he calculated to be only about five years (1977: 143, 139).

When Nordlinger sought to distinguish the paths through which military regimes were replaced by civilian rule, he included *voluntary* disengagement (with or without intra-military or civilian pressure) as 'by far' the most common path (*ibid.*: 141). Furthermore, the other two paths that he identified – countercoups and civilian opposition – seem only variations of the standard form of voluntary disengagement, differing only in form and/or in degree of voluntariness. For the several instances he mentioned of a countercoup's leading to the relinquishing of power by the new military government are also ultimately cases of voluntary withdrawal by the military; the distinctive feature is one of *form* in the sense of there being a two-stage process initiated by a countercoup. As for the military being 'forced to relinquish their power by extensive civilian opposition', such opposition is described as 'civilian pressures, demonstrations, strikes, and riots', not armed insurrection, and Nordlinger's two examples also involved military disunity and the refusal of some officers to support their leaders' retention of power (*ibid.*: 139). In fact he argued that no military regime supported by a united officer corps determined to retain power had ever been overthrown by civilians alone.

The military's relinquishing of power is usually described as its withdrawal or disengagement from power or politics. In the early 1990s Welch concluded that there was still no widely accepted 'paradigm' for the study of military withdrawal/ disengagement even though there had been over 80 cases of military disengagement in the 1940s–80s, of which more than a third were 'through a scheduled, planned withdrawal after holding elections' (Welch, 1992: 324, 334).

However, theorists of military dictatorship have long been aware of the issue of withdrawal/disengagement and have addressed it within their wider discussions of military rule. Long before Nordlinger raised the issue, Finer in 1962 had discussed

TABLE 8.1

The calculus of military retention of power – Factors leading to *relinquishing and transferral*

Motives (discouraging retention)	*Means (decline in)*	*Opportunity (decline in)*
Ideological/national interest	1. Disintegration of original conspiratorial/ruling group of officers because of policy differences and/or personal rivalries (Finer, 1976)	1. Mass civilian protest (Finer, 1976; Sundhaussen, 1985; Clapham and Philip, 1985; Welch, 1987) that may become an organised and occasionally armed challenge (Finer, 1988; Sundhaussen, 1985; Clapham and Philip, 1985; Welch, 1987)
1. Fulfilling promises (Finer, 1976) or intention (Nordlinger, 1977) of only temporary stay in power		
2. Ideological/legitimacy problems – for a longer than temporary stay (Huntington, 1968)	2. Diverging interests of: (a) military governors and (b) rest of officer corps (Finer, 1976)	2. Withdrawal (actual or threatened) of foreign support (Sundhaussen, 1985; Finer, 1988; Clapham and Philip, 1985)
3. Belief in civil supremacy (Sundhaussen, 1985; Finer, 1988)	3. Decline in (political) self-confidence (Finer, 1988; Sundhaussen, 1985; Nordlinger, 1977)	3. National-security problems or failures (Sundhaussen, 1985; Finer, 1988)
Corporate self-interest	4. Demonstration effect (domino, snowball) of global/regional democratisation decreases military's (political) self-confidence (Starr, 1991)	4. Negative economic trends (Welch, 1987; Epstein, 1984; Haggard and Kaufman, 1995)
1. Political difficulties of governing the country (Finer, 1976; Huntington, 1968; Nordlinger, 1977; Sundhaussen, 1985)		
2. Public reputation besmirched by unpopular/ineffective military rule (Nordlinger, 1977)		5. Electoral overconfidence (O'Donnell and Schmitter, 1986)
3. Politicisation/factionalism arising from policy-making (Nordlinger, 1977; Sundhaussen, 1985; Clapham and Philip, 1985; Finer, 1988; Welch, 1987)		6. Demonstration effect (domino, snowball) of global/regional democratisation increases civilians' (political) self-confidence (Starr, 1991)
4. Military police/intelligence units becoming too powerful and autonomous (O'Donnell and Schmitter, 1986)		
Individual self-interest		
1. Military governors' political difficulties of governing the country (Nordlinger, 1977)		

the 'return to the barracks' (1976: 32, 174–8) and Huntington had explored the issue of retaining/relinquishing power in connection with the veto coups of mass praetorianism (1968: 233–7). By the 1980s there were more specialised discussions of the topic of withdrawal/disengagement, such as Clapham and Philip's (1985) analysis of the political dilemmas of military regimes, Sundhaussen's (1985) of military-regime stability in Southeast Asia, and Welch's of military disengagement in Africa and Latin America (1987: 20–4). Moreover, these writers from the 1960s to the 1980s identified a large number of different factors affecting withdrawal/disengagement, with its relinquishing and transferral of power to civilians (see Tables 8.1 and 8.2).

Many of the factors affecting military withdrawal/disengagement have been incorporated into systematic analyses of the issue. By the 1980s, Finer was applying his disposition/opportunity framework (see Chapter 3) to the military's withdrawal from power. Although it was Sundhaussen who had first suggested this application, he later preferred a reasons/preconditions framework for analysing military withdrawal (Sundhaussen, 1985: 272–5). Finer, too, abandoned the term 'opportunity' in favour of 'societal conditions which invite withdrawal', and he also revamped the notion of 'disposition' to include necessary conditions as well as motivations (Finer, 1988: 299–305). His framework was therefore less like a disposition/opportunity analysis than Nordlinger's examination of withdrawal had been, as the latter had focused on 'disengagement motives' and had included the opportunity-like proviso that these motives will motivate a withdrawal 'as soon as an acceptable transition to civilian rule can be arranged' (Nordlinger, 1977: 141).

Adapting the Finer-style motive/means/opportunity calculus of usurpation (see Chapter 3) to fit withdrawal would have several advantages, such as being able to apply the same framework to both the entrance and exit of the military from power. It would not cover exit from power, though, in such an involuntary and therefore 'motiveless' form as *expropriation* through defeat by foreign or domestic forces or misappropriation by a personalist ruler. Moreover, there appear to be so many difficulties in adapting the motive/means/opportunity framework to fit withdrawal/disengagement that it may be better to approach the issue from the perspective of *ceasing to retain* power

TABLE 8.2

The calculus of transferral of power –
Factors affecting when/how/to whom

Motive	Means	Opportunity
Ideological/national interest 1. Protecting national interest or ideological goals (Welch, 1987; Sundhaussen, 1985) 2. Protecting regime's work in pursuit of national interest or ideology (Sundhaussen, 1985; Finer, 1988)	1. Negative: division over issue of appropriate time to withdraw (Nordlinger, 1977) 2. Positive: internal consensus/cohesion to withdraw (Sundhaussen, 1985; Finer, 1988)	1. Civilian successors will not ignore interest/policy preferences of the military (Nordlinger, 1977; Sundhaussen, 1985; Finer, 1988; Welch, 1987) 2. Civilian successors are a potentially stable and peaceful party or party system (Sundhaussen, 1985; Finer, 1988; Welch, 1987)
Corporate self-interest 1. Protecting military and its corporate interests from retaliation/retribution (Huntington, 1968; Sundhaussen, 1985) 2. Protecting its corporate autonomy under future civilian government (O'Donnell and Schmitter, 1986)		
Individual self-interest 1. Protecting governing and internal-security officers from retaliation/retribution (Huntington, 1968; Sundhaussen, 1985; O'Donnell and Schmitter, 1986)		

rather than that of withdrawal from power. Instead of looking at the loss of power, this framework would be concerned with the continuing or discontinuing *retention* of usurped power.

The Calculus of Retention

Any calculus of retention will differ significantly in content – in motives and factors – from the calculus of usurpation described in earlier chapters. Rustow pointed out long ago that those 'factors that keep a democracy stable may not be the ones that brought it into existence', and the same could be said of dictatorships; he himself noted that military dictatorships 'typically originate in secret plotting and armed revolt but perpetuate themselves by massive publicity and alliances with civilian supporters' (Rustow, 1970: 346, 341). It is not only this 'means' aspect which will have changed as the military moves from usurping to retaining power. New individual and corporate self-interested motives are likely to develop as the military enjoy the fruits of office, and any initial commitment to ideological or national-interest motives may evaporate.

Moreover, new motives that actually discourage the retention of power will probably arise. Just as there are motives which inhibit the military from seizing power (see Chapter 3), so there are motives which discourage the military from retaining power (see Table 8.1). Therefore, as with the calculus of usurpation, there is a 'balance sheet' of motives 'for' and 'against'; when motives discouraging retention outweigh those favouring retention, the military is on balance motivated to relinquish power rather than to continue retaining it. Even if on balance there is a motive for retention, this may be too weak to motivate the military to retain power when it faces declines in the means and/or opportunity for retention.

A balance-sheet approach also has to be taken to assessing the means of retaining power and the opportunity for retention. Analysts of military regimes usually mention only 'negative' factors, which detract from or produce a decline in the military's means/opportunity for retention of power (see Table 8.1). But, as Rustow pointed out, there are also factors that keep a (military) regime stable and that military dictatorships use to perpetuate themselves. These factors which favour or contribute to the retention of power can be presented in terms of means and opportunity, as being 'positive' means/opportunity factors that have to be weighed against the negative factors in order to arrive at a balanced assessment of the strength of a regime's means or opportunity. For example, Rustow's reference to military dictatorships' perpetuating themselves through civilian alliances can be viewed as a positive 'means' factor, favouring or contributing to retention. As for positive 'opportunity' factors, a substantial list of opportunity factors favouring retention can be produced by simply *reversing* well-recognised negative factors (see Table 8.1). For example, the negative factor of 'negative economic trends' can be reversed to become the positive factor of 'positive economic trends', which may or may not be present in any particular regime's balance of opportunity factors.

Therefore when analysing a particular regime, 'calculating' whether that regime will continue to retain power is a matter of assessing the overall balance of positive and negative motives, means and opportunity (see Figure 8.1). The same 'calculation' is required when analysing why a particular regime did not continue to retain power and instead relinquished it through a democratisation or other form of transferring power. Usually a few obvious changes in motives and/or factors can be readily identified as the likely cause of the shift from retention to relinquishment of power. The means/opportunity factors of the calculus of retention can also be used to help assess whether there will be, or why there was, an expropriation of the regime by domestic forces.

The Calculus of Transferral

The relinquishing of power, though, needs one further application of motive/means/opportunity – namely, to the actual *transferral* of power. For clearly the power must be relinquished *to* some other organisation, social group or person. A 'calculus of transferral' (see Table 8.2) provides a systematic examination of the issue of to whom the relinquished power is being transferred, such as to an allied party or to the people through free elections. Although the military's transferral of power is usually viewed in terms of democratisation, in the 1960s Finer and Huntington were interested in the decades-old Mexican example of the military actually building and transferring power to an

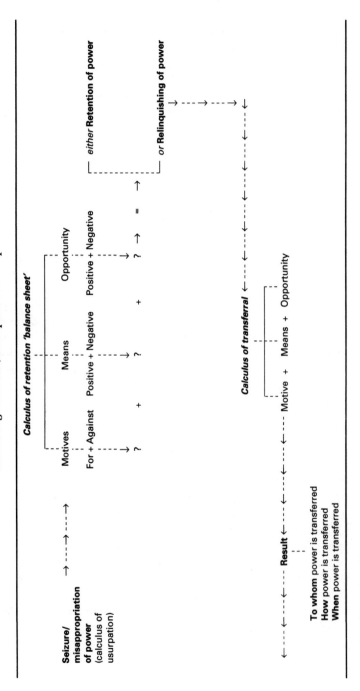

FIGURE 8.1
Calculating retention/relinquishment of power

official party – and since then there have been other examples of transferral to a party, such as in Cuba, Taiwan and Iraq (Finer, 1976: 180; Huntington, 1968: 239–62).

There is also the associated issue of *how* the transferral takes place. In the case of transferral of power to the people, for instance, this may be through

(a) elections that have been unilaterally scheduled, organised and supervised by the military; or
(b) a negotiated agreement with civilian representatives, covering the whole process of transition to democracy; or
(c) the military simply abandoning power and leaving it to civilians to sort out how democracy will be established.

Finally, there is the 'tactical' issue of *when* the relinquishment/transferral occurs. The military's basic motivation to relinquish power may be too weak to avoid delays and interruptions caused by negative factors in the calculus of transferral. Among these negative factors are the self-interested motive of protection from retribution, and the 'means' problem of the military itself being divided over whether it is the appropriate time to withdraw (see Table 8.2). There are also more positive factors to take into account, though, and in fact the calculus of transferral – with its open-ended questions of when, how and to whom – is in some respects the most complex application of the motive/means/opportunity framework.

Both the calculus of transferral and the calculus of retention are better suited to analysing a particular case than to categorising, comparing and contrasting a number of different cases. For there are simply too many possible combinations of particular motives and means/opportunity factors; the various combinations cannot be presented as a few general or schematic 'types' that can be used for classification and comparison/contrast on a global, regional or other basis. Such types can be found, though, in the classic study of transitions from dictatorship to democracy, and its typology of transition covers the transferral as well as relinquishment of power by the military.

Transitions to Democracy

There emerged in 1986 (O'Donnell, Schmitter and Whitehead) the massive collaborative study, *Transitions from Authoritarian Rule: Prospects for Democracy*, containing more than 20 contributions from a wide range of country, regional and thematic experts. Although these contributors usually referred to 'authoritarian' rather than specifically military regimes, virtually all the *Transitions* examples were of transitions from military regimes to democracy. Most of the country-studies included were of 1970s–80s (actual or likely) transitions from military rule, and encompassed a wide variety of cases drawn from southern Europe and Latin America. The *Transitions* study's 'tentative conclusions' were presented in a long essay by O'Donnell and Schmitter. As they acknowledged (1986: 38), their analysis was heavily influenced by Rustow's (1970) pioneering work on transitions to democracy.

He had categorised the transition to democracy into three phases:

1. prolonged struggle between polarised but evenly matched political forces;
2. the negotiation of a *compromise agreement* by the political forces' leaders which leads to the institutionalising of democratic procedures; and
3. the habituation of democratic procedures, which gradually enlarges the degree and range of consensus (1970: 352–8, 362–3).

O'Donnell and Schmitter followed Rustow in emphasising the role of compromise agreements – which they referred to as 'pacts' – in transitions to democracy, but they retailored his approach to better fit transitions from military rule. They defined a pact as an explicit compromise agreement that (a) seeks to redefine the political rules of the game and (b) is based on mutual guarantees that protect the vital interests of the pact-makers (1986: 37).

Pacted Transitions

A military extrication pact precedes any pacts made between political parties or social forces during the transition from military rule to democracy. The extrication aspect of the pact arises from the officers' desire to 'begin to extricate themselves from direct responsibility for ruling', and includes a growing awareness within the officer corps that the regime will soon – 'in the foreseeable future' – have to seek 'some degree or some form of electoral legitimation' (*ibid.*: 39, 16). The pacted aspect of the military's extrication arises from the mutual guarantees exchanged with civilians. In an extrication pact the military leaders guarantee civilian representatives that there will be a liberalising restoration of individual rights and of some opportunity for civilians to contest the military regime's policies. In exchange the military are guaranteed that civilians will (a) not seek retribution for repressive 'excesses' committed by military officers, and (b) not immediately or too insistently demand democratisation, let alone resort to disruptive or even violent measures against military rule (*ibid.*: 40).

The military extrication pact seems to arise in situations similar to those in Rustow's model of negotiated compromise between equally matched, stalemated political forces. But after the pact is made, the balance of power or political strength shifts dramatically in favour of the civilians. The military have initially conceded – through the extrication pact – only an immediate liberalisation of the regime and the prospect of limited, not full, democratisation: 'elections scheduled for an undefined future and, then, for insignificant offices only' (*ibid.*: 57). But this liberalisation leads to such a post-pact strengthening of the civilian public and weakening of the military that the regime is propelled into a full democratisation. For 'once a government signals that it is lowering the costs [in fear and actual injury] for engaging in collective action and is permitting contestation on issues previously declared off limits', it soon finds itself facing a 'repoliticized' society – what is termed a *resurrection of civil society* (*ibid.*: 48–9).

Although this may well involve the resurgence and/or establishment of political parties, most of the political mobilisation usually comes from social groups and organisations (*ibid.*: 49, 57). In particular, human-rights activists and organisations stimulate the public's ethical revulsion (often exacerbated by evidence of pervasive corruption) towards the regime's activities. Another particularly significant group is the working class, which has (re-)acquired a capacity for collective action and has been radicalised by its years of political and workplace subordination. Moreover, the various groups and organisations involved in this resurrection of civil society may join together to form what is termed a *popular upsurge*, in which 'all support each others efforts toward democratization and coalesce into a greater whole' – which calls itself 'the people' (*ibid.*: 53–4).

With or without a popular upsurge, the resurrection of civil society propels the military into bringing forward the pact-envisaged elections and extending their scope to produce a full rather than limited democratisation (*ibid.*: 57). In deciding to transfer power to the people, the now morally discredited military is opting for (relatively orderly) party politics instead of street politics, and it also seems to be calculating that instituting democratisation will enable it to divide and conquer opponents and garner support for its favoured candidate/party from a grateful public (*ibid.*: 57–8). More importantly, the military has no other realistic means of solving its political problem, for the resurrection of civil society has raised to unrealistic levels the 'perceived costs' of either a return to repression or a (counter)coup by hardline officers – even hardliners are 'likely to hesitate before the prospect of provoking a civil war' (*ibid.*: 53, 55).

However, although the *Transitions* conclusions lavished much attention on describing pacted transitions, there seem to be few actual *examples* of this type of transition among its country studies. The Introduction to its collection of Latin American country-studies admits that the only instances of explicit pacting occurred in Venezuela and Colombia in the late 1950s and, to a partial extent, in Uruguay in the early 1980s – where the agreement 'was barely implemented, if at all', and was 'extremely short-lived' (O'Donnell, 1986: 11–12). Nor did an explicit military-extrication pact occur in any of the transitions included in the southern European country-studies.

Other regions of the world seem just as bereft of military extrication pacts. Explicit pacts did not appear in the Asian 1980s–90s transitions from military rule to democracy: in Pakistan, Bangladesh, Thailand, the Philippines and South Korea.

Even the numerous African transitions do not show evidence of pacting: more than two dozen military regimes were democratised in 1990–95 but the 'phenomenon of elite pacting' had 'few echoes in Africa' (Wiseman, 1996: 158). The national conferences on constitutional matters that became quite common in parts of Africa in the early 1990s are only superficially similar to an extrication pact. In reality they differed from pacting in not only their size, procedure and wide range of civilian representatives, but also in their effect (*ibid.*: 84–94). For they tended either to be the medium for surrender agreements (for orderly expropriations of military regimes) or, in contrast, to be diversionary tactics by rulers who went on to thwart the conference's ambitions.

In fact, apart from Uruguay, the only 1970s–90s example of an explicit military-extrication pact seems to have occurred during the Polish communist regime's democratisation in 1989 (Stokes, 1993: ch. 4). As was noted earlier in the chapter, the military wing of the Communist Party had in December 1981 staged a dramatic military takeover aimed at attacking the country's economic crisis and eliminating Poland's massive independent trade-union movement, Solidarity (Brooker, 1995: 210–16). But in 1988 this by now 'civilianised' regime's party leader, General Jaruzelski, agreed to political negotiations with leaders of Solidarity in order to halt waves of (economically motivated) strikes.

The resulting roundtable negotiations eventually produced accords, announced in April 1989, which seem to be a military-extrication pact but one which contained more concessions than a 'typical' extrication pact. For an almost immediate limited-scope democratisation (with elections in which only 35 per cent of parliamentary seats could be contested by non-communist or non-puppet parties) was to be followed by full democratisation in 1993. However, in typical 'pacted' fashion, the limited-scope elections produced an unexpected situation that the regime could not control (though in parliament rather than the streets) as the regime lost control of its long-standing puppet parties. In August, President Jaruzelski accepted a non-communist prime minister and predominantly non-communist government, bringing to a close his military rule as well as the Polish communist regime.

The pacted transition would not seem so rare if it had been depicted in terms of political balance and compromise agreements between the military and their civilian opponents, rather than explicit pacts. Later analysts of transitions to democracy recognised that they often involve *implicit* or *tacit* negotiations and agreements (Huntington, 1991: 114, 139–40, 165–7; Haggard and Kaufman, 1995: 118); and the 'pacted' transition could readily be defined as arising from a situation where military and civilians are quite evenly matched in political strength, engage in explicit *or* implicit/tacit negotiations and compromise agreements, and see the agreed-upon liberalisation develop unexpectedly into democratisation.

Nevertheless, relatively few transitions from military rule to democracy begin with the military and its civilian opponents quite evenly matched in political strength. O'Donnell and Schmitter recognised that transitions may also begin when the military is in a politically weaker or stronger position than it enjoys at the outset of a pacted transition. They acknowledged that the military may be in such a weak political position that it relinquishes power without securing a pacted exchange of mutual guarantees (O'Donnell and Schmitter, 1986: 39). And they also pointed to situations where, in contrast, the military is in such a strong position that it can actually 'dictate the emerging rules of the game' rather than negotiate a compromise agreement (*ibid.*: 39). Therefore the *Transitions* conclusions offer three types of transition from military rule to democracy:

1. the dictated transition by a politically strong military;
2. the pacted transition by a military quite evenly matched with its civilian opponents; and
3. what might be termed the 'abdicated' transition by a politically weak military.

Other Types of Transition – The Abdicated and the Dictated

Although the abdicated and dictated types were only briefly described in the *Transitions* conclusions, at least there was a more explicit analysis of retention/transferral motives and means/opportunity factors than appeared in the description of the pacted type. The abdicated type of transition involves a relatively straightforward and quite familiar type of military relinquishment/transferral of power (O'Donnell and Schmitter, 1986: 39, 20–1, 35). It occurs when the military is discredited, in disarray, or under seemingly irresistible pressure (actual or potential) to relinquish power. In addition to these and other familiar means/opportunity factors, *Transitions* mentions various familiar aspects of the corporate self-interest motive – only one of which had not been identified by analysts of military withdrawal (see Table 8.1). What seems to distinguish this type of transition from the pacted type is that the military views immediate and full democratisation as an acceptable price to pay to enable it to escape a deteriorating situation. There may even be cases where the transition is actually imposed on the regime by its mobilised civilian opponents. On the other hand, *Transitions* acknowledged that even in an abdicated transition the process can be complicated by the military's (predictable calculus of transferral) concerns about its corporate autonomy under a civilian government, and about the fate of those officers directly responsible for repression (see Table 8.2).

The (Sub)types of Dictated Transition – the 'Relinquishing' and the 'Pacted-like'   The dictated type involves a more complex transition than the abdicated type, perhaps because there is less obvious reason for a politically strong military to relinquish power. In fact there seem to be two different types of dictated transition (see Figure 8.2). In the more straightforward, 'relinquishing' type the military initiates a fully intended relinquishment of public offices and powers through democratic elections – and its only pact-like feature is that the military is sometimes willing to negotiate with civilians over the details of the transition. In the other, 'pacted-like' type the military is initially seeking only some form or degree of electoral legitimacy – not a relinquishment of power – but this leads on to a full democratisation in a somewhat similar (though more controlled) fashion to a pacted transition. The relinquishing type is the more common of the two, and it was seen earlier that there were dozens of cases in the 1940s–80s of the military using elections to stage planned and scheduled relinquishments of power. Yet this type of dictated transition was not explored by the *Transitions* conclusions, which instead described the rarer and more pacted-like type of dictated transition from military rule.

O'Donnell and Schmitter's example of a military dictated transition, the one initiated by the 1964–85 Brazilian regime, was certainly not a case of planned and scheduled relinquishment

FIGURE 8.2

Three basic (non-personalist) types of transition to democracy
(original *Transitions* types with additions in italics or quotation marks)

Dictated	*Pacted*	*'Abdicated'*
Ruling military or party is politically stronger than (weak) opposition	Ruling military or party evenly matched in political strength with opposition → recognises it will shortly need to secure some electoral legitimacy	Ruling military or party is politically weaker than (powerful) opposition → recognises need to relinquish power through immediate and full democratisation

Dictated branch 1:

'Relinquishing' subtype seeks to relinquish power through (planned and scheduled) elections

→ *Pact-like negotiations with opposition about election details* → *Full democratisation*

Full democratisation

Dictated branch 2:

'Pacted-like' subtype seeks some electoral legitimacy → Liberalisation and limited democratisation → Resurrection of civil society (with possible mild and short popular upsurge) → Full democratisation

Pacted:

Explicit or *implicit* negotiations (mutual guarantees) and agreement – 'pact' → Liberalisation and promise of limited democratisation → Resurrection of civil society with perhaps 'popular upsurge' → Full democratisation

'Abdicated':

Relinquishment and full democratisation (without securing guarantees of its vital interests)

of power by means of elections. Instead, it was a case of the military's initially seeking some electoral legitimation through instituting limited democratisation or liberalising its democratic disguise, and ending up with a somewhat unexpected but still controlled relinquishment of power. (In Brazil the 1974 liberalisation of its democratic disguise was not followed by full democratisation until the later 1980s, as will be seen in Chapter 9.) In such cases as the Brazilian, one of the reasons for seeking some electoral legitimacy is that the socioeconomic success of the regime has resulted not only in 'a less active and aggressive opposition', but also in the regime being overconfident about the level of its public support, with the regime hoping to secure not just an electoral majority but a 'comfortable majority' (O'Donnell and Schmitter, 1986: 20).

However, this electoral overconfidence is not so much a motive as an opportunity factor, reducing the regime's opportunity for retaining power. For the overconfidence about its popular support encourages the regime to begin an electoral initiative that unexpectedly leads on to full democratisation. The actual motive for this initiative seems to be the desire for:

1. electoral legitimation of an internal succession to the regime's key office (in the Brazilian case it was one army general succeeding another as the country's President); and
2. the favourable response of international public opinion to the regime's leaders 'following through on their original claims to be preparing the country for a return to democracy' (*ibid.*).

Although the authors were doubtless well aware of the dominance of democratic ideology in Latin America (see Chapter 5), they do not mention the likely favourable response of domestic public opinion to an electoral initiative or mention the possibility that the military's claims of democratic intent may be quite genuine. In fact the *Transitions* conclusions never considered the possibility that authoritarian regimes may have ideological or national-interest motives for relinquishing power. Similarly, the *Transitions* conclusions did not consider the military regimes' tendency towards comparatively short-lived rule (when compared with other authoritarian regimes), even though this tendency was widely recognised by analysts of military regimes and would be recognised in later analyses of democratic transitions (Huntington, 1991: 117; Haggard and Kaufman, 1995: 11, 13).

The Global and Regional Distribution of Dictated Transitions   The dictated type seems to have been the prevalent type of transition in Asia during its 1980s wave of democratisation. The most complex example is Taiwan's long transition to democracy, which occurred against the backdrop of a military regime having gradually transferred power to its official party, the Kuomintang, which in turn was only gradually implementing a dictated transition – the martial-law decree inherited from the military regime was not revoked until 1986 (Cheng, 1989: 489)! This dictated transition also displayed some pact-like features, including a continual informal dialogue that led to formal negotiations between the regime and a civilian opposition which had occasionally used sizeable public demonstrations to support its position. The South Korean transition from military rule was a more straightforward case. It not only lacked the extra complications of a preceding military-to-party transferral but also occurred at a more rapid pace and was accompanied by more open or dramatic use of public demonstrations by the regime's civilian opponents. The dictated type also occurred in Pakistan and Thailand, and the only exception to the rule seems to have been the expropriation of Marcos's military-supportive regime in the Philippines by a combination of some military rebels and masses of 'people power'.

In comparison, the dictated type of transition was less prominent in South America's 1980s wave of democratisation. It appeared in Brazil and perhaps Peru (which was on the borderline with an implicitly pacted transition); but the Uruguayan transition was pacted, the Bolivian was a stop-go combination of pacted and abdicated, and the Argentinian was an abdicated transition. Moreover, Africa's 1990s wave of democratisation saw a huge number of transitions from military rule to democracy, but few examples of the dictated type of transition. African military regimes were 'more reticent about handing power back to civilians' than were their South American counterparts, and what have been termed 'managed transitions' were initiated 'either without great sincerity or in response to popular protest and pressures' (Bratton and Van de Walle, 1994: 481).

Even such a superficial 'global' survey of the incidence of dictated transitions shows the advantages of using the *Transitions* dictated/pacted/abdicated typology in global and regional comparisons. Moreover, *Transitions* could claim to have offered a whole new dimension to retention/transferral analysis of particular cases of transition by raising the issue of the relative strength of groups *within* the military.

Hardliners and Softliners

In a pacted type of transition 'there is no transition whose beginning is not the consequence – direct or indirect – of important divisions within the authoritarian regime itself, principally along the fluctuating cleavage between hard-liners and soft-liners' (O'Donnell and Schmitter, 1986: 19). A transition does not begin until the softliner faction, group or body of opinion is sufficiently strong to defeat, politically or militarily, the regime's hardliners (*ibid.*: 16).

The issue of internal divisions within the dictatorship was also raised by later analysts of transition. Huntington (1991) distinguished between 'standpatters' and liberal or democrat 'reformers' and viewed the relative strengths of the two groups as a crucial factor in determining what type of transition would occur. If reformers are in power, there will be transformation (dictated type); a political balance between them and standpatters will lead to transplacement (pacted type); and if standpatters are in power, there will be replacement (abdicated type or expropriation) (Huntington, 1991: ch. 3). The military's 'cohesion' was also an important issue in Haggard and Kaufman's (1995) analysis of transition. As they pointed out, a decline in the consensus within the military about the desirability of retaining power tends to lead to an attempt to negotiate an exit from power (Haggard and Kaufman, 1995: 12, 102).

However, both these later analyses of transition viewed the presence of personalist rule as being the most decisive internal – 'within regime' or 'within military' – political factor affecting transition. Haggard and Kaufman argued that military 'cohesion is greatest where personalist rulers have gained control over both the government and the military establishment', and that such personalist-based cohesion strengthens the military regime's capacity to withstand pressures to relinquish power

(1995: 12, 79). Huntington viewed personal dictatorships as a separate type of non-democratic regime and argued that 'leaders of personal dictatorships were less likely than those of military and one-party regimes to give up power voluntarily' (1991: 110–11, 120–1). And when *Transitions'* remarks about personalist rulers are examined, it appears that the dictated/pacted/abdicated typology will have to be expanded to accommodate the peculiarities of personalist rule.

Transitions from Personalist Rule

Within Military Regimes

In the *Transitions* conclusions, O'Donnell and Schmitter pointed out that none of the *personalist* military dictators mentioned in the country-studies had initiated transitions, which therefore had to wait for the dictator to die or be overthrown by a military countercoup (1986: 34–5). A famous example of transition following removal by death was the manner in which the Spanish transition to democracy took place only after General Franco's long-lasting personalist rule finally ended in 1975 with his death by natural causes. However, the personalist ruler's removal from power by death, incapacity or even retirement does not necessarily open the way for a transition to democracy. As was noted in Chapter 5, there are several instances of a personalist ruler heading a ruler-type military regime, in which the military as an organisation is *independently* committed to the permanence of some form of military rule. In such cases the military can hardly be expected to institute a transition to democracy just because the personalist ruler happens to have died or been incapacitated. For example, after Nasser's death in 1970 the Egyptian military backed the succession of another ex-officer, Sadat, and after his less personalist rule was ended by assassination in 1981, the military supported the succession of Vice-President and ex-General Mubarak – who in turn has established a new form of mildly personalist rule.

As for removal by a military countercoup, this is unlikely when the regime is so highly personalist that the military has lost its professional/corporate autonomy and become an instrument of personal rule. In fact O'Donnell and Schmitter noted that a civilian 'armed insurrection seems the only way for regime change and eventual democratization' in such 'sultanistic' dictatorships as the Somozas' former regime in Nicaragua (1986: 32–3). However, less highly personalist rulers are much more likely to be removed by the military (whether in a factional or corporate coup), and in fact this is the commonest form of countercoup-produced transition. Three of Nordlinger's four examples of countercoup-produced two-stage withdrawals involved the military removing personalist military dictators in 1955–58: Perón of Argentina, Rojas Pinilla of Colombia and Perez Jiménez of Venezuela (1977: 140). Nor has this been a solely 1950s phenomenon. In 1989 General Stroessner's long-standing personalist regime in Paraguay (see Chapter 6) was overthrown by a coup led by his senior army commander, who then presided over a long transition period that culminated in the 1993 elections. Such anti-personalist democratising countercoups are also to be found outside Latin America, as in the classic example that occurred in the African state of Mali in 1991–92 (Vengroff and Kone, 1995).

The countercoup which removes a personalist ruler is usually motivated by a desire to take the military out of politics in order to prevent any further erosion of its professional integrity (O'Donnell and Schmitter, 1986: 34–5). However, the question of motive is significant only when analysing particular cases, such as when applying the calculus of retention. The more important question is how to categorise these cases of a two-stage relinquishing of power produced by an anti-personalist democratising countercoup.

The Anti-Personalist and Personalist Types of Transition   Although it will add further complications to an already complex typology, an 'anti-personalist' type should be added to the dictated/ pacted/abdicated typology of transitions to democracy. After all, the countercoup that removes the personalist dictator is an integral part of two-stage transitions and may have as great an impact upon how the transition unfolds as an explicit pact does in a pacted type of transition. For example, the military's removal of a hated dictator may politically strengthen a formerly discredited and demoralised military, allowing it to carry out a dictated rather than abdicated style of transition. In contrast, the ending of a dictator's repressive rule may lead to a popular upsurge that leaves the military with little option but to seek an abdicated style of transition.

The *Transitions* typology of transitions has to be expanded anyway to incorporate a *personalist* type of transition. For although personalist rulers are typically reluctant to relinquish power, there have been occasions when a (not highly) personalist ruler has in fact initiated a transition from military rule. Among the more recent cases were Pinochet's 1988–89 democratising referendum and elections in Chile, and the young military leader of Ghana, Rawlings, completing a transition to democracy in 1992. Therefore, if it is to cover the full range of transitions from military rule to democracy, the *Transitions* typology needs to be expanded to include a 'personalist' as well as an 'anti-personalist' type (see Figure 8.3). In the latter type the removal of a personalist ruler begins what will become a dictated, pacted or abdicated style of transition; in the former type a personalist ruler himself begins what will become one of these styles of transition. Some new motives and factors will have to be added to the calculus of retention when it is applied to a case of personalist relinquishment of power, but such factors as the 'electoral option' are better described in relation to personalist transitions that involve a civilian personalist ruler and an official *party*.

Within Party Regimes

The general tendency of personalist rulers to refrain from relinquishing power is found among party as well as military dictatorships. And in fact by the 1990s there were analyses of transition focused specifically on neopatrimonial personalist types of regime, irrespective of whether the regime was military or civilian.

Snyder's (1992) analysis of the removal of these intransigent neopatrimonial personalist rulers, civilian as well as military, argued that an autonomous military is the most likely remover of a personalist dictator. He contended that only if 'the military lacks sufficient autonomy' to remove a (civilian or military) personalist ruler, is there then an opportunity for him to be removed by a revolutionary movement (Snyder, 1992: 380–1). In their later, regional study of African transitions from (civilian as well as military) neopatrimonial rule, Bratton and Van

FIGURE 8.3
Two additional (personalist) types of transition to democracy

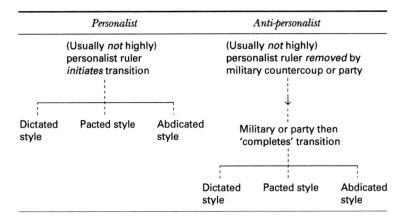

De Walle noted the general reluctance of neopatrimonial rulers to relinquish power, and confirmed that this reluctance is most pronounced in the most extreme case of neopatrimonial rule, the 'personal dictatorship' (1994: 462, 475). Therefore, African dictatorships' frequent tendency to degenerate into personalist rule may partly explain why Africa lagged behind other regions in shifting from dictatorship to democracy; its dictatorships' reluctance to relinquish power is what would be expected of personalist rulers (Wiseman, 1996: 18–19; Bratton and Van de Walle, 1994: 454, 459).

Anti-Personalist Transitions Within Party Regimes It was in the Eastern European communist state of Romania that a civilian personalist ruler paid the ultimate price for his reluctance to relinquish power (Stokes, 1993: 52–8, 158–66). By the 1980s the party boss, Ceausescu, had established a quasi-monarchical and repressive form of personalist rule, but his personalist regime quickly crumbled when in December 1989 he prodded the military into a bloody attempt to repress the public protests which had broken out in the city of Timisoara. A mixture of military opposition, internal revolt within the party, and quickly spreading popular uprising led to his execution on 25 December and the party rebels' NSF movement presiding over democratisation.

Some six weeks earlier, the much milder party boss of communist Bulgaria, the elderly Zhivkov, had been peacefully removed from power by senior communists in the first stage of an anti-personalist transition (Stokes, 1993: 147–8; Bell, 1993: 86–9). The new leaders soon publicly committed themselves to democratisation and in January the regime began roundtable negotiations about elections (held a few months later) with the Union of Democratic Forces, which had been formed by the now many pro-democracy parties and organisations – most of them created after Zhivkov's removal.

Personalist-type Transitions and the Electoral Option   In African party dictatorships, though, long-standing personalist rulers reluctant to relinquish power were pressured by the public into a personalist transition. By 1990 only four one-party states were still in the hands of their original and now aged founding leaders: Kaunda in Zambia, Banda in Malawi, Houphouet-Boigny in the Ivory Coast and Nyerere in Tanzania (who was soon to retire in favour of his deputy). In Zambia and Malawi the no-longer-popular founding leaders resisted for a time the growing pressure for democratisation, but eventually held democratic presidential and legislative elections in which they and their decrepit parties were defeated (Van Donge, 1995; Venter, 1995).

In contrast, founding leader Houphouet-Boigny of the Ivory Coast responded to public demands for multiparty elections by quickly initiating a dictated style of personalist transition that gave him a new degree of electoral legitimacy (Crook, 1995). As he was still respected and even admired by much of the public and had revitalised his party in the 1980s, he was in a strong electoral position and in fact went on to win over 80 per cent of the vote in the presidential election, and led his party to an even larger victory in the legislative elections.

Therefore the prospect, or even only the possibility, of winning democratic elections may be a major factor in personalist rulers' decisions to initiate dictated-style transitions or pressured abdicated-style transitions. It must be included as an opportunity factor whenever the calculus of retention is being applied to a personalist ruler. For just as a successful military regime's overconfidence about its popular support can lure it into an electoral initiative, so may a personalist ruler view competing in democratic elections as a more attractive option than continuing to struggle to hold on to power dictatorially. Some overconfidence about electoral prospects is likely to be found not only among the more successful personalist rulers, but also among those rulers whose backs are against the wall – irrational assessments of election prospects are understandable instances of wishful thinking in adversity (Przeworski, 1991: 65).

Moreover, the electoral option is also available to military personalist rulers. For example, in the earlier-mentioned case of Rawlings in Ghana he had good prospects for electoral success, having provided the country with a decade of 'purposive, effective, dynamic and relatively incorrupt personalist rule', and his electoral prospects were likely to decline if he did not soon fulfil his already frequent promises to 'pass power to the people' (Haynes, 1995: 99, 101). Similarly, when Pinochet held the (constitutionally prescribed) referendum on whether he should continue as President or hold democratic elections, he doubtless felt some hope of winning the referendum – and in fact he did manage to win some 44 per cent of the vote. It is in this somewhat paradoxical combination of (a) reluctance to relinquish power, and (b) hope of electorally regaining relinquished power that the personalist ruler, whether civilian or military, is more like a ruling party than a ruling military.

Democratisation of Party Dictatorships

The Durability of Party Dictatorships

Until the 1980s party dictatorships had displayed a marked reluctance to relinquish power. In contrast to the transitoriness of the common form of military regime, party regimes seemed more committed to retaining power and almost invariably were brought to an end only by armed force. The two fascist dictatorships had been destroyed by foreign invasion in the 1940s, and many of the African one-party states were overthrown by military coups from the 1960s onwards. Five of the newly established African one-party states had been removed in the mid-1960s and the attrition continued at a much reduced rate into the 1970s–80s (McKown and Kauffman, 1973: 56, 56 table 1; Decalo, 1989). But this had been a vulnerability to military coups, not to instituting transitions to democracy. (Only Senegal had seen a transition from one-partyism to a form of multiparty democracy and, as will be seen later, there was reason to be dubious about its democratic credentials.) Moreover, until the 1980s none of the world's many communist regimes had succumbed to military coup or democratisation, and in fact they appeared to be the most durable of dictatorships. There were no theories and analyses of party 'withdrawal' or 'disengagement' from power.

Such durability was not simply a result of the party regimes having become personalist and therefore displaying the typical reluctance of personalist rulers to relinquish power. It is true that most party dictatorships have degenerated into personalist rule, but those which escaped this trend (or revived after the death of their personalist ruler) have been no less reluctant to relinquish power. As has often been pointed out, the greater durability of the party regime, as compared to the common form of military regime, is partly due to the party's 'stronger' motivation to retain power, with a party usually differing from the military in its views of ideological rectitude, the national interest and corporate and individual self-interest (as was seen in earlier chapters).

What makes the party dictatorships' durability all the more striking is the party's relatively weak means of retaining power, when compared to the coercive capacity of a military regime. In most cases the party is similar to personalist rulers in having to rely on its control over the military to secure such a massive capacity for the use or threat of force. Therefore the party (and most personalist) dictatorships are vulnerable to expropriation by a military coup, as in the many African cases, and to expropriation by a revolution, as when the communist regimes in East Germany and Czechoslovakia were overthrown in late 1989 by two of history's very rare examples of peaceful and spontaneous revolution.

So it is likely that in some cases a decision to relinquish power was swayed by doubts about whether the military could be relied upon to defend the regime. The military's failure to do so during the collapse of communism in Eastern Europe has been likened to 'the proverbial "dog that did not bark"' (Bunce, 1995: 98). Such political unreliability must also have had a 'demonstration effect' that probably reached as far as Africa. In fact parties' and rulers' doubts about the political reliability of their military may have been one of the reasons why such a large proportion of the many party and party-personalist dictatorships that came to an end in the 1980s–90s did so through relinquishments of power.

Considering how many of the party regimes opted to relinquish power, it is not surprising that the *Transitions* approach (O'Donnell and Schmitter, 1986) was soon applied to analysing transitions from party dictatorship to democracy. The influence of the *Transitions* approach and terminology is evident in comparative studies of party dictatorships' transition to democracy (a) in Latin America, Southern and Eastern Europe, (b) in Central and Eastern Europe, and (c) in the Soviet Union (Karl and Schmitter, 1991; Welsh, 1994; Bova, 1991). There was a tendency, though, to focus on the pacted type of transition rather than applying all three basic types suggested by the *Transitions* approach. The basic dictated/pacted/abdicated typology, plus the occasional 'surrender' to expropriation, is in fact all that is required when classifying (non-personalist) party dictatorships' transitions to democracy; thankfully there is no need to develop any new types.

Applying the Calculus of Retention and Transferral

In contrast, the calculuses of retention and transferral require some significant changes to their lists of motives, means and opportunity when they are applied to party dictatorships. As was noted earlier, the party has different and stronger motivation than the military to retain power but has inherently weaker coercive means of doing so – having to rely on control over the military as its means of wielding military-style coercion. This inherent weakness in the party's coercive means of retaining power cannot be alleviated by the inherent strength of its non-coercive means, such as its possession of politically skilled personnel and an organisation specialising in political mobilisation and indoctrination. Therefore loss of control over the military will always be a crucial 'negative' factor that may nullify a party's means of retaining power and will dominate any party's calculus of retention.

Similarly, the differences between a ruling party's and a ruling military's 'life after dictatorship' have important implications for parties' retention/relinquishment as well as for the 'to whom, how, when' of transferral. A party which relinquishes power lacks the secure corporate role and individual careers awaiting an army which returns to the barracks. Moreover, the party will also lack the military's capacity to exercise indirect rule, from the barracks, over at least those policies that affect its corporate interests – as occurred in Brazil and, to varying degrees, in other Latin American countries after their 1980s democratisation (Stepan, 1988: chs 6–8; Pion-Berlin, 1992). Nor will the party usually have the military's at least potential capacity to return to power through a coup or the threat of a coup.

But, unlike the military, a party does have an immediate 'second chance' to regain power constitutionally; like a personalist ruler, it can use democratic means to reacquire public office and powers. In fact a party usually has better prospects than a personalist ruler of political survival under democracy; the party faces lower 'downside' risks and has better long-term prospects of eventual success. For even if a party loses the initial democratic elections, it may (1) win sufficient seats in parliament to participate in a coalition government or play a significant role in the legislature, and/or (2) survive 'to fight again another day' in later elections (Huntington, 1991: 120).

The Electoral Option

The electoral option can therefore be a particularly powerful factor in a party's decision to relinquish power, especially when accompanied by overconfidence or wishful thinking. It is very likely that the electoral option had a major influence on the earlier-mentioned Romanian and Bulgarian cases of civilian anti-personalist transition. And the Communist Party leaders who, respectively, rebelled against Ceausescu and removed Zhivkov saw their electoral expectations realised when their renamed and revamped parties duly won the first post-dictator elections. So it is not surprising to find ruling parties in *non*-personalist regimes, too, opting to relinquish power in the expectation or hope of regaining it through democratic means.

However, the Sandinista revolutionary regime in Nicaragua provides a classic example of electoral overconfidence (Vickers, 1990; Williams, 1994). The Sandinistas instituted a dictated transition in the late 1980s with every expectation of electoral triumph and hoping that an unquestionable democratisation would reassure potential foreign-aid donors, remove the threat of US military intervention and end the war with the counter-revolutionary Contras. In fact the party was so unprepared for defeat in the 1990 elections that a post-election pact had to be negotiated to ensure its smooth exit from office.

In Eastern Europe a similar result occurred when the communist regime in Hungary confidently sought a dictated type of transition (Stokes, 1993: 91, 100–1, 132–4; Swain and Swain, 1993: 69–74). Political reformers began to take over the regime in early 1989 and initially hoped to use a controlled transition to tame the burgeoning pro-democracy opposition and remain the country's most powerful political force. By June the Communist Party was seeking to secure its place in the transition by entering roundtable negotiations with the democratic parties, now united into the Opposition Roundtable. But it took until September to reach an agreement, and further controversy and revisions would see the election date put back until March/April 1990. The increasingly powerful democratic opposition was able to transform the drawn-out negotiations into a virtual surrender by the communists – leading to Hungary's democratisation being dubbed the 'negotiated revolution'. Moreover, although the communist leaders believed they could perform very well in democratic elections, their democratised and renamed party would actually win less than a tenth of the seats in the 1990 parliamentary elections.

In contrast, the African ruling parties proved remarkably successful in winning transition elections. The remaining handful of party dictatorships which had not fallen to military coups in the 1960s–80s and were free of personalist rule in the early 1990s were able to reacquire electorally their relinquished power. In Tanzania the recent successor of founding leader Nyerere quickly instituted in 1990 a preemptive-procrastinating dictated transition that preempted the development of pro-democracy opposition but inordinately prolonged the transition process, with elections not being held – and won – until 1995 (Baregu, 1994: 169–70). In neighbouring Kenya a much more established successor-leader, Moi, and his party were much more reluctant to begin transition but were still able to win the 1992 elections, thanks largely to the splitting of the opposition vote among three parties (Wiseman, 1996: 60–1, 108, 135–6). A similar approach was taken by the Cameroon ruling party and its well-established successor-leader, Biya, producing similarly unconvincing election victories that again relied largely on a splintering of the opposition vote (Van de Walle, 1994: 143–7).

However, not all the African party dictatorships completed a transition to democracy. In Sierra Leone the process was aborted in 1992 by a military coup, and in Angola it ended in the UNITA opposition claiming electoral fraud and returning to its civil war against the MPLA regime. Despite the Angolan debacle, one of the features of African transitions from dictatorship to democracy was the avoidance of state disintegration in a region that has suffered from ethnic/tribal divisions and even civil wars (Wiseman, 1996: 111; Clapham and Wiseman, 1995: 223–4). Although several African states did collapse into anarchy in the early 1990s, they did not do so while engaged in democratisation. The lack of state disintegration during democratisation was partly due to such 'technical' factors as the absence of federalism but, whatever the reason, the result was a striking contrast with the fate suffered by Yugoslavia and the Soviet Union as their communist regimes collapsed.

Democratisation and Disintegration – Yugoslavia and the Soviet Union   The communist regime in Yugoslavia had decentralised so much power down to the six republics comprising its federal state that democratisation proceeded separately in the various republics, with elections being held in March–April 1990 in Slovenia and Croatia, but not until December 1990 in Serbia, Montenegro, Macedonia and Bosnia. More importantly, democratisation quickly took on an ethnic-nationalist aspect as not only the regional remnants of the Communist Party (notably in Serbia under Milosevic's leadership) but also the democratic opposition played the nationalist card – with Bosnia seeing each of its three ethnic groups establish its own party. The separatist tendency led in 1991–92 to secessions by Slovenia, Croatia, Macedonia and Bosnia – producing a rump Yugoslavia comprising only Serbia and Montenegro.

The huge multiethnic federal state known informally as the Soviet Union (formally as the Union of Soviet Socialist Republics) did not survive the partial democratisation of its communist regime, disintegrating completely in 1991 into its

15 federated republics (see Exhibit 8.2). As will be described in the next chapter, not all the new states that emerged from the former Soviet Union would soon complete the transition to democracy – some would remain what will be termed 'protodemocracies'.

Protodemocracies

A protodemocracy arises when an emerging democracy suffers from serious limitations that prevent the transition to full democracy from being completed. These limitations raise concerns about whether democracy will in fact be attained and whether the country might even slide back into a form of dictatorship. A protodemocracy can continue in this state of limbo for several years, extending well beyond the period where the calculus of transferral is applicable, and the situation may involve undemocratic elements that played little or no part in the initial transition from dictatorship to protodemocracy. Therefore the forms of limited democracy associated with protodemocracy are quite different from the explicitly limited democratisation that may occur in the initial stages of transition from dictatorship, such as in the Soviet Union in the late 1980s, in Communist Poland in April–August 1989, and in the plans of a military regime instituting an explicitly pacted transition.

The question or issue of whether a country is protodemocratic rather than truly democratic arises mostly in transitions from party dictatorships, especially from personalist party regimes. The issue is particularly likely to arise when a former ruling party and/or personalist ruler wins the democratic elections which are meant to complete the transition to democracy. An early case of dubious and seemingly incomplete democratisation occurred in the West African Islamic country of Senegal. Years before the 1989–93 wholesale democratisation of party dictatorships, Senegal experienced a dictated, unpressured transition from one-party state to multiparty democracy. The transition had been initiated in the mid-1970s by the country's personalist leader and philosopher-poet, President Senghor, and had apparently been completed soon after his 1980 retirement by his protégé-successor, the technocratic President Diouf.

However, the massive electoral victories won by Diouf and

Exhibit 8.2   Disintegration of a Superpower: The Soviet Union

The most surprising and significant example of democratisation of a party dictatorship in the 1980s–90s occurred in the communist superpower, the Soviet Union; but the process was not completed before this federal state disintegrated into its constituent republics (most notably the republic of Russia), thereby ending a superpower as well as the oldest communist, and party, regime (Brown, 1996; Gill, 1994; Bova, 1991). The Union of Soviet Socialist Republics or 'Soviet Union' was a formally federal state comprising fifteen republics (often with a strong ethnic-national aspect) that was under the centralised control of the Communist Party of the Soviet Union. In the later 1980s the new party and regime leader, General Secretary Gorbachev, and his reform coalition instituted a revitalisation or reinvigoration of the Soviet system – including a liberalisation and limited democratisation. Within a few years there were indications of a personalist transition to democracy as Gorbachev moved to strengthen his personal position (culminating in 1990 with his indirect election to the powerful new state post of executive President), encouraged a weakening of the party's control, and sought to win over the party to a social-democratic rather than Leninist approach to politics.

But the limited democratisation of the late 1980s produced a 'democratic opposition' that became so splintered and diverted by ethnic-nationalist concerns that in 1990–91 the issue of separatism increasingly overshadowed democratisation. The separatist issue took on a constitutional as well as political aspect when the massive Russian republic declared its political sovereignty and the supremacy of its laws over those of the Soviet Union. As most other republics followed suit, by 1991 the Soviet Union was in danger of disintegrating into its component republics.

President Gorbachev was able in April–August 1991 to negotiate a treaty, with Russia and some other republics, which would have secured a continuing but much looser federalism. However, the formal signing of the treaty was preempted by the attempted anti-Gorbachev coup in August, which had the typically radicalising effect of a failed counter-revolutionary coup. Moreover, President Yeltsin of the Russian republic had become a hero as the leader of the widespread opposition to the coup, capitalising on his democratic prestige as Russia's directly elected President. Therefore Gorbachev was in no position to resist the pressure to wind up the Soviet Union. In December it was replaced by a loose confederation termed the Commonwealth of Independent States.

his party in the elections of 1983 and 1988 seemed to fall well short of the democratic ideal. In addition to opponents' claims of electoral malpractices (and to the biased ban on electoral coalitions), there was the more important issue of whether the state's patronage resources and opportunities had been used to reduce the competitiveness of elections. (As will be seen in Chapter 9, this subtle tactic has been used by democratically disguised dictatorships to ensure that their elections are only semi-competitive.) Even a sympathetic analyst of Senegalese democracy emphasised the role of the Senghor-constructed party machine – and the support it received from local Islamic leaders and organisations – in delivering the massive, crucial rural vote to Diouf (Wiseman, 1990: ch. 9). Less sympathetic analysts contended that the Senegalese electoral game was played with 'loaded dice' and pointed to the use of the state's patronage resources to 'buy' the electoral support of these locally influential Islamic figures (Tordoff, 1993: 116–7). Similarly, an account of Senegal's new 'semidemocracy' argued that democracy was limited by the influence of the state and by patron–client politics – and that local Islamic leaders maintained their hold on the countryside (Coulon, 1988).

The post-1988 wave of democratisation of party dictatorships brought many new cases of dubious, incomplete democratisation. For example, in addition to such debatable cases as the Bulgarian ex-Communist Party's election victory or Houphouet-Boigny's overwhelming victory in the Ivory Coast, there were several relatively clear-cut cases of elections falling short of democratic standards (Bell, 1993: 88–9; Crook, 1995: 13–20). In Europe, the Romanian ex-communists' National Salvation Front used undemocratic measures to help win overwhelming presidential and parliamentary victories (Stokes, 1993: 174–5). In Africa, the ex-ruling parties in Kenya and in Cameroon benefited from undemocratic practices as well as from the splitting of the opposition vote when they won their (earlier-cited) unconvincing election victories. These protodemocracies and their counterparts in the former Soviet Union are also examples of the wider notion of 'semidemocracy' which will be described in the following chapter.

9

Semi-Dictatorships and Semidemocracies

Some dictatorships have been so elaborately disguised as democracies that they can be difficult to distinguish from the partial or limited democracies, which became quite common during the 1980s–90s with the many transitions from dictatorship. The previous chapter mentioned two different forms of transitional limited democracy:

1. the limited democratisation that may occur in the initial stages of transition from dictatorship; and
2. the limitations on democracy that are to be found in a situation of protodemocracy, in which it is not clear whether a country will push on to full democracy or will relapse into dictatorship.

In addition to these transitional forms there are more stable or consolidated forms of limited democracy (including immobilised protodemocracies) that have lasted for decades. Distinguishing between democratically disguised dictatorships and these various forms of 'dictatorial' democracy can be difficult, but it is an important practical as well as academic issue.

A systematic analysis of this issue was provided by Diamond, Linz and Lipset (1989) as editors of a massive study of Third World democracies (see Figure 9.1). In their preface to this study they pointed out that the 'boundary between democratic and non-democratic is sometimes a blurred and imperfect one' but they identified a graduated range of 'less-than-democratic systems' within this border area (*ibid.*: xvii).

Figure 9.1
'Less-than-democratic' regimes (Diamond, Linz and Lipset, 1989)

Non-democratic ---→---→---→---→---→---→---→---→---→---→ *Near*-democratic		
1. Pseudodemocracy (and other types of authoritarian regime)	2. Hegemonic party system	3. Semidemocratic system – electoral outcomes deviate significantly from popular preferences

- At the clearly non-democratic end of the range they identified a type of authoritarian regime that they labelled 'pseudodemocracy', in which 'the existence of formally democratic political institutions, such as multiparty electoral competition, masks (often, in part, to legitimate) the reality of authoritarian domination' (*ibid.*: xviii).
- However, the editors acknowledged that pseudodemocracy in certain respects overlaps what they termed the 'hegemonic party system', which is not an authoritarian regime but also falls far short of being a democracy because its frequent use of state coercion and its 'pervasive electoral malpractices' deny opposition parties 'any real chance to compete for power' (*ibid.*: xvii). A hegemonic party system differs from a pseudodemocracy, though, in being more institutionalised and tending to be less personalised and coercive.
- Finally, at the near-democratic end of the range, the editors identified what they termed 'semidemocratic' regimes in which there are competitive elections but:

1. the outcome of these elections deviates significantly from the people's preferences because of
   - limits on the power of elected public officials,
   - restrictions on competition between political parties,
   - lack of freedom and fairness in the conduct of elections, and/or

2. there are limits on political and civil liberties which prevent some political orientations/interests from organising and expressing themselves (*ibid.*: xvii).

However, this analytical framework needs to be expanded in some areas and can be simplified in others. On the one hand, the conception of semidemocracy needs to be expanded to explicitly incorporate such transitional forms of limited democracy as protodemocracy and (pacted) limited democratisation – which can be viewed as transitional types distinct from the consolidated type of semidemocratic regime (see Figure 9.2). On the other hand, there is no need to adopt the conceptions of pseudodemocracy and hegemonic party system as two distinct but also overlapping conceptions of disguised dictatorship. Both are clearly undemocratic regimes, as even the hegemonic party system uses undemocratic means to deny opposition parties a chance to compete for power. That it is a less personalist and coercive system than pseudodemocracy may mean that it has a more convincing democratic disguise. But the key to any credible democratic disguise is the use of semi-competitive elections (see Chapter 5), and these appear to be present in pseudodemocracy as well as the hegemonic party system.

Therefore it is simpler to focus on the presence of semi-competitive elections as the distinctive and defining characteristic of the disguised dictatorships (see Figure 9.2). These semi-competitive (elections) dictatorships can be more concisely labelled 'semi-(competitive) dictatorships' or simply *semi-dictatorships*. They are *not* limited or partial forms of dictatorship; they are 'semi' dictatorships only in the sense of using *semi*-competitive elections to provide themselves with a more elaborate and convincing democratic disguise than if they had either refused to hold any form of election or allowed only non-competitive elections. The semi-dictatorship can therefore be distinguished typologically from the 'auto-dictatorship' and the 'mono-dictatorship' (see Figure 9.2). The auto-dictatorship refuses to hold *any* elections and seeks self-legitimation ('auto'-legitimation) by claiming to embody the popular will or to be preparing the country to attain or return to democracy. The mono-dictatorship allows only non-competitive elections, with only *one* candidate, party or list of candidates. In contrast, the semi-dictatorship goes so far in its search for democratic credibility and electoral legitimacy as to permit multiparty semi-competitive elections.

A semi-competitive election is much more credible and convincing than non-competitive elections, even if they are given a multiparty gloss by the use of regime-controlled, puppet

Figure 9.2
Semi-dictatorship and semidemocracy

Dictatorship		Semidemocracy (as in Figure 9.1)	
Auto-dictatorship = absence of elections with regime attempting *self-legitimation* by claiming to embody the popular will or to be preparing for democracy	*mono*-dictatorship = non-competitive elections with only *one* candidate, party, or list of candidates	*semi-dictatorship* = semi-competitive elections with limited competition against the official party	Consolidated
			Transitional: limited democratisation
			Transitional: protodemocracy

opposition parties (see Chapter 5). In semi-competitive elections the regime's official party actually competes for votes (to some degree) with other parties that are (to some degree) autonomous, not puppet, parties. The elections are only *semi*-competitive in the sense that the opposition parties are denied any chance of victory by the special advantages bestowed on the official party and/or by the various ways in which the other parties are hampered. The special advantages range from vote-rigging and other forms of electoral fraud, to vote-buying and other forms of electoral 'patron–client' relationship, such as the use of state-funded public works to secure electoral support. The hampering of the other parties ranges from the arrest of their leaders to restricting their access to the mass media.

The semi-dictatorship may further secure its position against undesired electoral results by ensuring that key public offices cannot even formally or constitutionally be acquired through victory at the polls. For example, some members of the legislature might be appointed rather than elected, and/or the executive President might be elected only indirectly, whether by the legislature or some other form of electoral college. However, preferring indirect election and/or appointment to public offices can wreck the regime's democratic disguise as effectively as allowing too little competitiveness in elections.

The Classic Example: Mexico

The party dictatorship in Mexico provides the most sophisticated as well as oldest example of semi-dictatorship. Although usually classified as an authoritarian regime, it has been described as 'more complex than practically any of the authoritarian regimes that have ruled over other Latin American, African, and Asian nations in recent decades' (Cornelius, 1987: 18). The complexity of the Mexican regime arises partly from its being a sophisticated semi-dictatorship, but also partly from its revolutionary heritage. The post-1946 PRI party-state regime is the most recent manifestation of a revolutionary regime that originated in the 1910–17 Mexican Revolution – a continuity that is symbolised by continuing allegiance to the Revolution's 1917 Constitution. In fact Mexico's is the oldest regime to have originated in a social revolution, as its only rival for revolutionary longevity disappeared from the scene with the demise of the Soviet Union.

The nature and goals of the Mexican Revolution ensured that any Mexican regime claiming a revolutionary heritage would be democratic, semidemocratic or a semi-dictatorship. The revolutionary programme expressed in the Revolution's 1917 Constitution included a commitment to liberal democracy as well as to various social goals. Moreover, the Constitution's prohibiting of presidential reelection expressed the revolutionaries' commitment (also expressed in the promise of 'effective suffrage; no reelection') to preventing Mexico from relapsing into a democratically disguised personal dictatorship like the 1876–1911 reign of President Diaz (Middlebrook, 1986: 129). Therefore, even if the post-1917 regimes' legitimacy depended primarily on commitment to the Revolution's principles rather than on winning competitive elections (Whitehead, 1994: 328), these principles required that outward, formal respect be shown to democracy and that dictatorship be convincingly disguised. The military and party dictatorships that have been established during the long history of post-Revolution Mexico have formally adhered to the democratic provisions of the Constitution, including the ban on reelection. Furthermore, political opponents have been allowed to operate within a *semi-competitive multiparty* system that is summed up by the formula 'you can be a party; but not a government', and in which the traditional role of the opposition parties has been 'to put up enough of a fight to make the ruling party's victory look credible' (Whitehead, 1994: 337; Cornelius, 1987: 32).

The regime's democratic disguise was less credible in the 1920s and 1930s when the military wing of the revolutionary movement had taken charge, but in the 1940s power was transferred to civilians and to the official party of the revolution, the Institutionalised Revolutionary Party (PRI). Founded by the military in 1928 as the National Revolutionary Party and known in 1938–46 as the Party of the Mexican Revolution, the party had already for many years enjoyed the special advantages of the official party within a semi-dictatorship. In addition to patronage opportunities, it had been able to rely on the electoral fraud perpetrated by Ministry of Government officials charged with administering the electoral system (Brooker, 1995: 222–3).

Civilianisation into a party-state regime did not bring an end to the use of electoral fraud and of extensive patronage opportunities, which were exploited by not only the PRI but also the party's huge labour and peasant organisations (Middlebrook, 1986: 129; Cornelius, 1987: 34). There was even the use of restrictive legislation to prevent such radical parties as the Mexican Communist Party from participating in elections and to hinder the forming of regional and local parties. Consequently, after more than 60 years of regular (semi-competitive) elections, Mexico still showed almost as much evidence of party monopoly as was to be found in the Soviet Union on the eve of its Gorbachev-led liberalisation. For in 1985 the PRI held the federal presidency, all the seats in the Senate, three-quarters of the seats in the Chamber of Deputies, all the state governorships, and control of 96 per cent of municipal governments (Cornelius, 1987: 15).

The PRI's overwhelming electoral dominance had in fact become politically counterproductive in the 1970s, forcing the regime to launch a series of political and electoral reforms aimed at creating a more credible opposition (Cornelius, 1987; Middlebrook, 1986). The opposition parties had become too disillusioned and weak to perform their traditional role of giving some democratic credibility to the official party's electoral victories. In 1976 the main opposition party, the conservative PAN, even failed to put up a presidential candidate, leaving a very embarrassed regime to conduct an uncontested presidential election. The public's disillusionment was evident in the steadily declining levels of voter participation, in middle-class discontent (symbolised and strengthened by the student demonstrators martyred in the 1968 massacre), and eventually in the emergence of leftist underground parties and short-lived urban and rural guerrilla movements. Therefore the reforming of the electoral system can also be seen as providing a safety valve for discontent and opposition (Tagle, 1993; Whitehead, 1994). The PRI had long employed a conciliatory strategy of safety valves and diversions, cooption and incorporation, to reduce its need to resort to crude repression.

The series of reforms in 1972, 1973 and 1977 assisted the opposition in quite the reverse fashion to the manner in which opposition parties are usually disadvantaged and hampered in a semi-dictatorship (Middlebrook, 1986; Cornelius, 1987; Tagle,

1993). Already, in 1963, a small element of proportional representation had been introduced into the electoral system to allow even the smaller of the opposition parties to be represented in the Chamber of Deputies, but now the threshold for representation was reduced from 2.5 per cent to only 1.5 per cent of the national vote, and the Chamber was expanded by a third to include 100 of these (non-PRI) proportional-representation 'party deputies'. Old and new leftist parties were now allowed to participate in elections, and a Federal Electoral Commission was established to oversee the electoral system and process. Furthermore, political parties were recognised as public-interest organisations, public funding was provided for their election campaigns, and they were guaranteed regular access to radio and television.

However, there were crucial limits on how far the electoral system would be reformed. Electoral fraud had certainly been reduced but in many rural areas 'the PRI conducted the elections much as it always had' and still engaged 'in various forms of electoral fraud' (Middlebrook, 1986: 136, 142). In fact the PRI's greatest electoral advantage was its control of the rural vote, which constituted as much as a third of the total vote and was overrepresented electorally thanks to the regime's unwillingness to adjust outdated constituency boundaries (Fox, 1994). Not only was fraud widespread in rural areas, but also they received little attention from opposition parties, leaving the vote to be mobilised by local political bosses exploiting their patronage opportunities – including the large-scale opportunities provided by road-building, school-building and other public works (Fox, 1994; Harvey, 1993).

Nevertheless, the 1970s reforms proved quite sufficient for the purpose of creating a more credible opposition and election contest. In the 1982 elections there was a wider range of parties, significant increase in voter participation, and a marked rise in the opposition's vote as well as congressional representation (Middlebrook, 1986). Thereafter, changes in the electoral rules no longer necessarily strengthened the opposition parties (Tagle, 1993). For example, although the 1986 revamping of electoral laws increased the number of proportional-representation seats in the Chamber of Deputies to 200 (out of 500), now the PRI as well as the opposition parties would be entitled to a share of these seats. Other electoral 'reforms' made at this time and in 1989–90 tended, on balance, to strengthen the PRI's ability to exert control over electoral results and to actually reverse the trend towards democratising electoral procedures.

For by the later 1980s Mexican politics had become too competitive for the semi-dictatorship's comfort. In the 1988 elections the PRI lost its two-thirds majority in the Chamber of Deputies, and without its new proportional-representation seats would have failed to secure an absolute majority – which in turn was needed to ratify the party's marginal and controversial presidential victory (Tagle, 1993). The electoral debacle was partly due to a split within the PRI, as a leftist faction opposed to their party's neo-liberal economic restructuring had broken away to support the presidential candidacy of their standard-bearer, Cardenas (Dresser, 1994). He became the joint candidate of a coalition of several leftist parties and groups that was later reformed into a new party, the PRD. The election result saw the PRI's presidential candidate, Salinas, officially win less than 50.4 per cent of the vote, and in such suspicious circumstances that the opposition candidates and large public demonstrations accused the government of electoral fraud. Salinas clearly depended upon the PRI-controlled rural vote for his victory, and most of the suspicious vote counts came from rural areas (Fox, 1994; Harvey, 1993).

In the following state and municipal elections the PRI remained true to its tradition of using fraud in rural areas, where 'official recognition of opposition victories was rarely won without protests and direct action' (Harvey, 1993: 213). But the regime also adopted more positive vote-winning strategies, such as the rapid development of an urban and rural National Solidarity Programme (PRONASOL) of poverty-alleviating public works projects. In theory they were proposed and administered by local communities but in practice the Solidarity projects established new patronage networks that were used for party-political purposes, if only to undercut support for leftists (Bruhn, 1996).

The 1991 congressional elections saw something of a PRI revival (Bruhn, 1996; Dresser, 1994). The party won over 60 per cent of the vote – and collapsed the leftist vote – without having to resort to massive fraud. Although the PRI revival seemed to have been based on weak foundations, the Mexican semi-dictatorship had at least avoided the disasters experienced in 1991 by the other long-lived revolutionary regime, the Soviet Union. By the late 1990s the Mexican regime finally seemed to be committed to real democratisation, as the PRI had accepted the loss of its majority in the Chamber of Deputies, the governorships of the six most modern states and the mayoralty of Mexico City (Klesner, 1998). But in the light of Mexico's long history of democratically disguised dictatorships, more than usual evidence of democracy would be required before sceptics accepted that this was much more than typical PRI conciliatory, safety-valve diversionary tactics.

The Historical Stronghold: Latin America

Mexico is only one of a number of countries in Latin America that have experienced semi-dictatorship. Both the other party regimes, the MNR's in 1950s–60s Bolivia and the Sandinistas' in 1970s–80s Nicaragua, were also semi-dictatorships, as were many of the longer-term military regimes. Their preference for disguised dictatorship has been particularly evident in Central America (Gilbert, 1988: 4; Rouquié, 1986: 117–9; Dunkerley, 1985). The Somoza family's 40-year rule over Nicaragua even saw political pacts being made with some opposition groups in order to secure more credible semi-competitive (fraudulent) elections. Semi-dictatorship was also employed in Panama from the late 1970s onwards to disguise the indirect personalist rule of a military leader – Torrijos until his death in 1981, and then Noriega until his removal by US invasion in 1989. And it was not only personalist regimes that favoured the semi-dictatorship approach; the military's rule in Guatemala and El Salvador was for decades disguised by semi-competitive elections, with El Salvador's official party having actually been modelled on the PRI in Mexico.

Semi-dictatorship has not been as common among military regimes in South America. However, General Stroessner's long-lived personalist regime in Paraguay developed a semi-competitive electoral system in the 1960s that was similar to the Somozas' arrangements with opponents. Two moderate opposition parties were encouraged to take part in the Stroessner regime's fraudulent elections and were legally guaranteed a third of the seats in parliament (Nickson, 1988: 241).

A far more famous case of semi-dictatorship emerged in Argentina from the conversion of General Juan Perón's democratic rule into a personalist semi-dictatorship. Having built up a large civilian following during his time as Minister of Labour and Welfare in the military government of 1943–45, Perón and his supporters had won the democratic presidential and congressional elections held in 1946. But President Perón and his party were not prepared to entrust their political fortunes to the unpredictable processes of uncontrolled democracy, and within a few years Argentina's democracy had been converted into semi-dictatorship. A wide range of often subtle undemocratic measures was used to hamper the opposition and assist the Peronist party (Brooker 1995: 175). Nevertheless, the Peronist claim to electoral legitimacy remained credible and, together with the popular following established by Perón and his wife Evita, this compensated for his weak hold on the military. Not until 1955 did the military finally overthrow a now widely unpopular Perón, who had never recovered politically from Evita's death three years earlier.

The Unusual Brazilian Case

Although less famous than Perón's regime, the Brazilian military's semi-dictatorship of the 1960s–80s was in certain respects no less significant or unusual. Unlike Perón's regime, it originated from a military coup, the 1964 'revolution', and did not develop into a personalist regime. The Brazilian military produced a succession of six one-term (or less) military presidents during the next two decades – finally approving the installation of a civilian president in 1985. However, the Brazilian military regime was similar to Perón's in having to respond to what has been termed the 'electoral imperative', which arose from the liberal, anti-authoritarian component of Brazil's 'ideological and institutional legacy' (Lamounier, 1989: 70).

This liberal, anti-authoritarian component was reflected in the military's justifications for abandoning its traditional 'restraint' (see Chapters 2 and 3) and resorting in 1964 to direct military rule. The 1964 coup against President Goulart's populism was depicted as a military-led revolution motivated by democratic ideals, and the regime committed itself to the long-term goal of establishing the economic and social preconditions for a 'true democracy' – for the evolution of stable and democratic institutions (Martins, 1986: 77). But Brazil's liberal legacy required more than just protestations of democratic intent; it also produced an electoral imperative that forced the military to combine this typical auto-dictatorship approach with a semi-dictatorship's use of semi-competitive elections (see Figure 9.2). In order to substantiate its claim to favour democracy, and to acquire some degree of electoral legitimacy, the military was forced to allow at least semi-competitive congressional elections.

Semi-dictatorship was institutionalised by the military in 1965. The president was from now on to be elected by Congress rather than by the people, and congressional politics, in turn, was to be reshaped by the indirect imposition of a two-party system. The new party system arose from the military's dissolving all existing parties and prohibiting any new party from being formed unless it was sponsored by at least 20 senators and 120 deputies (Schneider, 1991: 245–7). These measures not only opened the way for a new official party, the National Renovating Alliance (ARENA), to win the support of the defunct conservative party and a majority of the defunct centrist party, but also gave the various opposition elements little option except to form themselves into a single party, the Brazilian Democratic Movement (MDB) – which was confidently expected by the military to be a divided and incoherent opposition party (*ibid.*: 247–8).

However, in the 1970s the two-party semi-competitive electoral system developed an anti-regime momentum that posed an awkward problem for the Brazilian military. The opposition MDB's vote dramatically increased as many people who had cast invalid votes in 1966 and 1970 to protest against military rule now instead expressed their opposition by voting for the MDB (Lamounier, 1989: 58–9). Moreover, in 1974 a new president's move to soften the regime's highly repressive approach led to liberalising measures, such as relaxing press censorship and allowing the MDB unrestricted access to radio and television, that contributed to the dramatic increase in the MDB share of the vote – from 21 to 38 per cent – in that year's elections (Martins, 1986: 83). Therefore the military was now faced by the problem that the electoral process had become too credible and competitive; the opposition was likely to win an election victory that would force the military to reassess the whole structure and even purpose of its rule.

In response, the regime adopted a 'two steps forward; one step backwards' approach. While avoiding a return to the repressive approach of earlier years, it reduced both the competitiveness of elections and the constitutional implications of a possible electoral defeat. Controls were tightened before the 1976 municipal elections, and in the lead up to the 1978 congressional elections (a) the Senate was restructured to enable a third of its members to be indirectly elected, and (b) some state and municipal representation was introduced into the electoral college that chose the country's president (Martins, 1986: 83; Schneider, 1991: 279). Even the regime's later decision to abolish its two-party system in favour of a less restricted multipartyism has been seen as part of a strategy to encourage the creation of another, more moderate and 'reliable' opposition party (Martins, 1986: 85). However, these measures could not prevent the opposition winning a majority in the 1982 congressional elections and an opposition-backed civilian becoming president in 1985.

An Asian Example: Suharto's Indonesia

Semi-dictatorship has also occurred in other parts of the world than Latin America, as in the prominent Asian case of Suharto's Indonesia. The military regime established there in the late 1960s by General Suharto – who retained the Presidency until 1998 – became the longest-lived Asian example of semi-dictatorship.

The Indonesian regime was characterised by its unusually extensive and visible military presence, including having a hundred seats in parliament reserved for unelected military men (see Chapter 5). Moreover, the constitution inherited and preserved by the military specifies that the president be indirectly elected, by a People's Consultative Assembly comprising the members of parliament (including the swathe of appointed military members) and an equal number of appointees and delegates representing the regions and various political and social organizations (Brooker, 1995: 192). However, the military sought to win electoral legitimacy and to substantiate its claim of favouring (Pancasila) democracy by holding regular semi-competitive parliamentary elections during the 1970s–90s, in which the official party Golkar has won from 62 to 73 per cent of the vote.

But the Indonesian semi-dictatorship comes close to the borderline with mono-dictatorship in its refusal to allow opposition parties much more autonomy than a typical puppet party (*ibid.*: 185, 187). From the outset the military regime showed an inclination to exert control over the parties competing for votes with its own party, Golkar, and in the 1971 elections it not only prohibited any criticism of government policies but also interfered in opposition parties' internal affairs and disqualified hundreds of their candidates. After Golkar's election victory the regime forced all nine other parties to merge into two new parties, one Muslim (PPP) and the other nationalist (PDI), and the 1975 Political Parties Bill allowed only Golkar, the PDI and PPP to participate in elections. Unlike the indirect means used by the Brazilian regime to introduce a two-party system, this was a quite blatant restructuring of the party system to meet the military's requirements. The Indonesian regime justified its imposition of a three-party system by arguing that these three parties together provided sufficient facilities for channelling society's opinions and ideas. The parties themselves were warned not to be antagonistic to one another and behaved more like a three-party coalition than a bevy of political opponents.

The regime also placed various restrictions on the parties' activities. For example, the politically restrictive concept of the 'floating mass' was embodied in a legal prohibition on parties' establishing village-level branches in this still largely rural society (Rogers, 1988: 258). (Exponents of the floating-mass concept argued that the mass of villagers should be left to float free of political agitation and party contact between the country's brief election campaigns.) Restrictions on party activities were tightened in the 1980s and went so far as prohibiting the Muslim PPP from appealing to voters on the basis of religion (Suryadinata, 1989: 129–30).

Moreover, the regime strengthened Golkar's competitive advantage by exploiting its status as the regime's official party (Brooker, 1995: 187). The civil service was mobilised to support Golkar and it became formally obligatory for civil servants to campaign as well as vote for the party. Officials' influence over rural society was particularly important, with the Department of Internal Affairs being used to create a rural vote-winning patronage machine for Golkar. In addition to the various opportunities for using small-scale state patronage, public works projects, such as bringing electricity and clean water to the villages, provided opportunities for large-scale patronage (Suryadinata, 1989: 131). Furthermore, in the early 1980s village headmen were classified as civil servants, ensuring that these powerful grassroots figures would be Golkar activists. For example, in 1990 a village headman told the visiting Minister of Home Affairs that he would punish the small minority of his village that had not (yet) agreed to vote for Golkar (Vatikiotis, 1993: 103).

By the time of the 1987 elections the regime was actually becoming concerned about the weakness of the other two parties. If the PDI became so weak as to disappear, there would no longer be a 'buffer' between Golkar and the PPP, and if Golkar was to win every seat up for election, the regime's image would suffer both internationally and domestically (Suryadinata, 1989: 131). It was important to maintain a multiparty, democratic image not only in order 'to legitimize military power', but also to encourage the opposition from resorting to 'extra-parliamentary activities' (*ibid.*: 133–4). However, although Golkar did go on to win a record 73 per cent of the vote, the other parties performed their role sufficiently creditably to preempt any need for opposition-assisting reforms like those introduced in the 1970s in Mexico.

Distinguishing between Semi-Dictatorship and Semidemocracy

From this examination of a wide range of semi-dictatorships, from the classic Mexican case to an Indonesian case that borders on mono-dictatorship, it may appear that there is little difficulty in distinguishing between semi-dictatorship and semidemocracy. As was seen at the beginning of the chapter, the standard conception of semidemocracy points to a situation in which electoral outcomes 'deviate significantly' from popular preferences – as distinct from the more dictatorial situation in which opposition parties are denied 'any real chance of competing for power'. However, in practice distinguishing a deviation from a denial is not always as straightforward as it appears. And in a few cases distinguishing between these two situations also raises the awkward issue of whether a dictatorship can take the form of a misappropriation of power by more than one party.

It is at least conceivable that two or more leading parties might collude in jointly misappropriating power. This would take the form of (a) denying other parties any real chance of competing for power, and (b) sharing that power between themselves through coalitions or alternating periods in office. In a sense this is what occurred in the old-fashioned, nineteenth-century form of oligarchical democracy or semidemocracy, in which property qualifications or other restrictions denying the poor the right to vote also denied left-wing or populist parties any chance of electoral success. A modernised, more formally democratic version of this type of regime would see two or more parties using less obviously undemocratic measures to deny other parties any real chance of competing for power. As such a regime would involve semi-competitive elections in which there are two or more official parties, it could be termed a *joint-multiparty* semi-dictatorship.

Colombia has provided a modern example of two-party collusion and alternation in power which may be a specimen of joint semi-dictatorship, or may instead be one of the few examples of consolidated semidemocracy to have survived into recent times (Hartlyn, 1989). The regime has been categorised by some analysts as a form of democracy and by others as a form of authoritarian regime, but even those who prefer the democratic category have used such adjectives as 'controlled', 'oligarchical', 'restricted', 'limited' and 'semi' democracy (Hartlyn, 1989: 292–4). The regime arose in 1957 from the removal of the country's military dictator, General Rojas. The country's two major parties, the Conservatives and the Liberals, had joined together in an anti-Rojas National Front and agreed in a series of pacts to maintain their alliance during the early decades of the new democracy. There was to be coalition rule, with political parity between the two parties, and they would nominate a joint National Front candidate for president until at least 1974 (with the candidate being chosen alternately from each party).

This power-sharing arrangement between the two parties proved remarkably durable. Although the National Front was partially dismantled after 1968, the two parties continued to put forward a joint presidential candidate until 1974 and the coalitional approach actually continued on until 1986 when the Conservatives went into opposition. More importantly, for most of this time the coalition ruled the country under 'state of siege' emergency powers which restricted civil liberties and which were invoked against student protests and labour demonstrations as well as guerrilla movements. In fact, even the regime's milder critics have had to admit that 'the regime at times employed or condoned the use of undemocratic practices' and that 'many feel fraud' was used by the regime in 1970 to deny election victory to the ANAPO populist movement (Hartlyn, 1989: 310, 316). If such serious undemocratic practices as electoral fraud did occur, the Colombian case would have to be categorised not as a semidemocracy, but as a joint-multiparty form of semi-dictatorship.

A joint semi-dictatorship may be as rare among dictatorships as the dominant-party system is among democracies. What have been described as one-party dominant 'uncommon democracies' have arisen for a time in Japan, Sweden, Italy and Israel:

> In these countries, despite free electoral competition, relatively open information systems, respect for civil liberties, and the right of free political association, a single party has managed to govern alone or as the primary and ongoing partner in coalitions, without interruption for substantial periods of time, often for three to five decades. (Pempel, 1990: 1)

The 'uncommon dictatorships', the joint semi-dictatorships, would require a similar careful definition once a few likely specimens have been reliably identified. However, the identification of such specimens is bound to be controversial. In addition to the problems involved in researching and 'proving' charges of undemocratic practices, there is also room for argument in assessing the effect and even the intent of these practices.

Furthermore, difficult conceptual and even ethical issues arise when considering whether to categorise the racist regime that ruled South Africa until 1994 as having been a case of joint-multiparty dictatorship. Dating back to the founding 1910 Constitution, the Union of South Africa's bizarre racist system combined:

(a) multiparty democracy for the Dutch/British-origin settler communities; with

(b) the exclusion of the non-white races, nearly four-fifths of the population, from the right to vote.

Within the multiparty democracy reserved exclusively for whites, there was much more party competition than occurred between Colombia's colluding Liberals and Conservatives. After the racially segregationist (apartheid) Nationalist Party was first elected to government in 1948, it did not share power or alternate in power with any other white parties; it continued to compete against and defeat them in the racist elections that continued to be regularly held until the regime's demise nearly half a century later.

However, although these elections lacked the collusion found in a typical joint dictatorship, they were even less like the racist elections found in a typical ethnic/racial semidemocracy, in which one or more ethnic/racial groups are excluded in some fashion from otherwise competitive elections. For an ethnic or racial semidemocracy involves a social *minority*, not the great majority of the population, being prevented from expressing its preferences in election outcomes. The notion of a small racial minority enjoying democratic rights and powers that are denied to the rest of the population is quite different ethically as well as conceptually, and it also seems ethically and conceptually banal to blame only the political parties for such a racist regime. The regime is better described not as some form of joint-multiparty dictatorship, but as a dictatorship of the white minority over the other racial groups – a misappropriation of power by a racial minority. Although this conception of the South African case is stretching the notions of dictatorship and misappropriation of power, it is only a further step in the direction taken in categorising the Iranian regime as the clergy's semi-dictatorship (see Exhibit 9.1).

The racial or ethnic issue also arises when dealing with the seemingly more straightforward problem of distinguishing between (a) the *semidemocracy* that excludes or reduces the electoral effect of an ethnic minority's preferences, and (b) the *semi-dictatorship* in which a party exploits ethnic divisions to secure its misappropriation of power. This distinction is particularly

Exhibit 9.1   The Clergy's Semi-Dictatorship in Iran

The Iranian case of semi-dictatorship suggests that a modern form of non-democratic regime can be established by organisations other than parties or militaries, and in fact by groups that are hardly organisations at all. For in Iran a semi-dictatorship was established by a Shiite Muslim clergy that was only partially organised (Brooker, 1997). The fewer than 200 000 clergy (in the widest sense of the term) had a hierarchy of religious titles and spiritual authority, culminating in the few Grand Ayatollahs, and had a network of mosques, seminaries and other religious institutions, but they could not be described as an 'organisation' comparable to a party or the military. The lack of organisational coherence was displayed in the open political divisions that emerged within the clergy as the more politicised members and their secular allies took charge of government, parliament and party politics after the 1978–79 Islamic revolution.

The clergy-led Islamic revolution produced a semi-democratic Islamic Republic that incorporated several constitutional safeguards against democracy's overriding the Islamic nature of the Republic. For example, a clergy-dominated Council of Guardians vetted electoral candidates' Islamic qualifications. Within a few years of the Revolution it appeared that the Islamic Republican Party had established a party semi-dictatorship, but the IRP was only a party-political vehicle for the clergy and was dissolved in 1987, having outlived its usefulness now that all other competing parties had been removed from the scene. The regime continued to be dominated by the personalist rule of (Grand) Ayatollah Khomeini, who was not only spiritual leader of the 1978–79 revolution, but also holder of the powerful constitutional office of Rahbar (leader) and Supreme Faqih (religious judge) of the Islamic Republic.

After Khomeini's death in 1989 a clergy-dominated collective leadership took over, and despite continuing factional divisions, carried the regime through the 1990s. Although the clergy's presence in parliament and government had declined, the key posts of Rahbar-Faqih and President continued to be held by clerics. And while there was no longer an official party, the competitiveness of presidential and parliamentary elections was restricted by the clergy's control over candidature and issues. The clerics and their political allies were still divided into various factions – conservative, populist, pragmatic and even liberal – but their parliamentary and electoral rivalries were not allowed to undermine the clergy's hold on power.

relevant when categorising the Malaysian regime, perhaps the best-known example of an 'ambiguous' authoritarian/democratic regime. Like the similarly ambiguous Singapore regime, it is also a leading example of what some East Asian thinkers and leaders referred to in the early 1990s as an 'Asian' form of democracy as distinct from the more individualist Western-style democracy (Jones, 1995: 41–2).

Two Ambiguous Cases: Malaysia and Singapore

Malaysia

Ever since independence from British colonial rule in 1957, the constitutional monarchy of Malaysia has been ruled by a coalition of parties, known as the Alliance and then (from 1974) as the Barisan Nasional. It has regularly won more than two-thirds of the seats in the parliamentary elections that have been regularly held every five or four years since independence. The coalition presents a combined slate or ticket of candidates at the country's parliamentary elections and has been multiethnic since its inception as an Alliance that combined the United Malays National Organisation (UMNO) with a party representing the large Chinese minority and another representing the small Indian minority (Means, 1991: 1–2). When refounded in 1974 as the Barisan Nasional (National Front), the coalition organisation contained no fewer than eight parties but was now even more dominated by UMNO – which held well over half of the BN's seats in parliament – and was 'in effect a facade for UMNO rule' (*ibid.*: 30–32; Crouch, 1996: 34).

Therefore, unlike in the Colombian case of coalition, one party within the coalition has always dominated the government and in fact UMNO leader Mahathir has been the country's continual and dominating Prime Minister ever since becoming the party's leader in 1981. If Malaysia is a semi-dictatorship rather than a semidemocracy, it is not so much a joint-multiparty dictatorship as an UMNO semi-dictatorship.

It is widely acknowledged that the Malaysian regime does not follow standard democratic procedures, and even the regime itself depicts Malaysian politics as differing from the 'Western' model of democracy. While constantly asserting that

Malaysia is democratic, official spokesmen – notably Prime Minister Mahathir – have also emphasised that Malaysia had a different definition of democracy than Western countries (Munro-Kua, 1996: 151, 123). Mahathir has argued that Western-style democracy and its preoccupation with individual rights is inappropriate for Malaysian circumstances, and that Third World or Asian conceptions of democracy are no less valid than Western conceptions (Means, 1991: 140; Jones, 1995: 42).

However, although analysts of semidemocracy have categorised Malaysia as semidemocratic (Diamond, Linz and Lipset, 1989; Case, 1996), it has also been described as a case of authoritarian populism (Munro-Kua, 1996). Furthermore, the Malaysian regime has been labelled as 'ambiguous' not only because it combines democratic and authoritarian elements, but also because it can be categorised either as semidemocratic or as a more authoritarian type of regime, as a hegemonic party system (Crouch, 1996: 6). In fact the regime would seem to have gone well beyond the semidemocracy's level of electoral deviation if it has employed a 'wide range of authoritarian controls' which 'make it very difficult to envisage the defeat of the ruling party at the polls', and has 'actually routinely manipulated the electoral process to ensure its own victories' (*ibid.*: 5, 240).

If the Malaysian regime is a semidemocracy rather than a semi-dictatorship, it is a case of (Malay) ethnic semidemocracy. Incorporating Chinese and Indian parties in the UMNO-dominated governing coalition shrewdly disguised an electoral bias against these ethnic minorities which significantly reduced the electoral impact of their political preferences. The regime's ethnic bias is evident in the targeting of the regime's authoritarian controls as well as in the ethnic nature of its electoral gerrymandering. The 'sensitive issues' which were banned (by constitutional amendments) from public and even parliamentary discussion included Malays' special rights and privileges, as well as the status of Malay as the sole national language, and the status of Islam (the religion of most Malays) as the official religion (Means, 1991: 14–15).

But it was the gerrymandering of the electoral constituencies which was crucial in reducing the electoral effect of the minorities. For by this means the Malays' (barely) absolute majority of the electorate was transformed into potentially a more than two-thirds majority of the seats in parliament. The gerrymander used the simple method of ensuring that the rural constituencies, which are disproportionately populated by Malays, were increasingly overrepresented in parliament – so that by 1984 Malays were in the absolute majority in nearly three-quarters of the country's constituencies (Crouch, 1996: 57–9; Means, 1991: 135). Thanks to this ethnic gerrymandering, the governing coalition has been able to achieve its target of a two-thirds majority in parliament despite the fact that substantial numbers of Malays as well as Chinese vote for parties that oppose the BN coalition. Such a large parliamentary majority has enabled the government to make its many constitutional amendments and also provides useful insurance for UMNO against a parliamentary revolt by the coalition's non-Malay parties.

In addition to the electoral bias, there is striking circumstantial evidence of ethnic semidemocracy, namely the ethnically biased New Economic Policy that has been implemented since 1971. Although under colonial rule and in Malaysia's Constitution Malays had enjoyed some 'special rights', the NEP expanded these rights, job quotas and educational opportunities and also included an ambitious programme to raise Malays to full partnership in the nation's Chinese-dominated economic life – specifically by achieving the goal of '30 per cent Malay ownership and participation in all industrial and commercial activities by 1990' (Means, 1991: 24). This was a very ambitious goal considering that Malays then owned less than 2 per cent of the country's share capital, but two decades of energetic pursuit of the NEP's goals produced a 'veritable revolution' in the reallocation of wealth and jobs (*ibid.*: 27, 265). In light of this huge policy bias in favour of the Malays, the regime does seem a clear-cut case of reducing the minorities' electoral influence in order to safeguard the benefits flowing to the ethnic majority through its control of the government.

However, the Malaysian regime can also be viewed as a party semi-dictatorship based upon ethnic factors rather than as an ethnic semidemocracy. From this perspective the UMNO party has been able to misappropriate power by exploiting the country's ethnic divisions and, in particular, by presenting itself as the political standard-bearer and benefactor of the Malay majority. It can claim to have brought Malays the benefits of the NEP and to be the political means of protecting Malays' privileged position. As Prime Minister Mahathir argued in 1989, Malays had not yet achieved the NEP's goals and still had to protect their position through political success and specifically through UMNO's success (*ibid.*: 270).

There is much evidence of a specifically UMNO *party* (rather than simply Malay ethnic) bias in the regime's operations, particularly in its use of authoritarian controls and in its electoral practices. The regime's armoury of authoritarian controls, which included legal powers to deregister organisations, ban publications and impose preventive detention, 'were sometimes used mainly to strengthen the government against the opposition or even one government faction against another', as in the 1987 arrest and detention of more than a hundred people (Crouch, 1996: 112, 109–113). The controls over the mass media were particularly advantageous to the UMNO government. In conjunction with state or BN ownership of television and radio, the deterrent effect of these controls ensured that the mass media would present UMNO leaders and policies to the public in a solely and overly positive light (Means, 1991: 137–9, 292; Munro-Kua, 1996: 123–5).

Furthermore, as in Indonesia, there was a range of restrictions on party activities, such as a ban on public rallies, that hampered the opposition parties more than the government party (Means, 1991: 88; Munro-Kua, 1996: 122). Another similarity with the Indonesian regime was the massive use of state patronage opportunities to improve electoral performance. In addition to promises of local development projects, there was a village-level use of material benefits to secure political loyalty – in fact the village head was quite often the chairman of the local branch of UMNO (Crouch, 1996: 61, 40–1).

With these electoral and other competitive advantages, UMNO has been able to dominate the Malay vote and to prevent Malay opposition parties from capitalising on their ethnic electoral advantages. Even when faced in the 1990 elections with an UMNO breakaway party and an electoral pact among the opposition parties, UMNO was able to lead the BN coalition to another sweeping electoral victory (*ibid.*: 125–7). The coalition retained a two-thirds majority in parliament despite a fall in the overall BN vote to 53 per cent, and in the next election its vote rebounded to a record 65 per cent. But UMNO's electoral resilience begs comparison with the PRI's in Mexico, just as UMNO's competitive advantages beg comparison with Golkar's in Indonesia. And the regime as a whole seems no less comparable to semi-dictatorship than to semidemocracy.

Singapore

The Singapore regime, like the Malaysian, has emphasised that it has developed a form of democracy that suits its country's circumstances, and has argued that it is important to retain this 'dominant-party system' (Rodan, 1993a: 78). However, among Western analysts Singapore is usually seen as less than democratic, and the issue is whether this ambiguous regime should be categorised as a semidemocracy or as effectively a one-party state (Case, 1996; Rodan, 1993a: 78, 86, 103).

The People's Action Party (PAP) regime in Singapore developed in quite different fashion from its Malaysian counterpart, UMNO. The PAP came to power in 1959, in a British decolonising election, by mobilising mass support from the Chinese ethnic majority, but it was a socialist rather than a communal or ethnic party and sought support from the Malay and Indian ethnic minorities as well as from the Chinese majority. Moreover, in 1961 the party's communist-sympathising (and mass-mobilising) faction broke away from the PAP and formed the Barisan Sosialis (BS) party. The BS was 'seriously crippled', though, in 1963 when more than a hundred leading leftists fell victim to anti-communist preventive detention measures (Chan, 1976: 198), and later in the year a now rebuilt PAP handed the BS a heavy electoral defeat. Within a decade the BS had declined into obscurity, leaving the PAP with an unchallenged electoral dominance. Although in the 1970s–80s elections there were always five or more opposition parties contesting elections with the PAP, it won every parliamentary seat in the 1970s and thereafter retained all but a few seats, despite its share of the vote falling to 61–63 per cent.

In fact the development of the PAP regime shows some resemblances with that of African one-party states (see Chapter 4). Like them, the PAP exploited the unique organisational and electoral opportunity presented by decolonising elections. As Singapore's first mass party the PAP was the first party to establish a link with the bulk of ethnic-majority Chinese voters, and therefore once the challenge from the breakaway BS had been defeated the party had an impregnable electoral advantage over 'fledgling' competing parties (Chan, 1976: 229, 218). Another similarity with the African pattern was the use of cooption and coercion to consolidate the party's monopoly, but the PAP's commitment to a formally multiparty system meant that the cooption/coercion was aimed at parties' potential leaders and activists rather than the parties themselves. Influential or potential local leaders were appointed to the Citizens Consultative Committees – where they were at least 'quarantined' from the opposition parties – while fears of retribution deterred career-conscious individuals from becoming election candidates, or even visible supporters, of opposition parties (Chan, 1976: 144, 219; Milne and Mauzy, 1990: 93).

A further similarity with the African one-party states was the manner in which the 'founding' head of government elected during the decolonising transition went on to establish a powerful personal position within the post-independence regime. Although he shared power with a small team of other senior ministers/party-leaders, Singapore's founding Prime Minister (and founding PAP Secretary-General) Lee Kuan Yew dominated party and state until his retirement in 1990, and thereafter retained a 'crucial' personal role as privileged Senior Minister and wielder of 'considerable influence through less formal means' (Milne and Mauzy, 1990: 103–4; Tillman, 1989: 54–7; Cotton, 1993: 9, 14, 11).

However, Singapore also shows some similarities with neighbouring Malaysia in its form of authoritarian controls and in its resort to gerrymandering parliamentary constituencies. Singapore's own Internal Security Act has allowed preventive detention for prejudicing the country's security and public order, there have been government-favouring restrictions on party activities such as the ban on election campaigning outside the official campaign period, and there has been firm control over the mass media, to the extent of moving against such international publications as *Time* magazine when they offended the government (Tremewan, 1994: 201, 169; Chan, 1976: 205–6; Rodan, 1993a: 91).

Gerrymandering has taken two different forms. The older, ethnic form saw the government use the re-delineation of constituency boundaries, rehousing programmes and other measures to break up (and prevent the reforming) of Malay-majority constituencies, in which PAP dominance had been threatened by communal voting for Malay parties (Chan, 1976: 210; Tremewan, 1994: 65). The newer form arose from the 1988 creation of some large three-member winner-take-all parliamentary constituencies that could absorb and shore up endangered PAP single-member seats by combining them with neighbouring safer seats (Tremewan, 1994: 167).

Nevertheless, there are difficulties in classifying Singapore as a semi-dictatorship rather than a semidemocracy. The PAP can point to an impressive record of economic performance and administrative competence to support its claim that the party's electoral triumphs have been based on voters' recognition of, and gratitude for, its unparalleled record of 'good government'. More importantly, the opposition parties lack of any real chance since the 1960s to compete for power appears to be due more to such historical factors as the PAP's decolonising organisational/electoral advantage and Lee's founding-father prestige than to undemocratic measures aimed at guaranteeing victory for the official party. The PAP itself has long been concerned that what it terms a 'freak' election result will remove it from power, and in 1991 the party moved to protect itself against some of the effects of a possible future election defeat by transforming the formerly ceremonial presidency into an elected and more powerful office whose holder can be reliably expected to be a PAP sympathiser and protector thanks to the stringent legal restrictions on who can be a presidential candidate (Tremewan, 1994: 173–5; Rodan, 1993a: 100).

Finally, it is worth noting that although Singapore, Malaysia and even Indonesia were sometimes depicted in the early 1990s as examples of a distinctive 'Asian' form of democracy (Jones, 1995: 42), these three regimes differ quite markedly from one another in terms of the semi-dictatorship/semidemocracy issue. The Indonesian regime was a military semi-dictatorship close to the borderline with mono-dictatorship; the Malaysian regime was a party semi-dictatorship or an ethnic semidemocracy; and the Singaporean regime was probably more of a semidemocracy than a party semi-dictatorship.

It is true that in addition to presiding over what are at least semi-competitive elections, the three regimes have shown a common tendency towards long-lasting personalist rule and ideological legitimation. In addition to experiencing the personalism of respectively Suharto, Mahathir and Lee, the three regimes have shown a concern for ideological legitimation, as expressed:

1. in the Indonesian Pancasila (Five Principles) ideology;
2. in Malaysia's Pancasila-like Rukunegara ideology and the Malay-nationalist NEP doctrines that were reinforced by ideologue Mahathir when he eventually became UMNO leader; and
3. in Singapore's ideology of 'survivalism' (emphasising the threats posed by communism, inter-ethnic friction and lack of economic resources) and its later attempt to develop a Pancasila-like national ideology based on Asian rather than Western values (Means, 1991: 12–13, 23–5, 83–4; Munro-Kua, 1996: 113–16; Jones, 1995: 72–3; Brown, 1995: 147; Rodan, 1993a: 90).

But these personalist and ideological as well as electoral similarities should not obscure the important differences between these sophisticated examples of semi-dictatorship and semidemocracy.

Protodemocracy in Russia and Central Asia

As was noted earlier, the standard conception of semidemocracy can incorporate several different categories of regime, transitional as well as consolidated. These transitional forms, too, are sometimes difficult to distinguish from semi-dictatorship, and often this distinction is of great practical importance. Serious consequences may arise from mistaking a shift from auto- to semi-dictatorship as being a shift to the limited democratisation that occurs during the initial stages of some transitions from dictatorship. There may also be serious consequences if an emerging semi-dictatorship is mistaken for a transitional protodemocracy. A protodemocracy has gone beyond the stage of removing the former dictatorship but has a successor regime or situation that is not fully democratic and may relapse into dictatorship (or even be consolidated as a semidemocracy) rather than evolve into a democracy. Although the term proto*democratic* implies that democracy is the most likely outcome of this transitional situation, a semi-dictatorship may emerge and consolidate itself while using the notion of protodemocracy to excuse its 'excesses' and 'failings'.

For example, it seemed for a time in 1993 that President Yeltsin might establish a personalist semi-dictatorship in Russia under the guise of dealing with protodemocratic 'growing pains'. During that year the struggle for power between parliament and President had developed into a constitutional crisis. In March parliament sought to strip Yeltsin of the powers that it had temporarily delegated to him in 1991, but his resistance and democratic credibility were buoyed by an April referendum in which a clear majority of voters expressed confidence in him and his policies.

The 1993 crisis came to a head in September–October when Yeltsin suspended the Constitution, dissolved parliament, and decreed that parliamentary elections would be held in December. On 3–4 October a strongly anti-Yeltsin group of parliamentarians and their supporters resorted to direct action and Yeltsin was forced to rely on the military, whom he ordered to storm the parliament building. Although Yeltsin in a sense had more democratic or popular legitimacy than his parliamentary opponents, his suspension of the Constitution and dissolution of parliament – let alone the military's storming of the parliament building – indicated a likely relapse into some form of dictatorship, probably a military-supported personalist semi-dictatorship.

Yet although some parties and movements were now suspended or banned from taking part in elections, Yeltsin did not establish a widely or permanently repressive regime. A December referendum approved a new, more presidential Constitution that provided him with a constitutional basis for his powerful presidency. But the new Constitution did not strip parliament (renamed the Federal Assembly) of all its powers. The lower house, the State Duma, remained the country's legislature and could refuse to endorse Yeltsin's choice of prime minister on three successive occasions (before being automatically dissolved for new elections).

Yeltsin's lack of control over Russian politics was evident in the unfavourable result of the December elections for the State Duma. The two parties explicitly supporting Yeltsin's appointed government won less than a quarter of the vote while the explicitly opposition parties won well over 40 per cent. Further-more, although the new parliament did not adopt an antagonistic or even consistently oppositional stance, neither did it become a tame organ of presidential rule. Yeltsin's lack of dictatorial control was evident again in the 1995 Duma elections. The explicitly opposition parties, particularly the communists, fared much better than the NDR 'government party' of Yeltsin's Prime Minister, Chernomyrdin. Then, in the 1996 presidential elections, Yeltsin failed to win an absolute majority and therefore had to enter a run-off election (which he won comfortably) with the communist leader, Zyuganov.

On the other hand, even after these well-contested presidential elections, it was still argued by an authority on Russian politics that democracy had not yet been consolidated and that Yeltsin was still displaying 'his own type of authoritarianism' in an 'authoritarian democracy', whose degeneration 'into some uglier form of dictatorship could not be excluded' (Sakwa, 1996: 171). This notion of authoritarian democracy referred to a protodemocratic situation of 'incomplete democratisation', in which the 'response to governmental inadequacy and the weakness of the social base of democracy' was one of intensified or renewed authoritarianism, 'not acting directly against democracy but as its accompaniment' (*ibid.*: 46). The authoritarian democrats' rationalisation for the lack of democracy was apparently that the shift from communism to democracy required an intervening authoritarian stage in which a strong state established the liberal economy and society appropriate for a full democracy, and meanwhile protected the emerging democracy from less democratic forms of authoritarianism (*ibid.*: 47). But this begs the question of *how long* the protodemocratic stage can be expected to last – at what point must it be deemed to have instead evolved into stable semidemocracy?

The authoritarian-democratic approach was apparently also to be found in other parts of the former Soviet Union, such as the newly independent states of Central Asia (*ibid.*: 47). As in Russia, in these five states the presidency was the focus of political events and usually continued to be held by the 1991 incumbent. In fact three of the five new states show enough similarities for a Central Asian 'model' of presidential rule to be discernable (Hiro, 1995; Atkin, 1997; Gleason, 1997; Huskey,

1997; Olcott, 1997; Nissman, 1997). The Central Asian model was for the incumbent President

1. to have once been the territory's Communist Party boss;
2. to have established a more repressive personalist rule than Yeltsin's;
3. to have installed the former Communist Party (in a new, nationalist and supposedly democratic guise) as effectively the official party; and
4. to have had his tenure in the presidency extended to the year 2000 or beyond by an overwhelmingly supportive referendum held in the mid-1990s.

Turkmenistan and Uzbekistan are the prime examples and Kazakhstan differed from the model only in having a president who had cut his ties with the former Communist Party. The two other Central Asian states had quite different protodemocratic experiences. Tajikistan suffered a bloody civil war that led to the victors overseeing a dubious presidential election in 1994. Kyrgyzstan (renamed the Kyrgyz Republic) differed from the other four states in having a relatively liberal president, who had not been a Communist Party boss, did not favour the former Communist Party, and did not prolong his tenure by referendum (but had entered into a potentially dangerous alliance with regional administrators and political bosses).

Only the last of these five Central Asian cases seemed to be likely to evolve into even consolidated semidemocracy, let alone actual democracy. In the other Central Asian cases there was a danger that the notion of protodemocracy would conceal the emergence and consolidation of new semi-dictatorships. The problem here was how *soon* could the period of protodemocracy be said to be over, and for it to be acknowledged that these transitions had ended in a relapse into dictatorship.

10

The Failure and Extinction of Dictatorship?

Failure

By the time of their mass demise in the 1980s and early 1990s the dictatorships had in most cases failed to meet their own standards of performance and to outperform the democracies (see Chapter 7). Over the decades military regimes had failed to lay the foundations of stable democracy and had been no more than average managers of modernisation and the economy. As for the party dictatorships, in the communist cases they had eventually failed to bring about rapid economic progress towards communism, and in the African cases they had consistently failed to promote economic development.

Nevertheless, a 'devil's advocate' argument on behalf of the dictatorships could be made by concentrating on the issue of political development and, somewhat paradoxically, the development of democratic institutions and procedures. Such an argument was quite commonly heard in the 1960s and seemed to be at least implicitly supported by some Western theorists of political development, as when emphasising the need to develop authoritative, effective state machinery, apparently even at the cost of abandoning support for (ineffective and unstable) democracy and taking a more positive view of dictatorship (Huntington, 1968: 7–8). It was suggested that the frequency of military intervention in Third World politics indicated that military rule might be 'an inseparable part of political modernisation' (*ibid*.: 192).

Some political-development justifications for dictatorship also emphasised how long it had taken the feudal and monarchical governments of Western Europe to establish the strong 'nation-state' foundation for modern democracy. A further twist in the argument was to point to how the problem of establishing nation-states was aggravated, particularly in Africa, by the host of different ethnic-tribal communities incorporated together in the new territorial 'nation' states formed through colonisation and decolonisation. Indeed it was argued in the 1960s that the African one-party states would perform a vital nation-building role by implanting a national solidarity that would override ethnic-tribal divisions and rivalries (see Chapter 5). The importance of nation-building in the development of democracy was confirmed by Rustow's model of transitions to democracy, which included the existence of national unity (without secessionist aspirations) as the sole background condition for democracy (1970: 350–1).

The political-development arguments lost all credibility when it became increasingly obvious in the 1970s–80s that most Third World dictatorships, especially the African examples, had been ineffective state-builders (see Chapter 7) and ineffective nation-builders (Young, 1982b). Therefore, if the political-development justification or apology for dictatorship is revived, it will probably take the 'heads I win, tails you lose' form of arguing that by their transition to democracy these ineffective dictatorships in the 1980s–90s had a nation-building effect that outweighed their previous failings. For in Africa 'democratisation has provided the means through which some form of national political community has been re-established' (Clapham and Wiseman, 1995: 223–4). In fact the terms 'second independence' and 'second liberation' have been widely used to highlight the similarity between Africans' successful struggle for democracy and their nationally unifying struggle for independence and liberation from colonial rule in the 1940s–50s (Wiseman, 1996: 83 n. 95). Moreover, the many Latin Americans, Asians and Europeans who experienced a 'popular upsurge' during their country's transition to democracy in the 1970s–80s (see Chapter 8) will have likely experienced a comparable strengthening of their national political community. The final twist to the argument would be to emphasise how the democratic hypocrisy of modern dictatorships, their public commitment to democratic ideals and practices, has helped to keep alive the notion that democracy is the most legitimate form of government.

The simplest reply to such a specious argument is to accept its premises and point out that as the dictatorships therefore have now completed their 'historical mission', they have outlived whatever usefulness is claimed for them. The remaining examples can with clear conscience shuffle off the political stage and not delay the inevitable extinction of a type of rule that has proved to be in most cases a mediocre or poor performer of the duties of government.

Extinction?

The question of whether these dictatorships are indeed inevitably headed for the scrapheap of history is not as clear-cut as it once seemed to be. In the mid-1990s the conventional wisdom was that the remaining dictatorships were living on borrowed time, but after the widespread democratisation in Africa in the early 1990s the global 'third wave' of democratisation lost its momentum and by the end of the decade seemed to have left the Middle East and parts of Asia 'high and dry'. As Huntington noted, though, when expressing his pessimism in 1990 about the prospects of the third wave soon reaching Africa, it is difficult to rule out any possibility (1991: 312). Moreover, it is difficult to see any factors that would (continue to) preserve the world's remaining dictatorships. A mid-1990s study of eight dictatorships that had survived democratisation could find no common factor apart from their having taken a defiant stand against their countries' military or political foes (Brooker, 1997).

But a more important question than the survival of the remaining dictatorships is whether there is likely to be a global revival of dictatorship. For in the past whenever it has seemed that democracy has triumphed on a global scale, dictatorship has found a way of spoiling the party. Within a few years of the First World War being fought and won to 'keep the world safe for democracy', the communist and fascist forms of dictatorship had emerged in Russia and Italy. Similarly, within a few years of the Second World War's destruction of the fascist threat, communism had expanded into Eastern Europe and

East Asia and was presenting democracy with what was seen at the time as being a major political, ideological and military threat. Moreover, Huntington has pointed out that the first two waves of global democratisation were each followed by a 'reverse wave', in 1922–42 and 1958–75, during which the globally predominant form of regime change was from democracy to authoritarianism (1991: 16–21, 290). The notion of a cyclical pattern of democratisation and authoritarianism is confirmed on a regional basis by Latin America's long experience with military interventions and rule. For example, in the democratising 1955–61 era no fewer than 11 of the region's 12 military regimes came to an end, but this was soon followed in the mid-1960s to mid-1970s by another wave of military rule, which in turn succumbed in the 1980s to the third wave of democratisation (Rouquié, 1986: 109).

Huntington has identified some potential causes of a future third, 'reverse wave' of authoritarianism and has also identified the forms of authoritarianism that might reappear (1991: 292–4). Among the causes were a decline in democracy's performance legitimacy, an international economic crisis similar to the Great Depression, and a 'snowballing' demonstration effect of some new democracies' reverting to dictatorship. Among the various forms of non-democratic regime that might reemerge are:

1. authoritarian nationalism;
2. religious dictatorship;
3. communal dictatorship (based on ethnic or religious divisions); and
4. populist dictatorships.

He also suggested that a new, technocratic electronic form of dictatorship might emerge.

Any revival of dictatorship will probably be hidden behind a democratic disguise, employing the semi-competitive elections of the semi-dictatorship (see Chapter 9). Behind this democratic disguise may hide any of the prospective forms of dictatorship identified by Huntington. The democratic disguise has already been used by the new nationalist regimes in Central Asia, by the religious dictatorship in Iran, by the communal (ethnic) regime in Malaysia, and by the long-standing populist dictatorship in Mexico. Nor is it difficult to imagine how a future technocratic electronic dictatorship could develop the West's present elections into an effective democratic disguise.

Therefore the most prescient or prophetic theorist of dictatorship seems to have been Arendt. Her theory of totalitarianism may be too extreme or narrow (see Chapter 1), but her later reference to the 'banality of evil', as embodied in the bureaucrats who organised totalitarianism and its crimes, now seems to sum up a historical tendency which will see any new non-democratic regimes opt for banal (democratically disguised) semi-dictatorship. There will be no new counterparts of fascism or communism, nor many blatant examples of military regime. If a democracy comes to an end, it will likely end not in a bang but in a whimper.

Further Reading

Chapter 1

On totalitarianism see the classic theories of Arendt (1962) and Friedrich and Brzezinski (1961); on second-generation theories see Schapiro (1972) and Friedrich (1969). For a 1980s reconsideration see Menze (1981), and for a 1990s application of Friedrich and Brzezinski's theory to North Korea see Kim (1995). On authoritarianism see Linz (1970), O'Donnell (1979) and Perlmutter (1981). For a comparative description of both totalitarianism and authoritarianism see Linz (1975).

Chapter 2

On party dictatorships see Tucker (1961) and Huntington (1970); on military dictatorships see Huntington (1968), Finer (1976) and Nordlinger (1977); on personalist types see Weber (1964), Roth (1968), Linz (1975), Theobald (1982) and Jackson and Rosberg (1982a).

Chapter 3

On the calculus of intervention see Finer (1976 or 1988) and Nordlinger (1977); on capacity see Janowitz (1964); on coup techniques and tactics see Luttwak (1968) and Farcau (1994).

Chapter 4

On the revolution method in general see Calvert (1990) and Skocpol (1979); on the communist revolution in Russia, including the civil war, see Pipes (1991 and 1994); on the civil war aspect of the communist revolution in China see Dreyer (1995); and on the Italian

Fascists' 'revolutionary' coup and subsequent misappropriation of power
see Lyttelton (1973). On the electoral method in Africa see Coleman
and Rosberg (1964) and Zolberg (1966); and on its use in Nazi Germany see Childers (1983) and Bracher (1973).

Chapter 5

On communist claims to legitimacy see Holmes (1986), and on some
other dictatorships' ideological claims to legitimacy see Brooker (1995),
which also covers their means of control. On the communist means
of party control developed in the Soviet Union see Schapiro (1970).
On West African one-party states' ideology and means of control see
Zolberg (1966). On mass organisations see Kasza (1995).

Chapter 6

For examples of African and a wide range of other personalist rulers
see Jackson and Rosberg (1982a) and Brooker (1995 and 1997). On
Stalin see Tucker (1990) and Volkogonov (1991); on Hitler see Broszat
(1981) and Peterson (1969); and on Saddam Hussein see Karsh and
Rautsi (1991).

Chapter 7

On communist policies see Kornai (1992) and White and Nelson (1986);
on African one-party states' policies see Young (1982a); and on Nazi
policies see Schoenbaum (1967). On successful economic performance by authoritarian regimes see Haggard (1990).

Chapter 8

On theories of transition to democracy see O'Donnell and Schmitter
(1986), Huntington (1991), Przeworski (1991) and Haggard and
Kaufman (1995). On Latin America see O'Donnell *et al.* (1986); on
Eastern Europe see Stokes (1993); on the Soviet Union see Brown
(1996) and Gill (1994); on Africa see Wiseman (1996).

Chapter 9

The key works are Diamond, Linz and Lipset (1989) and, for a different perspective, Case (1996). For a brief description of semi-competitive elections in Perón's Argentina and Suharto's Indonesia, see Brooker (1995). On the Brazilian case of disguised dictatorship see Lamounier (1989), and on the Malaysian ambiguous case see Crouch (1986). For several analyses of Mexico's 1980s non-transition to democracy see Harvey (ed.) (1993).

References

Aguirre, B. E. (1989) 'The Conventionalization of Collective Behavior in Cuba', in I. L. Horowitz (ed.), *Cuban Communism*, 7th edn (New Brunswick, N.J.: Transaction).

Alagappa, M. (1995) *Political Legitimacy in Southeast Asia* (Stanford: Stanford University Press), chs 1–3.

al-Khalil, S. (1989) *Republic of Fear: Saddam's Iraq* (London: Hutchinson Radius).

Allen, W. S. (1984) *The Nazi Seizure of Power*, rev. edn (New York: F. Watts).

Andrain, C. F. (1964) 'Guinea and Senegal: Contrasting Types of African Socialism', in W. H. Friedland and C. G. Rosberg (eds), *African Socialism* (Stanford: Stanford University Press).

Apter, D. E. (1965) *The Politics of Modernization* (Chicago: University of Chicago Press).

Arendt, H. (1962) *The Origins of Totalitarianism* (first published 1951) (Cleveland and New York: Meridian).

Ash, T. G. (1997) *The File: A Personal History* (London: HarperCollins).

Atkin, M. (1997) 'Tajikistan: Reform, Reaction, and Civil War', in I. Bremmer and R. Taras (eds), *New States, New Politics: Building the Post-Soviet Nations* (Cambridge: Cambridge University Press).

Azarya, V. and Chazan, N. (1987) 'Disengagement from the State in Africa: Reflections on the Experience of Ghana and Guinea', *Comparative Studies in Society and History*, 29, 1.

Baker, R. W. (1978) *Egypt's Uncertain Revolution under Nasser and Sadat* (Cambridge, Mass.: Harvard University Press).

Barber, B. R. (1969) 'Conceptual Foundations of Totalitarianism', in C. J. Friedrich, M. Curtis and B. R. Barber, *Totalitarianism in Perspective: Three Views* (London: Pall Mall Press).

Baregu, M. (1994) 'The Rise and Fall of the One-Party State in Tanzania', in J. A. Widner (ed.), *Economic Change and Political Liberalization in Sub-Saharan Africa* (Baltimore: Johns Hopkins University Press).

Barkan, J. D. and Okumu, J. J. (1978) '"Semi-Competitive" Elections, Clientelism, and Political Recruitment in a No-Party State: The Kenyan Experience', in G. Hermet, R. Rose and A. Rouquié (eds), *Elections Without Choice* (Basingstoke: Macmillan).

Bell, J. D. (1993) 'Bulgaria', in S. White, J. Batt and P. G. Lewis (eds), *Developments in East European Politics* (Basingstoke: Macmillan).

Berglund, S. and Dellenbrant, J. A. (1991) 'The Breakdown of

Authoritarianism in Eastern Europe', in S. Berglund and J. A. Dellenbrant (eds), *The New Democracies in Eastern Europe* (Aldershot: Edward Elgar).

Bienen, H. (1970a) *Tanzania: Party Transformation and Economic Development* (Princeton: Princeton University Press).

Bienen, H. (1970b) 'One-Party Systems in Africa', in S. P. Huntington and C. H. Moore (eds), *Authoritarian Politics in Modern Society: The Dynamics of Established One-Party Systems* (New York: Basic Books).

Bova, R. (1991) 'Political Dynamics of the Post-Communist Transition: A Comparative Perspective', *World Politics*, 44, 1.

Bowie, L. (1976) 'Charisma, Weber and Nasir', *Middle East Journal*, 30, 2.

Bracher, K. D. (1973) *The German Dictatorship: The Origins, Structure and Consequences of National Socialism* (Harmondsworth: Penguin).

Bratton, M. and Van de Walle, N. (1992) 'Popular Protest and Political Reform in Africa', *Comparative Politics*, 24, 4.

Bratton, M. and Van de Walle, N. (1994) 'Neopatrimonial Regimes and Political Transitions in Africa', *World Politics*, 46, 4.

Brooker, P. (1991) *The Faces of Fraternalism: Nazi Germany, Fascist Italy, and Imperial Japan* (Oxford: Oxford University Press).

Brooker, P. (1995) *Twentieth-Century Dictatorships: The Ideological One-Party States* (Basingstoke: Macmillan).

Brooker, P. (1997) *Defiant Dictatorships: Communist and Middle-Eastern Dictatorships in a Democratic Age* (Basingstoke: Macmillan).

Broszat, M. (1981) *The Hitler State* (London: Longman).

Brown, A. (1996) *The Gorbachev Factor* (Oxford: Oxford University Press).

Brown, D. (1995) 'Democratization and the Renegotiation of Ethnicity', in D. A. Bell, D. Brown, K. Jayasuriya and D. M. Jones (eds), *Towards Illiberal Democracy in Pacific Asia* (Basingstoke: Macmillan).

Bruhn, K. (1996) 'Social Spending and Political Support: The "Lessons" of the National Solidarity Program in Mexico', *Comparative Politics*, 28, 2.

Bunce, V. (1995) 'Comparing East and South', *Journal of Democracy*, 6, 3.

Calvert, P. (1990) *Revolution and Counter-Revolution* (Milton Keynes: Open University Press).

Carter, G. M. (1962) 'Introduction', in G. M. Carter (ed.), *African One-Party States* (Ithaca: Cornell University Press).

Case, W. F. (1996) 'Can the "Halfway House" Stand? Semidemocracy and Elite Theory in Three Southeast Asian Countries', *Comparative Politics*, 28, 4.

Chan, H. C. (1976) *The Dynamics of One Party Dominance: The PAP at the Grass Roots* (Singapore: Singapore University Press).

Cheng, T-j. (1989) 'Democratizing the Quasi-Leninist Regime in Taiwan', *World Politics*, 41, 4.

Childers, T. (1983) *The Nazi Voter: The Social Foundations of Fascism in Germany, 1919–1933* (Chapel Hill: University of North Carolina Press).

Clapham, C. and Philip, G. (1985) 'The Political Dilemmas of Military Regimes', in C. Clapham and G. Philip (eds), *The Political*

Dilemmas of Military Regimes (Beckenham: Croom Helm).

Clapham, C. and Wiseman, J. A. (1995) 'Conclusion', in J. A. Wiseman (ed.), *Democracy and Political Change in Sub-Saharan Africa* (London and New York: Routledge).

Coleman, J. S. and Rosberg, C. G. (1964) 'Conclusions', in J. S. Coleman and C. G. Rosberg (eds), *Political Parties and National Integration in Tropical Africa* (Berkeley: University of California Press).

Collier, D. (ed.) (1979) *The New Authoritarianism in Latin America* (Princeton: Princeton University Press).

Cornelius, W. A. (1987) 'Political Liberalization in an Authoritarian Regime: Mexico, 1976–1985', in J. Gentleman (ed.), *Mexican Politics in Transition* (Boulder: Westview).

Cotler, J. (1986) 'Military Interventions and "Transfer of Power to Civilians" in Peru', in G. O'Donnell, P. C. Schmitter and L. Whitehead (eds), *Transitions from Authoritarian Rule: Latin America* (Baltimore and London: Johns Hopkins University Press).

Cotton, J. (1993) 'Political Innovation in Singapore: The Presidency, the Leadership and the Party', in G. Rodan (ed.), *Singapore Changes Guard* (Melbourne: Longman Cheshire).

Coulon, C. (1988) 'Senegal: The Development and Fragility of Semidemocracy', in L. Diamond, J. J. Linz and S. M. Lipset (eds), *Democracy in Developing Countries: Africa* (Boulder: Lynne Rienner).

Crook, R. C. (1995) 'Côte d'Ivoire – Multi-Party Democracy and Political Change: Surviving the Crisis', in J. A. Wiseman (ed.), *Democracy and Political Change in Sub-Saharan Africa* (London and New York: Routledge).

Crouch, H. (1978) *The Army and Politics in Indonesia* (Ithaca: Cornell University Press).

Crouch, H. (1979) 'Patrimonialism and Military Rule in Indonesia', *World Politics*, 31, 4.

Crouch, H. (1996) *Government and Society in Malaysia* (Ithaca: Cornell University Press).

Curtis, M. (1969) 'Retreat from Totalitarianism', in C. J. Friedrich, M. Curtis and B. R. Barber, *Totalitarianism in Perspective: Three Views* (London: Pall Mall Press).

Decalo, S. (1989) 'Modalities of Civil-Military Stability in Africa', *Journal of Modern African Studies*, 27, 4.

Decalo, S. (1990). *Coups and Army Rule in Africa*, 2nd edn (New Haven: Yale University Press).

Dekmejian, R. H. (1971) *Egypt under Nasir: A Study in Political Dynamics* (Albany: State University of New York Press).

Dekmejian, R. H. (1976) 'Marx, Weber and the Egyptian Revolution', *Middle East Journal*, 30, 2.

Diamond, L., Linz, J. J. and Lipset, S. M. (1989) 'Preface', in L. Diamond, J. J. Linz and S. M. Lipset (eds), *Democracy in Developing Countries* (Boulder: Lynne Rienner).

Doornbos, M. (1990) 'The African State in Academic Debate: Retrospect and Prospect', *Journal of Modern African Studies*, 28, 2.

Dresser, D. (1994) 'Embellishment, Empowerment, or Euthanasia of the PRI? Neoliberalism and Party Reform in Mexico', in M. L. Cook, K. J. Middlebrook and J. M. Horcasitas (eds), *The Politics of Economic Restructuring: State-Society Relations and Regime Change in Mexico* (San Diego: University of California).

Dreyer, E. L. (1995) *China at War, 1901–1949* (London and New York: Longman).

Dunkerley, J. (1985) 'Central America: Collapse of the Military System', in C. Clapham and G. Philip (eds), *The Political Dilemmas of Military Regimes* (Beckenham: Croom Helm).

Easter, G. M. (1997) 'Preference for Presidentialism: Postcommunist Regime Change in Russia and the NIS', *World Politics*, 49, 2.

Eastman, L. E. (1984) *Seeds of Destruction: Nationalist China in War and Revolution 1937–1949* (Stanford: Stanford University Press).

Eisenstadt, S. N. (1973) *Traditional Patrimonialism and Modern Neopatrimonialism* (Beverly Hills: Sage).

Epstein, E. C. (1984) 'Legitimacy, Institutionalization, and Opposition in Exclusionary Bureaucratic-Authoritarian Regimes', *Comparative Politics*, 17, 1.

Fainsod, M. (1958) *Smolensk Under Soviet Rule* (Cambridge, Mass: Harvard University Press).

Fall, B. B. (1967) *The Two Viet-Nams: A Political and Military Analysis* (New York: Praeger).

Farcau, B. W. (1994) *The Coup: Tactics in the Seizure of Power* (Westport, Conn.: Praeger).

Ferguson, J. (1988) *Papa Doc, Baby Doc: Haiti and the Duvaliers*, rev. edn (Oxford: Blackwell).

Finer, S. E. (1974) *Comparative Government* (Harmondsworth: Penguin).

Finer, S. E. (1976) *The Man on Horseback: The Role of the Military in Politics*, 2nd edn (first published 1962) (Harmondsworth: Penguin).

Finer, S. E. (1988) *The Man on Horseback: The Role of the Military in Politics*, 2nd rev. edn (Boulder: Westview).

First, R. (1970) *The Barrel of a Gun: Political Power in Africa and the Coup d'État* (London: Allen Lane).

Forrest, J. B. (1988) 'The Quest for State "Hardness" in Africa', *Comparative Politics*, 20, 4.

Fox, J. (1994) 'Political Change in Mexico's New Peasant Economy', in M. L. Cook, K. J. Middlebrook and J. M. Horcasitas (eds), *The Politics of Economic Restructuring: State-Society Relations and Regime Change in Mexico* (San Diego: University of California).

Friedrich, C. J. (1969) 'The Evolving Theory and Practice of Totalitarian Regimes', in C. J. Friedrich, M. Curtis and B. R. Barber (eds), *Totalitarianism in Perspective: Three Views* (London: Pall Mall Press).

Friedrich, C. J. and Brzezinski, Z. K. (1961) *Totalitarian Dictatorship and Autocracy* (first published 1956) (New York: Praeger).

Garretón, M. A. (1986) 'The Political Evolution of the Chilean Military Regime and Problems in the Transition to Democracy', in G. O'Donnell, P. C. Schmitter and L. Whitehead (eds), *Transitions from Authoritarian Rule: Latin America* (Baltimore: Johns Hopkins University Press).

Getty, J. A. (1985) *Origins of the Great Purges: The Soviet Communist Party Reconsidered, 1933–1938* (Cambridge: Cambridge University Press).

Gilbert, D. (1988) *Sandinistas: The Party and the Revolution* (Oxford: Blackwell).

Gill, G. (1994) *The Collapse of a Single-Party System: The Disintegration of the Communist Party of the Soviet Union* (Cambridge: Cambridge University Press).

Gleason, G. (1997) 'Uzbekistan: the politics of national independence', in I. Bremmer and R. Taras (eds), *New States, New Politics: Building the Post-Soviet Nations* (Cambridge: Cambridge University Press).

Grundy, K. W. (1964) 'Mali: The Prospects of "Planned Socialism"', in W. G. Friedland and C. G. Rosberg (eds), *African Socialism* (Stanford: Stanford University Press).

Haggard, S. (1990) *Pathways from the Periphery: The Politics of Growth in the Newly Industrializing Countries* (Ithaca: Cornell University Press).

Haggard, S. and Kaufman, R. R. (1995) *The Political Economy of Democratic Transitions* (Princeton: Princeton University Press).

Hammond, T. T. (1975a) 'A Summing Up', in T. T. Hammond (ed.), *The Anatomy of Communist Takeovers* (New Haven: Yale University Press).

Hammond, T. T. (1975b) 'The History of Communist Takeovers', in T. T. Hammond (ed.), *The Anatomy of Communist Takeovers* (New Haven: Yale University Press).

Hamrin, C. L. (1992) 'The Party Leadership System', in K. G. Lieberthal and D. M. Lampton (eds), *Bureaucracy, Politics, and Decision Making in Post-Mao China* (Berkeley: University of California Press).

Hartlyn, J. (1989) 'Colombia: The Politics of Violence and Accommodation', in L. Diamond, J. J. Linz and S. M. Lipset (eds), *Democracy in Developing Countries: Vol. 4, Latin America* (Boulder: Lynne Rienner).

Harvey, N. (1993) 'The Limits of Concertation in Rural Mexico', in N. Harvey (ed.), *Mexico: Dilemmas of Transition* (London: British Academic Press).

Haynes, J. (1995) 'Ghana – From Personalist to Democratic Rule', in J. A. Wiseman (ed.), *Democracy and Political Change in Sub-Saharan Africa* (London and New York: Routledge).

Helliwell, J. F. (1994) 'Empirical Linkages Between Democracy and Economic Growth', *British Journal of Political Science*, 24, 2.

Hiden, J. and Farquharson, J. (1989) *Explaining Hitler's Germany: Historians and the Third Reich*, 2nd edn (London: Batsford).

Hiro, D. (1995) *Between Marx and Muhammad: The Changing Face of Central Asia* (London: HarperCollins).

Holmes, L. (1986) *Politics in the Communist World* (Oxford: Oxford University Press).

Hough, J. F. (1977) *The Soviet Union and Social Science Theory* (Cambridge, Mass.: Harvard University Press).

Hough, J. F. and Fainsod, M. (1979) *How the Soviet Union Is Governed* (Cambridge, Mass.: Harvard University Press).

Huntington, S. P. (1967) *The Soldier and the State: The Theory and Politics of Civil-Military Relations* (first published 1957) (Cambridge, Mass.: Harvard University Press).

Huntington, S. P. (1968) *Political Order in Changing Societies* (New Haven: Yale University Press).

Huntington, S. P. (1970) 'Social and Institutional Dynamics of One-Party Systems', in S. P. Huntington and C. H. Moore (eds), *Authoritarian Politics in Modern Society: The Dynamics of Established One-Party Systems* (New York: Basic Books).

Huntington, S. P. (1991) *The Third Wave: Democratization in the Late Twentieth Century* (Norman: University of Oklahoma Press).

Huskey, E. (1997) 'Kyrgyzstan: the politics of demographic and economic frustration', in I. Bremmer and R. Taras (eds), *New States, New Politics: Building the Post-Soviet Nations* (Cambridge: Cambridge University Press).

Im, H. B. (1987) 'The Rise of Bureaucratic Authoritarianism in South Korea', *World Politics*, 39, 2.

Jackman, R. W. (1976) 'Politicians in Uniform: Military Governments and Social Change in The Third World', *American Political Science Review*, 70, 4.

Jackson, R. H. and Rosberg, C. G. (1982a) *Personal Rule in Black Africa: Prince, Autocrat, Prophet, Tyrant* (Berkeley: University of California Press).

Jackson, R. H. and Rosberg, C. G. (1982b) 'Why Africa's Weak States Persist: The Empirical and the Juridical in Statehood', *World Politics*, 35.

Jalal, A. (1995) *Democracy and Authoritarianism in South Asia* (Cambridge: Cambridge University Press).

Janos, A. C. (1970) 'The One-Party State and Social Mobilization: East Europe between the Wars', in S. P. Huntington and C. H. Moore (eds), *Authoritarian Politics in Modern Society: The Dynamics of Established One-Party Systems* (New York: Basic Books).

Janowitz, M. (1964) *The Military in the Political Development of New Nations: An Essay in Comparative Analysis* (Chicago: University of Chicago Press).

Johnson, J. J. (1964) *The Military and Society in Latin America* (Stanford: Stanford University Press).

Jones, D. M. (1995) 'Democracy and Identity: The Paradoxical Character of Political Development', in D. A. Bell, D. Brown, K. Jayasuriya and D. M. Jones (eds), *Towards Illiberal Democracy in Pacific Asia* (Basingstoke: Macmillan).

Jones, T. (1976) *Ghana's First Republic, 1960–1966: The Pursuit of the Political Kingdom* (London: Methuen).

Joseph, R. A. (1987) *Democracy and Prebendal Politics in Nigeria* (Cambridge: Cambridge University Press).

Karl, T. L. and Schmitter, P. C. (1991) 'Modes of Transition in Latin America, Southern and Eastern Europe', *International Social Science Journal*, 128. Reprinted in G. Pridham (ed.), *Transitions to Democracy* (Aldershot: Dartmouth, 1995).

Karsh, E. and Rautsi, I. (1991) *Saddam Hussein: A Political Biography* (London: Brassey's).

Kasza, G. J. (1995) *The Conscription Society: Administered Mass Organizations* (New Haven: Yale University Press).

Kaufman, R. R. (1979) 'Industrial Change and Authoritarian Rule in Latin America: A Concrete Review of the Bureaucratic-Authoritarian Model', in D. Collier (ed.), *The New Authoritarianism in Latin America* (Princeton: Princeton University Press).

Kautsky, J. H. (1962) 'An Essay in the Politics of Development', in J. H. Kautsky (ed.), *Political Change in Underdeveloped Countries* (New York: Wiley).

Kebschull, H. G. (1994) 'Operation "Just Missed": Lessons from Failed Coup Attempts', *Armed Forces and Society*, 20, 4.

Kennedy, C. H. and Louscher, D. J. (1991) 'Civil-Military Interaction: Data in Search of a Theory', *Journal of Asian and African Studies*, 26, 1–2.

Kershaw, I. (1983) *Popular Opinion and Political Dissent in the Third Reich: Bavaria 1933–1945* (Oxford: Oxford University Press).

Kershaw, I. (1987) *The 'Hitler Myth': Image and Reality in the Third Reich* (Oxford: Oxford University Press).

Kim, H. (1995) 'On the Nature of the North Korean State', *Korea and World Affairs*, 19, 4.

Kirkpatrick, J. (1979) 'Dictatorships and Double Standards', *Commentary*, 68, 5.

Klesner, J. L. (1998) 'An Electoral Route to Democracy?: Mexico's Transition in Comparative Perspective', *Comparative Politics*, 30, 4.

Koehl, R. (1960) 'Feudal Aspects of National Socialism', *American Political Science Review*, 54, 4.

Kornai, J. (1992) *The Socialist System: The Political Economy of Communism* (Princeton: Princeton University Press).

Lamounier, B. (1989) '*Authoritarian Brazil* Revisited: The Impact of Elections on the Abertura', in A. Stepan (ed.), *Democratizing Brazil* (Oxford: Oxford University Press).

Leslie, W. J. (1993) *Zaire: Continuity and Political Change in an Oppressive State* (Boulder: Westview).

Liebenow, J. G. (1962) 'Liberia', in G. M. Carter (ed.), *African One-Party States* (Ithaca: Cornell University Press).

Linz, J. J. (1970) 'An Authoritarian Regime: Spain', in E. Allardt and S. Rokkan (eds), *Mass Politics* (first published 1964) (New York: Free Press).

Linz, J. J. (1975) 'Totalitarian and Authoritarian Regimes', in F. I. Greenstein and N. W. Polsby (eds), *Macropolitical Theory: Handbook of Political Science: Vol. 3* (Reading, Mass.: Addison-Wesley).

Linz, J. J. (1990) 'The Perils of Presidentialism', *Journal of Democracy*, 1.

Lipset, S. M. (1959) 'Some Social Requisites of Democracy: Economic Development and Political Legitimacy', *American Political Science Review*, 53, 1.

Luckham, R. (1971) *The Nigerian Military: A Sociological Analysis of Authority & Revolt 1960–67* (Cambridge: Cambridge University Press).

Luttwak, E. (1968) *Coup d'État: A Practical Handbook* (London: Allen Lane).

Lyttelton, A. (1973) *The Seizure of Power: Fascism in Italy, 1919–1929* (London: Weidenfeld and Nicolson).

Malloy, J. M. (1971) 'Revolutionary Politics', in J. M. Malloy and R. S. Thorn (eds), *Beyond the Revolution: Bolivia Since 1952* (Pittsburgh: University of Pittsburgh Press).

Markoff, J. and Duncan Baretta, S. R. (1985) 'Professional Ideology and Military Activism in Brazil: A Critique of a Thesis of Alfred Stepan', *Comparative Politics*, 17, 2.

Martin, D. (1978) 'The 1975 Tanzanian Elections: the Disturbing 6 per cent', in G. Hermet, R. Rose and A. Rouquié (eds), *Elections Without Choice* (Basingstoke: Macmillan).

Martins, L. (1986) 'The "Liberalization" of Authoritarian Rule in Brazil', in G. O'Donnell, P. C. Schmitter and L. Whitehead (eds), *Transitions from Authoritarian Rule: Latin America* (Baltimore: Johns Hopkins University Press).

Matthews, B. (1989) 'Sri Lanka in 1988: Seeds of the Accord', *Asian Survey*, 29, 2.

Matthews, B. (1990) 'Sri Lanka in 1989: Peril and Good Luck', *Asian Survey*, 30, 2.

McKinlay, R. D. and Cohan, A. S. (1975) 'A Comparative Analysis of the Political and Economic Performance of Military and Civilian Regimes: A Cross-National Aggregate Study', *Comparative Politics*, 8, 1.

McKinlay, R. D. and Cohan, A. S. (1976) 'Performance and Instability in Military and Nonmilitary Regime Systems', *American Political Science Review*, 70, 3.

McKown, R. E. and Kauffman, R. E. (1973) 'Party System as a Comparative Analytic Concept in African Politics', *Comparative Politics*, 6, 1.

Means, G. P. (1991) *Malaysian Politics: The Second Generation* (Singapore: Oxford University Press).

Medard, J-F. (1982) 'The Underdeveloped State in Tropical Africa: Political Clientelism or Neo-patrimonialism?', in C. Clapham (ed.), *Private Patronage and Public Power* (London: Pinter).

Menze, E. A. (1981) 'Totalitarianism: An Outmoded Paradigm?', in E. A. Menze (ed.), *Totalitarianism Reconsidered* (Port Washington, N.Y.: Kennicat).

Middlebrook, K. J. (1986) 'Political Liberalization in an Authoritarian Regime: The Case of Mexico', in G. O'Donnell, P. C. Schmitter and L. Whitehead (eds), *Transitions from Authoritarian Rule: Latin America* (Baltimore: Johns Hopkins University Press).

Migdal, J. S. (1988) *Strong Societies and Weak States: State-Society Relations and State Capabilities in the Third World* (Princeton: Princeton University Press).

Milne, R. S. and Mauzy, D. K. (1990) *Singapore: The Legacy of Lee Kuan Yew* (Boulder: Westview).

Munro-Kua, A. (1996) *Authoritarian Populism in Malaysia* (Basingstoke: Macmillan).

Nelson, J. M. (1990) 'Conclusions', in J. M. Nelson (ed.), *Economic Crisis and Policy Choice: The Politics of Adjustment in the Third World* (Princeton: Princeton University Press).

Nickson, R. A. (1988) 'Tyranny and Longevity: Stroessner's Paraguay', *Third World Quarterly*, 10, 1.

Nissman, D. (1997) 'Turkmenistan: Just like Old Times', in I. Bremmer and R. Taras (eds), *New States, New Politics: Building the Post-Soviet Nations* (Cambridge: Cambridge University Press).

Nordlinger, E. A. (1977) *Soldiers in Politics: Military Coups and Governments* (Englewood Cliffs: Prentice-Hall).

Nove, A. (1977) *The Soviet Economic System* (London: Allen and Unwin).

Nursey-Bray, P. (1983) 'Consensus and community: the theory of African one-party democracy', in G. Duncan (ed.), *Democratic Theory and Practice* (Cambridge: Cambridge University Press).

Obando, E. (1996) 'Fujimori and the Military: A Marriage of Convenience', *NACLA Report on the Americas*, 30, 1.

O'Donnell, G. (1979) *Modernization and Bureaucratic Authoritarianism: Studies in South American Politics* (first published 1973) (Berkeley: University of California Press).

O'Donnell, G. (1986) 'Introduction to the Latin American Cases', in G. O'Donnell, P. C. Schmitter and L Whitehead (eds), *Transitions from Authoritarian Rule: Latin America* (Baltimore: Johns Hopkins University Press).

O'Donnell, G. (1994) 'Delegative Democracy', *Journal of Democracy*, 5.

O'Donnell, G. and Schmitter, P. C. (1986) *Transitions from Authoritarian Rule: Tentative Conclusions about Uncertain Democracies* (Baltimore: Johns Hopkins University Press).

O'Donnell, G., Schmitter P. C. and Whitehead, L. (eds) (1986) *Transitions from Authoritarian Rule: Prospects for Democracy* (Baltimore: Johns Hopkins University Press).

O'Kane, R. H. T. (1981) 'A Probabilistic Approach to the Causes of Coups d'Etat', *British Journal of Political Science*, 11, 3.

Olcott, M. B. (1997) 'Kazakhstan: Pushing for Eurasia', in I. Bremmer and R. Taras (eds), *New States, New Politics: Building the Post-Soviet Nations* (Cambridge: Cambridge University Press).

Overy, R. (1995) *Why the Allies Won* (London: Jonathan Cape).

Pempel, T. J. (1990) 'Introduction', in T. J. Pempel (ed.), *Uncommon Democracies: The One-Party Dominant Regimes* (Ithaca: Cornell University Press).

Perlmutter, A. (1974) *Egypt, the Praetorian State* (New Brunswick: Transaction Books).

Perlmutter, A. (1977) *The Military and Politics in Modern Times: On Professionals, Praetorians, and Revolutionary Soldiers* (New Haven: Yale University Press).

Perlmutter, A. (1981) *Modern Authoritarianism: A Comparative Institutional Analysis* (New Haven: Yale University Press).

Perthes, V. (1995) *The Political Economy of Syria under Asad* (London: I. B. Tauris).

Peterson, E. N. (1969) *The Limits of Hitler's Power* (Princeton: Princeton University Press).

Phadnis, U. (1989) 'Sri Lanka: Crises of Legitimacy and Integration', in L. Diamond, J. J. Linz and S. M. Lipset (eds), *Democracy in Developing Countries: Vol. 3, Asia* (Boulder: Lynne Rienner).

Philip, G. (1985) 'Military Rule in South America: The Dilemmas of Authoritarianism', in C. Clapham and G. Philip (eds), *The Political Dilemmas of Military Regimes* (London and Sydney: Croom Helm).

Pion-Berlin, D. (1992) 'Military Autonomy and Emerging Democracies in South America', *Comparative Politics*, 25, 1.

Pipes, R. (1991) *The Russian Revolution* (New York: Knopf).

Pipes, R. (1994) *Russia under the Bolshevik Regime 1919–1924* (London: Harper Collins).

Porter, G. (1993) *Vietnam: The Politics of Bureaucratic Socialism* (Ithaca: Cornell University Press).

Pravda, A. (1978) 'Elections in Communist Party States', in G. Hermet, R. Rose and A. Rouquié (eds), *Elections Without Choice* (Basingstoke: Macmillan).

Przeworski, A. (1991) *Democracy and the Market: Political and Economic Reforms in Eastern Europe and Latin America* (Cambridge: Cambridge University Press).

Pye, L. W. (1962) 'Armies in the Process of Political Modernization', in J. J. Johnson (ed.), *The Role of the Military in Underdeveloped Countries* (Princeton: Princeton University Press).

Rabinovich, I. (1972) *Syria Under the Ba'th 1963–66: The Army-Party Symbiosis* (Jerusalem and New York: Israel University Press).

Remmer, K. L. (1989) 'Neopatrimonialism: The Politics of Military Rule in Chile, 1973–1987', *Comparative Politics*, 21, 2.

Remmer, K. L. (1991) 'New Wine or Old Bottlenecks? The Study of Latin American Democracy', *Comparative Politics*, 23, 4.

Rigby, T. H. (1972) '"Totalitarianism" and Change in Communist Systems', *Comparative Politics*, 4, 3.

Rivière, C. (1977) *Guinea: The Mobilization of a People* (Ithaca: Cornell University Press).

Rodan, G. (1993a) 'Preserving the One-Party State in Contemporary Singapore', in K. Hewison, R. Robison and G. Rodan (eds), *Southeast Asia in the 1990s* (North Sydney: Allen and Unwin).

Rodan, G. (1993b) 'Introduction: Challenges for the New Guard and Directions in the 1990s', in G. Rodan (ed.), *Singapore Changes Guard* (Melbourne: Longman Cheshire).

Rogers, M. L. (1988) 'Depoliticization of Indonesia's Political Parties: Attaining Military Stability', *Armed Forces and Society*, 14, 2.

Roth, G. (1968) 'Personal Rulership, Patrimonialism, and Empire-Building in the New States', *World Politics*, 20, 2.

Rouquié, A. (1986) 'Demilitarization and the Institutionalization of Military-dominated Polities in Latin America', in G. O'Donnell, P C. Schmitter and L. Whitehead (eds), *Transitions from Authoritarian Rule: Comparative Perspectives* (Baltimore: Johns Hopkins University Press).

Rouquié, A., trans. P. E. Sigmund (1987) *The Military and the State in Latin America* (Berkeley: University of California Press).

Rustow, D. A. (1970) 'Transitions to Democracy: Toward a Dynamic Model', *Comparative Politics*, 2, 3.

Sakwa, R. (1996) *Russian Politics and Society*, 2nd edn (London and New York: Routledge).

Salamé, G (ed.) (1994) *Democracy Without Democrats?: The Renewal of Politics in the Muslim World* (London and New York: I. B. Tauris).

Salisbury, H. E. (1993) *The New Emperors: Mao and Deng: A Dual Biography* (London: Harper Collins).

Sandbrook, R. (1985) *The Politics of Africa's Economic Stagnation* (Cambridge: Cambridge University Press).

Schamis, H. E. (1991) 'Reconceptualizing Latin American Authoritarianism in the 1970s: From Bureaucratic-Authoritarianism to Neoconservatism', *Comparative Politics*, 23, 2.

Schapiro, L. (1970) *The Communist Party of the Soviet Union* (London: Eyre and Spottiswoode).

Schapiro, L. (1972) *Totalitarianism* (London: Pall Mall).

Schmitter, P. C. (1974) 'Still the Century of Corporatism?', *The Review of Politics*, 36, 1.

Schneider, R. M. (1991) *'Order and Progress': A Political History of Brazil* (Boulder: Westview).

Schoenbaum, D. (1967) *Hitler's Social Revolution* (New York: Anchor Books).

Sera, J. (1979) 'Three Mistaken Theses Regarding the Connection Between Industrialization and Authoritarian Regimes', in D. Collier (ed.), *The New Authoritarianism in Latin America* (Princeton: Princeton University Press).

Shaw, W. H. (1986) 'Towards the One-Party State in Zimbabwe: A Study in African Political Thought', *The Journal of Modern African Studies*, 24, 3.

Shils, E. (1962) 'The Military in the Political Development of the New States', in J. J. Johnson (ed.), *The Role of the Military in Underdeveloped Countries* (Princeton: Princeton University Press).

Sigmund, P. E. (1977) *The Overthrow of Allende and the Politics of Chile, 1964–1976* (Pittsburgh: University of Pittsburgh Press).

Skocpol, T. (1979) *States and Social Revolutions: A Comparative Analysis of France, Russia and China* (Cambridge: Cambridge University Press).

Snyder, R. (1992) 'Explaining Transitions from Neopatrimonial Dictatorships', *Comparative Politics*, 24, 4.

Sondrol, P. C. (1991) 'Totalitarian and Authoritarian Dictators: A Comparison of Fidel Castro and Alfredo Stroessner', *Journal of Latin American Studies*, 23, 3.

Sondrol, P. C. (1992) 'The Paraguayan Military in Transition and the Evolution of Civil-Military Relations', *Armed Forces and Society*, 19, 1.

Starr, H. (1991) 'Democratic Dominoes: Diffusion Approaches to the Spread of Democracy in the International System', *Journal of Conflict Resolution*, 35, 2.

Stepan, A. (1973) 'The New Professionalism of Internal Warfare and Military Role Expansion', in A. Stepan (ed.), *Authoritarian Brazil* (New Haven: Yale University Press).

Stepan, A. (1978) *The State and Society: Peru in Comparative Perspective* (Princeton: Princeton University Press).

Stepan, A. (1988) *Rethinking Military Politics: Brazil and the Southern Cone* (Princeton: Princeton University Press).

Stephens, R. (1971) *Nasser: A Political Biography* (London: Allen Lane).

Stokes, G. (1993) *The Walls Came Tumbling Down: The Collapse of Communism in Eastern Europe* (Oxford: Oxford University Press).

Sundhaussen, U. (1985) 'The Durability of Military Regimes in South-East Asia', in Z. H. Ahmad and H. Crouch (eds), *Military-Civilian Relations in South-East Asia* (Singapore: Oxford University Press).

Suryadinata, L. (1989) *Military Ascendancy and Political Culture: A Study of Indonesia's Golkar* (Athens: Ohio University Press).

Swain, G. and Swain, N. (1993) *Eastern Europe Since 1945* (Basingstoke: Macmillan).

Tagle, S. G. (1993) 'Electoral Reform and the Party System, 1977–90', in N. Harvey (ed.), *Mexico: Dilemmas of Transition* (London: British Academic Press).

Talmon, J. L. (1952) *The Origins of Totalitarian Democracy* (London: Secker and Warburg).

Theobald, R. (1982) 'Patrimonialism', *World Politics*, 34, 4.

Thompson, W. R. (1980) 'Corporate Coup-Maker Grievances and Types of Regime Targets', *Comparative Political Studies*, 12, 4.

Tigrid, P. (1975) 'The Prague Coup of 1948: The Elegant Takeover', in T. T. Hammond (ed.), *The Anatomy of Communist Takeovers* (New Haven: Yale University Press).

Tillman, R. O. (1989) 'The Political Leadership', in K. S. Sandhu and P. Wheatley (eds), *Management of Success: The Moulding of Modern Singapore* (Singapore: Institute of Southeast Asian Studies).

Tordoff, W. (1993) *Government and Politics in Africa*, 2nd edn (Basingstoke: Macmillan).

Tremewan, C. (1994) *The Political Economy of Social Control in Singapore* (Basingstoke: Macmillan).

Trimberger, E. K. (1978) *Revolution from Above: Military Bureaucrats and Development in Japan, Turkey, Egypt and Peru* (New Brunswick: Transaction Books).

Tucker, R. C. (1961) 'Towards a Comparative Politics of Movement-Regimes', *American Political Science Review*, 55, 2.

Tucker, R. C. (1990) *Stalin in Power: The Revolution from Above 1928–1941* (New York and London: Norton).

Unger, A. L. (1974) *The Totalitarian Party: Party and People in Nazi Germany and Soviet Russia* (London: Cambridge University Press).

van Dam, N. (1979) *The Struggle for Power in Syria: Sectarianism, Regionalism and Tribalism in Politics, 1961–1978* (London: Croom Helm).

Van de Walle, N. (1994) 'Neopatrimonialism and Democracy in Africa, with an Illustration from Cameroon', in J. A. Widner (ed.), *Economic Change and Political Liberalization in Sub-Saharan Africa* (Baltimore: Johns Hopkins University Press).

Van Donge, J. K. (1995) 'Zambia – Kaunda and Chiluba: Enduring Patterns of Political Culture', in J. A. Wiseman (ed.), *Democracy and Political Change in Sub-Saharan Africa* (London and New York: Routledge).

Vatikiotis, M. R. J. (1993) *Indonesian Politics under Suharto: Order, Development and Pressure for Change* (London and New York: Routledge).

Vengroff, R. and Kone, M. (1995) 'Mali – Democracy and Political Change', in J. A. Wiseman (ed.), *Democracy and Political Change in Sub-Saharan Africa* (London and New York: Routledge).

Venter, D. (1995) 'Malawi – The Transition to Multi-Party Politics', in J. A. Wiseman (ed.), *Democracy and Political Change in Sub-Saharan Africa* (London and New York: Routledge).

Vickers, G. R. (1990) 'A Spider's Web', *NACLA Report on the Americas*, 24, 1.

Volkogonov, D. (1991) *Stalin: Triumph and Tragedy*, ed. and trans. H. Shukman (London: Weidenfeld and Nicolson).

Weber, M. (1964) *The Theory of Social and Economic Organization*, trans. A. M. Henderson and T. Parsons (first published 1947) (New York: Free Press).

Welch, C. E. (1987) *No Farewell to Arms? Military Disengagement from Politics in Africa and Latin America* (Boulder: Westview).

Welch, C. E. (1992) 'Military Disengagement from Politics: Paradigms, Processes, or Random Events', *Armed Forces and Society*, 18, 3.

Welsh, H. A. (1994) 'Political Transition Processes in Central and Eastern Europe', *Comparative Politics*, 26, 4.

White, S. (1986) 'Economic Performance and Communist Legitimacy', *World Politics*, 38, 3.

White S. and Nelson D. (eds). (1986) *Communist Politics: A Reader*, part 5 (Basingstoke: Macmillan).

Whitehead, L. (1994) 'Prospects for a "Transition" from Authoritarian Rule in Mexico', in M. L. Cook, K. J. Middlebrook and J. M. Horncasitas (eds), *The Politics of Economic Restructuring: State-Society Relations and Regime Change in Mexico* (San Diego: University of California).

Williams, P. J. (1994) 'Dual Transitions from Authoritarian Rule: Popular and Electoral Democracy in Nicaragua', *Comparative Politics*, 26, 2.

Wiseman, J. A. (1990) *Democracy in Black Africa: Survival and Renewal* (New York: Paragon House).

Wiseman, J. A. (1996) *The New Struggle for Democracy in Africa* (Aldershot: Avebury).

Young, C. (1982a) *Ideology and Development in Africa* (New Haven: Yale University Press).

Young, C. (1982b) 'Nationalizing the Third-World State: Categorical Imperative or Mission Impossible?', *Polity*, 15, 2.

Zhou, X. (1995) 'Industry and the Urban Economy', in R. Benewick and P. Wingrove (eds), *China in the 1990s* (Basingstoke: Macmillan).

Zolberg, A. R. (1966) *Creating Political Order: The Party-States of West Africa* (Chicago: Rand McNally).

Zuk, G. and Thompson, W. R. (1982) 'The Post-Coup Military Spending Question: A Pooled Cross-Sectional Time Series Analysis', *American Political Science Review*, 76, 1.

Index